THE ART OF PRAYER

THE ART OF PRAYER

An Orthodox Anthology

Compiled by
**IGUMEN CHARITON
OF VALAMO**

Translated by
E. KADLOUBOVSKY
and
E. M. PALMER

Edited with an Introduction by
TIMOTHY WARE

FARRAR, STRAUS AND GIROUX

NEW YORK

Farrar, Straus and Giroux
18 West 18th Street, New York 10011

Printed in the United States of America
Originally published in 1966 by Faber and Faber Limited, Great Britain
Published in the United States by Farrar, Straus and Giroux
This paperback edition (with revised bibliography), 1997

ISBN: 978-0-571-19165-9

www.fsgbooks.com

2123 25 27 29 30 28 26 24 2222

TABLE OF CONTENTS

TABLE OF CONTENTS

INTRODUCTION

Father Chariton and his monastery

'What is prayer? What is its essence? How can we learn to pray? What does the spirit of the Christian experience as he prays in humility of heart?'[1]

Such are the questions which this book sets out to answer. It presents a picture of prayer in its various degrees, from ordinary oral prayer to unceasing prayer of the heart; above all, however, it is concerned with one particular prayer, known in the Orthodox Church as the Jesus Prayer. One of the simplest of all Christian prayers, this consists in a single brief sentence, 'Lord Jesus Christ, Son of God, have mercy upon me.' Ten words in English, in other languages it is even shorter—in Greek and Russian, no more than seven words. Yet around these few words many Orthodox over the centuries have built their spiritual life, and through this one prayer they have entered into the deepest mysteries of Christian knowledge. The present anthology helps to explain how men have come to discover so much in so short a phrase.

The compiler, Igumen[2] Chariton, was a Russian Orthodox monk, a member of the ancient and historic community of Valamo, situated on an island in Lake Ladoga, on the borders between Finland and Russia. Entering the community at the turn of the

---

[1] See below, p. 51 (Bishop Nikon).

[2] *Igumen* (ἡγούμενος): the title used in Greek and Russian for the superior of a monastic community.

century, he became superior during the period between the two world wars, at a time when Valamo still stood outside the limits of the Soviet Union.

Father Chariton's anthology springs directly from his own monastic experience. On his first entry to the monastery—following the normal custom in Orthodox religious communities —he was placed under the supervision of a *staretz*,[1] who instructed the young novice in the practice of the Jesus Prayer, and at the same time in other forms of prayer and ascetic effort. On the death of his *staretz*, Chariton—in the absence of a living teacher—turned to books for guidance. It was his custom to copy down in a special notebook the passages which particularly impressed him, and so in course of time he compiled an anthology on the art of prayer. The idea came to him that the words which he himself had found helpful would also help others—not only monks but lay people in the outside world—and so in 1936 he decided to publish the material in his notebook. Deliberately self-effacing, he added no comments or connecting links of his own—'not daring even to presume', as he puts it, that he had 'achieved Inner Prayer'[2]—but he left the authors to speak entirely for themselves.

The Art of Prayer, then, represents the fruit of careful reading over many years in the monastic life. It contains authors of widely differing dates, extending from the fourth to the twentieth centuries, but the bulk of the extracts come from Russian writers during the second half of the last century. Taken as a whole, Father Chariton's anthology sets before the reader the spiritual teaching of the Orthodox Church in its classic and traditional form. There are other books which attempt, in various ways, to fulfil the same task, but few of them are framed in such unusually direct and vivid terms.

Living in the great monastery of Valamo, Father Chariton

---

[1] *Staretz* (plural *startsi*), literally an 'elder': a monk (occasionally a lay person) distinguished for his saintliness, long experience in the spiritual life, and special gift for guiding the souls of others.

[2] p. 40.

could not but feel himself the inheritor of a rich and ancient tradition, extending back over many centuries. When he first entered the community, Valamo was still at the height of its prosperity, with 300–400 monks and four churches within the main enclosure, besides many lesser chapels: it was a place of pilgrimage honoured throughout Russia, with a guest house large enough for 200 visitors at the same time. But it was not so much the outward glory that attracted a monk such as Chariton: his interest lay rather in the tradition of asceticism and inner prayer for which Valamo stood, and it is this invisible and spiritual heritage that he seeks to make available to others through his anthology.

Valamo had long been famous as a missionary centre: during the Middle Ages members of the monastery travelled throughout the surrounding district of Karelia preaching to the pagan tribes, while in 1794 it was nine monks from Valamo who were chosen to go to Alaska as the first Orthodox missionaries in the New World. Although he speaks to Christians, not pagans, in his way Igumen Chariton is also a missionary—not through direct preaching, but through the printed word. He tells of that inner kingdom of the heart, unknown to most Christians, which every baptized member of Christ's Body can discover within himself through the art of prayer.

The sources of the anthology

During the nineteenth century the Russian Orthodox Church witnessed an outstandingly rich flowering of the spiritual life. It was on two of the greatest writers in this movement that Chariton chiefly drew when compiling his notebook—on Bishop Theophan 'the Recluse' (in Russian, *Zatvornik*) and on Bishop Ignatii Brianchaninov. Extracts from the former comprise by far the greater part of *The Art of Prayer*.

Theophan the Recluse (1815–94), known in the world as George Govorov, was born at Chernavsk, near Orlov, in the central Russian province of Viatka. His father was a parish priest, and like many sons of the clergy in pre-revolutionary Russia he was himself trained for the priesthood, being sent to study in a seminary. His later characteristics were already apparent at this early stage in his life: the seminary teachers described him as 'disposed to solitude, gentle and silent'. After seminary he spent four years at the Theological Academy of Kiev (1837–41). Here in the city of Kiev he came to know the monastic life at first hand, paying frequent visits to the Petchersky Lavra, the cradle of Russian monasticism, and passing under the influence of one of the *startsi* in the community, Father Parthenii.[1]

On graduating from the Academy, Theophan took monastic vows and was ordained priest. Intellectually gifted, scholarly by natural inclination, he became professor at the seminary of Olonetz and later at the Academy of St. Petersburg. Next he spent seven years (1847–54) in the Near East, especially in Palestine, where he served in the Russian Spiritual Mission. During this time he acquired an excellent mastery of Greek and became thoroughly familiar with the Fathers—knowledge which he was to put to good use in later life. Returning to Russia, he became rector of the St. Petersburg Academy. In 1859 he was raised to the episcopate, serving as Bishop, first of Tambov, and then of Vladimir.

But Theophan's heart lay, not in the active work of diocesan administration, but rather in a life of prayer and seclusion: and so in 1866, after only seven years as a bishop, he resigned his position and retired to a modest provincial monastery at Vyshen, where he stayed until his death twenty-eight years later. At first he took part in the services at the monastery church, but from 1872 onwards he remained strictly enclosed, never going outside, seeing no one except his confessor and the superior of the monastery. He lived with the utmost simplicity in two poorly furnished rooms, while in his little domestic chapel everything was reduced to the barest essentials, and there was not even an iconostasis.[2] Here, after his enclosure, he celebrated the Holy

---

[1] See below, p. 110.
[2] Screen of icons, which normally divides the sanctuary in an Orthodox church from the rest of the building.

Liturgy,[1] at first on Saturdays and Sundays only, but during the last eleven years of his life daily. He performed the service by himself, without a server, with no reader to make the responses —in the words of one biographer, 'all alone, in silence, concelebrating with the angels'.

As a recluse, Theophan divided his time between prayer and literary work: in particular he spent many hours each day answering the vast correspondence which came to him from every corner of Russia, mainly from women. By way of relaxation he painted icons and did a little carpentry. His diet was of great austerity: in the morning, a glass of tea with some bread; around 2 p.m. an egg (if it was not a fast day) and another glass of tea; in the evening, tea again and bread. That was all.

Of all the Russian monastic authors, Theophan is probably the most highly educated. Into his retreat at Vyshen he took with him a well-stocked library, including works of contemporary western philosophy, but consisting primarily in the Fathers: among his books was the complete Patrology of Migne. His reverence for the Fathers is evident in everything that he wrote: although explicit quotations are comparatively infrequent, he always keeps extremely close to their teaching.

As a visible monument to his three decades in seclusion, Theophan left a substantial body of writings. He prepared editions in Russian of various Greek spiritual works[2] and composed several volumes of commentaries on the Epistles of St. Paul. But his chief legacy is his correspondence, partially published in ten volumes, and it is from this that Father Chariton mostly quotes in his anthology. Despite his scholarly background, Theophan had a special gift for expressing himself in direct and lively language. He wrote in answer to practical questions and specific personal problems; and so he wrote simply, in terms that could penetrate straight to the heart of these spiritual children whom he had never met, yet understood so

[1] The Liturgy: the usual Orthodox term for the Communion Service or Mass.

[2] Some of these editions are available in English translation: see the Bibliography.

well. Deeply rooted in the tradition of the past, and at the same time through his correspondence kept closely in touch with contemporary problems, Theophan represents much of what is best in the ascetic and spiritual teaching of the Orthodox Church. It has been rightly said, 'We cannot understand Russian Orthodoxy unless we understand the celebrated Recluse.'[1]

The author whom, next to Theophan, Chariton most frequently cites—Ignatii Brianchaninov (1807–67)—followed a career that was in several respects parallel. Like Theophan, Ignatii became a bishop, and like Theophan he served as such for only a short time, voluntarily resigning and retiring into seclusion, so as to devote his full energies to writing and spiritual direction. The two came, however, from different social backgrounds: while Theophan's father was a parish priest, Dimitri (as Ignatii was named before he became a monk) was a member of the nobility, the son of a provincial landowner.

In nineteenth-century Russia it was far from usual for a member of the aristocracy to be ordained or to become a monk. Dimitri's father intended his son to follow the way of life normal for one of his class, and so in 1822 the boy was sent to the Pioneer Military School at St. Petersburg. Here he proved an exemplary pupil—gifted and industrious—and during an inspection he was specially noticed by Grand Duke Nicolas Pavlovich (soon to ascend the throne as Emperor Nicolas I). But Dimitri's heart was not in his military studies. From an early age he felt a deep inner longing for the monastic life, and at one point during his time at the Pioneer School he even asked for his release, but this was refused by Emperor Nicolas. In 1827 he was commissioned as an officer, but at the end of that year he fell seriously ill, passing through a physical and spiritual crisis, and he was allowed to apply for his discharge from the Army. At once he became a novice and spent the next four years in several different monasteries, eventually taking his vows and receiving the priesthood in a small community near Vologda.

But Father Ignatii—as he was now known—was not allowed

1 S. Tyszkiewicz, S. J., in *Orientalia Christiana Periodica*, xvi (1950), p. 412.

14

to remain there for long. About this time the Tsar visited the Pioneer School and (unaware of Ignatii's discharge from the army) he asked the Director what had happened to Brianchaninov. 'He is now a monk,' came the answer. 'Where?' Nicolas demanded; but the Director did not know. After making further inquiries Nicolas learnt of Ignatii's retreat near Vologda, and immediately gave orders for him to return to the capital. Convinced that a good officer would scarcely prove a bad monk, Nicolas promptly appointed Ignatii—at the early age of twenty-six—to be Archimandrite (superior) of the important St. Sergii Monastery in Petersburg. This stood not far from the Palace, and so enjoyed imperial patronage: the Tsar instructed Ignatii to transform it into a model community, where visitors to the court could go in order to learn what a true monastery should be. Here Ignatii remained for the next twenty-four years. In 1857 he was consecrated Bishop of Stavropol, but resigned in 1861, withdrawing for the last six years of his life to the Nicolo-Babaevski monastery in the Kostroma diocese.

Ignatii, like Theophan, was a prolific writer, and the collected edition of his works runs to five weighty volumes. Most of his books are intended specifically for a monastic audience. Among other things he composed a treatise on the Jesus Prayer.[1] He was steeped, as Theophan was, in the tradition of the Fathers. Neither of them sought to be 'original', but they saw themselves rather as guardians and spokesmen of a great ascetic and spiritual heritage received from the past. At the same time they did far more than mechanically repeat earlier writers: for this tradition inherited from the past was also something which they had themselves experienced creatively in their own inner life. This combination of tradition and personal experience gives to their writings a particular value and authority.

Apart from Theophan and Ignatii, Father Chariton also quotes on occasion from other Russian authorities of the late nineteenth or early twentieth century, such as Bishops Justin and Nikon, and St. John of Kronstadt. As well as these Russian writers, he

[1] Translated into English (see the Bibliography).

includes a number of Greek texts—for example, passages from St. Mark the Monk and the Homilies of St. Makarios (5th cent.), from Sts. Barsanouphios and John (6th cent.), St. Simeon the New Theologian (11th cent.), Sts. Gregory of Sinai and Gregory Palamas (14th cent.). A few Syriac Fathers make their appearance, such as St. Ephraim (4th cent.) and St. Isaac (6th cent.); also a Latin Father, St. John Cassian (5th cent.).

Most of these non-Russian authors Chariton had consulted in the great collection of spiritual texts entitled *Philokalia* ('Love of Beauty'), first edited in Greek by St. Nicodemus of the Holy Mountain in 1782: a Slavonic version, by the Russian *staretz* Paissy Velichkovsky, appeared ten years later, while a much expanded Russian edition, prepared by Theophan the Recluse, was published in five volumes during 1876–90 under the title *Dobrotolubiye*.[1] It was this last that Chariton consulted. On the whole, however, he does not include many extracts from the *Philokalia*, perhaps out of a desire to keep his anthology as simple and intelligible as possible: he may have feared that the *Philokalia* would prove too difficult for many readers. He turned, therefore, to the works of Theophan and Ignatii, which contain precisely the same basic teaching as the Greek texts in the *Philokalia*, but present it in a form that can be more easily assimilated by Christians of the twentieth century. In Bishop Ignatii's own words (of course he is not in fact speaking of himself, but what he says applies also to him and Theophan): 'The writings of Russian Fathers are more accessible to us than those of the Greek authorities, owing to their particular clarity and simplicity of exposition, and also because they are closer to us in time.'[2]

The mind, the spirit, and the heart

The basic definition of prayer laid down in Father Chariton's anthology is exceedingly simple. Prayer is essentially a state of *standing before God*. In the words of St. Dimitri of Rostov (17th

[1] Large parts of this have appeared in English: see the Bibliography.
[2] p. 107.

cent.): 'Prayer is turning the mind and thoughts towards God. To pray means to stand before God with the mind, mentally to gaze unswervingly at Him and to converse with Him in reverent fear and hope.'[1] This notion of 'standing before God' recurs again and again in Theophan: 'The principal thing is to stand with the mind in the heart before God, and to go on standing before Him unceasingly day and night, until the end of life.'[2] 'We shall not contradict the meaning of the Holy Fathers' instructions, if we say: Behave as you wish, so long as you learn to stand before God with the mind in the heart, for in this lies the essence of the matter.'[3] This state of standing before God may be accompanied by words, or it may be 'soundless': sometimes we speak to God, sometimes we simply remain in His presence, saying nothing, but conscious that He is near us, 'closer to us than our own soul'.[4] As Theophan puts it: 'Inner prayer means standing with the mind in the heart before God, either simply living in His presence, or expressing supplication, thanksgiving, and glorification.'[5]

While St. Dimitri speaks of 'standing before God *with the mind*', Theophan is more precise, and says 'standing before God *with the mind in the heart*'. This notion of being 'with the mind in the heart' constitutes a cardinal principle in the Orthodox doctrine of prayer. To appreciate the implications of this phrase, it is first necessary to look briefly at the Orthodox teaching on man's nature.

Theophan and other authors in *The Art of Prayer* speak of three elements in man—body, soul, and spirit—which Theophan describes as follows: 'The body is made of earth; yet it is not something dead but alive and endowed with a living soul. Into this soul is breathed a spirit —the spirit of God, intended to know God, to reverence Him, to seek and taste Him, and to have its joy in Him and nothing else.'[6] The soul, then, is the basic principle of

[1] p. 50. [2] p. 63. [3] pp. 62–63.
[4] A phrase of the Greek writer, Nicolas Cabasilas (14th cent.): Migne, P. G. (*Patrologia Graeca*), cl. 712A.
[5] pp. 70–71.
[6] pp. 60–61.

life—what makes a human being something alive, as opposed to an inanimate mass of flesh. But while the soul exists primarily on the natural plane, the spirit brings us into contact with the order of divine realities: it is the highest faculty in man, and that which enables him to enter into communion with God. As such, man's spirit (with a small 's') is closely linked with the Third Person of the Trinity, the Holy Spirit or Spirit of God (with a capital 'S'); but though connected, the two are not identical—to confuse them would be to end in pantheism.

Body, soul, and spirit have each their special way of knowing: the body, through the five senses; the soul, through intellectual reasoning; the spirit, through the conscience, through a mystical perception that transcends man's ordinary rational processes.

Alongside the elements of spirit, soul, and body, there is another aspect of man's nature which lies outside this three-fold classification—the *heart*. The term 'heart' is of particular significance in the Orthodox doctrine of man. When people in the west today speak of the heart, they usually mean the emotions and affections. But in the Bible, as in most ascetic texts of the Orthodox Church, the heart has a far wider connotation. It is the primary organ of man's being, whether physical or spiritual; it is the centre of life, the determining principle of all our activities and aspirations. As such, the heart obviously includes the affections and emotions, but it also includes much else besides: it embraces in effect everything that goes to comprise what we call a 'person'.

The Homilies of St. Makarios develop this idea of the heart: 'The heart governs and reigns over the whole bodily organism; and when grace possesses the ranges of the heart, it rules over all the members and the thoughts. For there, in the heart, is the mind, and all the thoughts of the soul and its expectation; and in this way grace penetrates also to all the members of the body . . . Within the heart are unfathomable depths. There are reception rooms and bedchambers in it, doors and porches, and many offices and passages. In it is the workshop of righteousness and of wickedness. In it is death; in it is life. . . . The heart is Christ's palace: there Christ the King comes to take His rest, with the angels and the spirits of the saints, and He dwells there, walking within it and placing His Kingdom there.

'The heart is but a small vessel: and yet dragons and lions are there, and there poisonous creatures and all the treasures of wickedness; rough, uneven paths are there, and gaping chasms. There likewise is God, there are the angels, there life and the Kingdom, there light and the apostles, the heavenly cities and the treasures of grace: all things are there.'[1]

Understood in this all-embracing sense, the heart clearly does not fall within any one of the three elements in man—body, soul, spirit—if taken singly, but it is linked with all of them at once:

(1) The heart is something existing on the material level, a part of our *body*, the centre of our organism from the physical point of view. This material aspect of the heart must not be forgotten: when Orthodox ascetic texts speak of the heart, they mean (among other things) the 'carnal heart', 'a piece of muscular flesh',[2] and they are not to be understood solely in a symbolical or metaphorical sense.

(2) The heart is connected in a special way with man's psychic composition, with his *soul*: if the heart stops beating, we know from this that the soul is no longer in the body.

(3) Most important of all for our present purpose, the heart is linked with the *spirit*: in Theophan's words, 'The heart is the innermost man, or spirit. Here are located self-awareness, the conscience, the idea of God and of one's complete dependence on Him, and all the eternal treasures of the spiritual life.'[3] There are times, he continues, when the word 'heart' is to be understood, 'not in its ordinary meaning, but in the sense of "inner man". We have within us an inner man, according to the Apostle Paul, or a hidden man of the heart, according to the Apostle Peter. It is the God-like spirit that was breathed into the first man, and it remains with us continuously, even after the Fall.'[4] In this connection Greek and Russian writers are fond of

[1] *Hom.* xv. 20, 32, 33; xliii. 7.
[2] p. 191 (Theophan).   [3] p. 190.
[4] p. 191.

quoting the text, 'The inner man and the heart are very deep'.[1]
This 'deep heart' is equivalent to man's spirit: it signifies the core
or apex of our being, what the Rhineland and Flemish mystics
termed the 'ground of the soul'. It is here, in the 'deep heart',
that a man comes face to face with God.

It is now possible to understand, in some small measure, what
Theophan means when he describes prayer as 'standing before
God with the mind in the heart'. So long as the ascetic prays with
the mind in the head, he will still be working solely with the
resources of the human intellect, and on this level he will never
attain to an immediate and personal encounter with God. By the
use of his brain, he will at best know *about* God, but he will not
know God. For there can be no direct knowledge of God without an
exceedingly great love, and such love must come, not from the
brain alone, but from the whole man—that is, from the heart.
It is necessary, then, for the ascetic to descend from the head
into the heart. He is not required to abandon his intellectual
powers—the reason, too, is a gift of God—but he is called to
descend *with the mind* into his heart.

Into the heart, then, he descends—into his natural heart first,
and from there into the 'deep' heart—into that 'inner closet'
of the heart which is no longer of the flesh. Here, in the depths of
the heart, he discovers first the 'godlike spirit' which the Holy
Trinity implanted in man at creation, and with this spirit he
comes to know the Spirit of God, who dwells within every
Christian from the moment of baptism, even though most of us
are unaware of His presence. From one point of view the whole
aim of the ascetic and mystical life is the rediscovery of the
grace of baptism. The man who would advance along the path of

[1] Psalm lxiii. 7 according to the Septuagint numbering; Psalm lxiv. 6 in the
Book of Common Prayer. The Orthodox Church uses the numbering of Psalms
as given in the Greek translation of the Old Testament known as the Septuagint;
the same numbering is also given in the Latin Vulgate. In the case of most
Psalms, this differs slightly from the numbering of the Hebrew text, which is
followed by the Anglican Book of Common Prayer and the Authorised Version.

In the case of this present text, we have translated directly from the Hebrew
rather than from the Septuagint, where the sense is somewhat obscure.

inner prayer must in this way 'return into himself', finding the kingdom of heaven that is within, and so passing across the mysterious frontier between the created and the uncreated.

Three degrees of prayer

Just as there are three elements in man, so there are three main degrees of prayer[1]:

(1) Oral or bodily prayer
(2) Prayer of the mind
(3) Prayer of the heart (or 'of the mind in the heart'): spiritual prayer.

Summarizing this threefold distinction, Theophan observes: 'You must pray not only with words but with the mind, and not only with the mind but with the heart, so that the mind understands and sees clearly what is said in words, and the heart feels what the mind is thinking. All these combined together constitute real prayer, and if any of them are absent your prayer is either not perfect, or is not prayer at all.'[2]

The first kind of prayer—oral or bodily—is prayer of the lips and tongue, prayer that consists in reading or reciting certain words, in kneeling, standing, or making prostrations. Clearly such prayer, if it is merely oral and bodily, is not really prayer at all: besides reciting sentences it is also essential for us to concentrate inwardly on the meaning of what we say, to 'confine our mind within the words of prayer'.[3] Thus the first degree of prayer develops naturally into the second: all oral prayer, if it is to be worthy of the name 'prayer', must be in some measure inward prayer or prayer of the mind.

As prayer grows more interior, the outward oral recitation

---

[1] Prayer is a living reality, a personal encounter with the living God, and as such it is not to be confined within the limits of any rigid analysis. The scheme of classification given here, like all such schemes, is intended only as a general guide. Careful readers of this anthology will observe that the Fathers are not absolutely consistent in their use of terminology.

[2] p. 67.

[3] p. 67.

becomes less important. It is enough for the mind to pray the words inwardly without any movement of the lips; sometimes, indeed, the mind prays without forming any words at all. Yet even those who are advanced in the ways of prayer will usually still wish on occasion to use ordinary oral prayer: but their oral prayer is at the same time an inner prayer of the mind.

It is not sufficient, however, merely to reach the second degree of prayer. So long as prayer remains in the head, in the intellect or brain, it is incomplete and imperfect. It is necessary to descend from head to heart—to 'find the place of the heart', to 'bring down the mind into the heart', to 'unite the mind with the heart'. Then prayer will become truly 'prayer of the heart'—the prayer not of one faculty alone, but of the *whole* man, soul, spirit, and body: the prayer not only of our intelligence, of our natural reason, but of the spirit with its special power of direct contact with God.

Observe that prayer of the heart is not only prayer of the soul and spirit but also of the body. It must not be forgotten that the heart signifies, among other things, a bodily organ. The body has also a positive rôle to play in the work of prayer. This is clearly indicated in the lives of Orthodox saints whose bodies during prayer have been outwardly transfigured by Divine Light, just as Christ's body was so transfigured on Mount Tabor.[1]

Prayer of the heart takes two forms—the one (in Theophan's words) '*strenuous*, when man himself strives for it', and the other '*self-impelled*, when prayer exists and acts on its own'.[2] In the first or 'strenuous' stage, the prayer is still something that a man offers by his own conscious effort, assisted, of course, by the grace of God. At the second stage, the prayer offers itself spontaneously, being bestowed upon man as a gift: he is, as it were, 'taken by the hand and forcibly led from one room to another'[3]—it is no longer he that prays, but the Spirit of God that prays in him. Such prayer, 'bestowed as a gift', may be something that comes to a

[1] See p. 66; and compare p. 156, where Theophan speaks of the 'spiritualization of soul *and body*'.

[2] p. 71.

[3] p. 65 (Theophan).

man only from time to time, or it may be unceasing. In the second case, the prayer continues within him whatever he is doing, present when he talks and writes, speaking in his dreams, waking him up in the morning. Prayer in such a man is no longer a series of acts but a state; and he has found the way to fulfil Paul's command, 'Pray without ceasing' (1 Thess. v. 17). In the words of St. Isaac the Syrian: 'When the Spirit takes its dwelling-place in a man he does not cease to pray, because the Spirit will constantly pray in him. Then, neither when he sleeps nor when he is awake, will prayer be cut off from his soul; but when he eats and when he drinks, when he lies down or when he does any work, even when he is immersed in sleep, the perfumes of prayer will breathe in his heart spontaneously.'[1] As the Bible expresses it, 'I sleep, but my heart waketh' (Song of Solomon, v. 2).

From this point onwards prayer of the heart begins to take the form of 'mystical prayer' in the narrower sense—what Theophan terms 'contemplative prayer', or prayer 'which goes beyond the limits of consciousness'.[2] 'The state of contemplation', he says, 'is a captivity of the mind and of the entire vision by a spiritual object so overpowering that all outward things are forgotten, and wholly absent from the consciousness. The mind and consciousness become so completely immersed in the object contemplated that it is as though we no longer possess them.'[3] Theophan also terms this state of contemplation 'prayer of ecstasy' or 'ravishment'. Not much, however, is said in Chariton's anthology about these higher levels of prayer. Those without personal experience of such prayer will not understand what is said, while those who have themselves experienced it will have little further need of books.

The passions and the imagination

As the ascetic seeks to advance from oral prayer to prayer of the mind in the heart, he faces two chief obstacles: the passions and the imagination.

[1] *Mystic Treatises*, ed. A. J. Wensinck, Amsterdam, 1923, p. 174.
[2] pp. 52, 64.   [3] p. 64.

INTRODUCTION

'The most important ascetic undertaking', writes Theophan, 'is to keep the heart from passionate movements, and the mind from passionate thoughts.'[1] By the passions Orthodox writers do not mean simply lust and anger—the things which today spring to most people's minds when the word 'passion' is employed. They mean something wider—every evil longing and desire whereby the devil seeks to lead men into sin. Traditionally the passions are classified into eight 'demons' or evil thoughts: gluttony, lust, avarice, sorrow,[2] anger, 'accidie',[3] vainglory, and pride.[4] All eight spring in the last resort from the same root—self-love (φιλαυτία), the placing of self first, and of God and our neighbour second; and so, of the eight, perhaps pride may be regarded as the most fundamental.

'Blessed are the pure in heart: for they shall see God' (Matt. v. 8). The vision of God and purity of heart go hand in hand: no one, then, can hope to ascend on the ladder of prayer unless he engages in a bitter and persistent struggle against the passions. As Theophan insists, 'There is only one way to begin: and that is by taming the passions.'[5] The way to pure prayer is a moral way, involving a discipline of the will and character. That is the reason why such a long section in *The Art of Prayer* is devoted to the theme of the 'war with passions'.

But parallel with the moral discipline there must also be a disciplining of the mind. It is not only passionate thoughts that are an obstacle to inner prayer, but *all* images, whether accompanied by passion or not. According to the teaching of eastern Christendom, the imagination (φαντασία)—the faculty whereby we form mental pictures, more or less vivid according to our capacity—has at best only a very restricted place in the work of prayer; and

---

[1] p. 185. [2] This includes envy.

[3] This has no exact equivalent in modern English. It is a form of sloth, listlessness, and depression.

[4] This list goes back to Evagrios of Pontus, a monk of Egypt in the 4th century. Taken over by the west and slightly adapted, it became the 'seven deadly sins'. Some Fathers use a different classification—for example, St. Mark the Monk with his 'three spiritual giants' (p. 201).

[5] p. 200.

many (including Theophan) would claim that it has really no place at all.[1]

In prayer, so Theophan teaches, we must 'hold no intermediate image between the mind and the Lord': 'The essential part is to dwell in God, and this walking before God means that you live with the conviction ever before your consciousness that God is in you, as He is in everything: you live in the firm assurance that He sees all that is within you, knowing you better than you know yourself. This awareness of the eye of God looking at your inner being must not be accompanied by any visual concept, but must be confined to a simple conviction or feeling.'[2]

'Do not permit yourself any concepts, images, or visions'[3]; 'dispel all images from your mind'[4]; 'in prayer the simplest rule is not to form an image of anything'.[5] Such is the standard teaching of the eastern Fathers: as one of them put it, 'Whoever sees nothing in his prayer, sees God.' Our mind, which is normally dispersed abroad among a wide variety of thoughts and ideas, must be 'unified'. It must be brought from multiplicity to simplicity and emptiness, from 'diversity' to 'scantiness': it must be stripped naked of every mental picture and intellectual concept, until it is conscious of nothing save the presence of the invisible and incomprehensible God. Orthodox writers describe this state as 'pure prayer'—pure, that is, not only from sinful thoughts but from all thoughts. In the west a partial equivalent may be found in what is sometimes termed 'prayer of simple regard' or 'prayer of loving attention'.

But while insisting on the exclusion of all images, Theophan and other writers in The Art of Prayer are not so exacting in regard to feelings. On the contrary, they emphasize that prayer of the

[1] Contrast the methods of discursive meditation widely recommended in the Roman Catholic Church since the Counter-Reformation, which depend very extensively on the use of the imagination. On the difference here between Orthodox and modern western spirituality, see Professor H. A. Hodges in his introduction to Unseen Warfare (translated by E. Kadloubovsky and G. E. H. Palmer), London, 1952, especially pp. 34–35.

[2] p. 100.   [3] p. 101.   [4] p. 101.   [5] p. 183.

heart is a prayer of feeling, and this is one of the things that distinguish it from prayer of the mind.

Among the feelings which Theophan and the others mention, three are of particular interest:

(1) The sense of 'soreness' in the heart.[1] This would seem to be predominantly penitential—a feeling of compunction, of being 'pricked' to the heart.

(2) The sentiment of 'warm tenderness' or *umilenie*.[2] Here the feeling of compunction, of human unworthiness, is still present, but it is overshadowed by a sense of loving and responsive joy.

(3) Most important of all is the sense of spiritual warmth—the 'burning of the spirit' within us, the 'flame of grace' kindled in the heart.[3] Closely related to this experience of flame or fire is the vision of Divine Light which many Orthodox saints have received, entering into the mystery of the Transfiguration: but to this there are only a few passing allusions in *The Art of Prayer*.

These references to 'feelings', to 'warmth' and 'light', while they are not to be explained away as mere metaphors, must also not be understood in too gross and material a sense. The Light which the saint sees around him and within, the warmth that he feels in his heart—these are indeed a real, objective light and warmth, perceptually experienced through the senses. But at the same time they are a *spiritual* light and warmth, different in kind from the *natural* warmth and light that we normally feel and see; and as such they can only be experienced by those whose senses have been transformed and refined by divine grace.

While attaching great importance to feelings, Theophan is also sharply conscious of the dangers that may follow from pursuing feelings of the wrong kind. It is necessary to distinguish with the utmost care between natural and spiritual feelings: the former are not necessarily harmful, but they are of no particular value, and must not be regarded as the fruit of God's grace. We should watch carefully to ensure that our feelings in prayer are not polluted by any tinge of sensual pleasure[4]; the unwary fall only

[1] p. 127.   [2] p. 124.   [3] pp. 65, 108–10, 149–63.
[4] pp. 94–95.

too easily into a spiritual hedonism, desiring 'sweetness' in prayer as an end in itself[1]—one of the more pernicious forms of 'illusion' (*prelest*).[2] 'The principal fruit of prayer is not warmth and sweetness, but fear of God and contrition.'[3]

The Jesus Prayer

In theory the Jesus Prayer is but one of many possible ways for attaining inner prayer; but in practice it has acquired such influence and popularity in the Orthodox Church that it has almost come to be identified with inner prayer as such. In one spiritual authority after another, the Jesus Prayer is specially recommended as a 'quick way' to unceasing prayer, as the best and easiest means for concentrating the attention and establishing the mind in the heart. Such references to the Jesus Prayer as 'easy' must not of course be pressed too far. To pray in spirit and in truth is never easy, least of all in the initial stages. To use a Russian expression, prayer is a *podvig*—an act of ascetic struggle, a 'feat' or 'exploit'; prayer, in Bishop Ignatii's phrase, is a 'hidden martyrdom'.[4] If the Jesus Prayer is termed 'easy', this is only in a relative sense.

The Jesus Prayer is usually said in the form 'Lord Jesus Christ, Son of God, have mercy upon me.' The words 'a sinner' may be added at the end, or the prayer may be said in the plural, 'have mercy upon us'; and there are other variations. What is essential and constant throughout all the forms is the invocation of the Divine Name. As a help in the recitation of the Jesus Prayer it is common to employ a rosary (in Greek, κομβοσχοίνιον; in Russian, *vervitsa*, *lestovka*, or *tchotki*). This Orthodox rosary differs in structure from that used in the west: normally it is a knotted cord of wool or other material, so that unlike a string of beads it makes no noise.

The general division of prayer into three degrees—of the lips, of the mind, and of the heart—applies also to the Jesus Prayer:

[1] On 'sweetness' and its dangers, see pp. 128, 160.
[2] On *prelest*, see p. 40, n. 2. [3] p. 131 (Theophan).   [4] p. 216.

(1) To begin with, the Jesus Prayer is an oral prayer like any other: the words are prayed aloud by the voice, or at least formed silently by the lips and tongue. At the same time by a deliberate act of will the attention must be concentrated on the meaning of the Prayer. During this initial stage, the attentive repetition of the Prayer often proves a hard and exhausting task, calling for humble persistence.

(2) In course of time the Prayer becomes more inward, and the mind repeats it without any outward movement of lips or tongue. With this increasing inwardness, the concentration of the attention also becomes easier. The Prayer gradually acquires a rhythm of its own, at times singing within us almost spontaneously, without any conscious act of will on our part. As *staretz* Parthenii put it, we have within us 'a small murmuring stream'.[1] All this is a sign that a man is approaching the third stage.

(3) Finally the Prayer enters into the heart, dominating the entire personality. Its rhythm is identified more and more closely with the movement of the heart, until finally it becomes unceasing. What originally required painful and strenuous effort is now an inexhaustible source of peace and joy.

During the earlier stages, when the Prayer is still recited with a deliberate effort, it is usual for a person to set aside an allotted part of the day—perhaps no more than quarter or half an hour to start with, perhaps longer, each according to the direction of his *staretz*—during which his undivided attention is given to the repetition of the Jesus Prayer, to the exclusion of all other activities. But those who have acquired the gift of unceasing prayer find that the Jesus Prayer continues uninterrupted within them, even when they are engaged in external activities—in Theophan's phrase, 'The hands at work, the mind and heart with God'.[2] Even so, most people will naturally wish to set aside as much of their time as possible for the undistracted recitation of the Prayer.

Historically the roots of the Jesus Prayer extend back to the New Testament, and even earlier still. The Jews of the Old Testament had a special reverence for the Name of God—the

[1] p. 110. [2] p. 92.

28

tetragrammaton which, according to later Rabbinic tradition, none might pronounce aloud. God's Name was seen as an extension of His Person, as a revelation of His being and an expression of His power. Continuing this same tradition, Christianity has from the start shown respect for the Name which God took at His Incarnation—JESUS.[1] Three New Testament texts are of particular importance here:

(1) The declaration of Our Lord at the Last Supper: 'Hitherto have ye asked nothing in my name. . . . Whatsoever ye shall ask the Father in my name, he will give it you' (John xvi. 24, 23).

(2) The solemn affirmation of St. Peter before the Jews: after mentioning 'the name of Jesus Christ of Nazareth', he proclaims, 'There is none other name under heaven given among men, whereby we must be saved' (Acts iv. 10, 12).

(3) St. Paul's familiar words: 'Wherefore God also hath highly exalted him, and given him a name which is above every name: that at the name of Jesus every knee should bow, of things in heaven, and things in earth, and things under the earth' (Phil. ii. 9–10). It is easy to understand how, on the basis of Scriptural passages such as these, there developed in time the practice of the invocation of the divine Name in the Jesus Prayer.[2]

Besides the actual Name, the other parts of the Prayer also have a Biblical foundation. Two prayers in the Gospel may be noted: that of the blind men, 'Jesus, thou Son of David, have mercy on me' (Luke xviii. 38)[3]; and that of the Publican, 'God be merciful to me a sinner' (Luke xviii. 13). In Christian usage 'Son of David' naturally became 'Son of God'. Thus the developed

[1] The Name of 'Jesus' carries the special sense of 'Saviour': 'Thou shalt call his name JESUS: for he shall save his people from their sins' (Matt. i. 21).

[2] There are, of course, many other Scriptural passages of significance for the development of the Jesus Prayer: for example, 1 Cor. xii. 3: 'No man can say, Lord Jesus, but by the Holy Ghost'; and 1 Cor. xiv. 19: 'I had rather speak five words with my understanding . . . than ten thousand words in an unknown tongue'. In traditional Orthodox exegesis, the 'five words' have been taken to mean the Prayer 'Lord Jesus Christ, have mercy upon me', which in Greek and Russian is exactly five words (see below, p. 91).

[3] Compare Matt. ix. 27; also xx. 31, 'Have mercy on us, O Lord, thou Son of David.'

formula of the Jesus Prayer—'Lord Jesus Christ, Son of God, have mercy upon me a sinner'—is taken entirely from Scripture.

But while the constituent elements are all clearly present in the New Testament, it seems to have been some time before they were actually combined into a single prayer. It is clear that the early Christians reverenced the Name of Jesus: whether they also practised continual invocation of the Name, and if so in what form, we cannot say. The first clear development towards the Jesus Prayer, as we know it today, comes with the rise of monasticism in fourth-century Egypt. The Desert Fathers gave great prominence to the ideal of continual prayer, insisting that a monk must always practise within him what they termed 'secret meditation'[1] or 'the remembrance of God'. To help them in this task of perpetual recollection, they took some short formula which they repeated over and over again: for example, 'Lord, help,'[2] 'O God, make speed to save me; O Lord make haste to help me,'[3] 'Lord, the Son of God, have mercy upon me,'[4] 'I have sinned as a man, do Thou as God have mercy.'[5] In the earliest monastic period there was a considerable variety of these ejaculatory prayers.

Such was the *milieu* in which the Jesus Prayer developed. Initially it was but one among many short formulae, but it had an incomparable advantage over all the rest—the fact that it contained within it the Holy Name. Hence it is not surprising that in course of time it came to be used more and more in preference to the others. Even so—for Orthodoxy is a religion of freedom— the original variety never entirely ceased: and on occasion in *The Art of Prayer* Theophan recommends other short formulae, observing: 'The power is not in the words but in the thoughts and feelings.'[6] Elsewhere, however, he qualifies this, attributing

[1] On this, see p. 75.
[2] Recommended by St. Makarios (died 390): *Apophthegmata* 19 (P.G. xxxiv. 249A).
[3] Recommended by St. John Cassian: *Collat.* x. 10.
[4] *Vitae Patrum*, V. v. 32: P. L. (Migne, *Patrologia Latina*), lxxiii, 882BC.
[5] *Apophthegmata* (P.G. lxv), Apollo 2.
[6] p. 62.

a special efficacy to the Holy Name: 'The words: "Lord Jesus Christ, Son of God, have mercy upon me" are only the instrument and not the essence of the work; but they are an instrument that is very strong and effective, for the Name of the Lord Jesus is fearful to the enemies of our salvation and a blessing to all who seek Him.'[1] 'The Jesus Prayer is like any other prayer. It is stronger than all other prayers only in virtue of the all-powerful Name of Jesus, Our Lord and Saviour.'[2]

At what date does the developed text of the Jesus Prayer first emerge in a clearly recognizable form? The earliest monastic sources (4th cent.), while mentioning other formulae, do not speak of the Invocation of the Name. The first writers to refer explicitly to such invocation or 'remembrance' of the Name of Jesus are St. Diadochos of Photike (several times cited in *The Art of Prayer*) and St. Neilos of Ancyra (both 5th cent.); they do not, however, explain exactly what form this invocation took. But the full text—'Lord Jesus Christ, Son of God, have mercy upon me'—is found in a work of slightly later date (6th–7th cent.: possibly early 6th cent.), the Life of Abba Philemon, an Egyptian hermit.[3] Thus there is no explicit and definite evidence for the Prayer, in its fully developed form, before the sixth century: but its origins go back to the veneration of the Name in the New Testament.

In time there grew up around the Jesus Prayer a body of traditional teaching—partly written, but mainly oral—usually designated by the name 'Hesychasm', those who follow this teaching

---

[1] pp. 100–1.   [2] p. 99.

[3] Father Chariton quotes the decisive passage (pp. 76–77). Other early authorities, important for the history of the Jesus Prayer, are the Life of St. Dositheos (Palestine, early 6th cent.), the spiritual letters of Sts. Barsanouphios and John (Palestine, early 6th cent.), and the works of Sts. John Climacus and Hesychios (Sinai, 6th–7th cent.): none of these, however, give the Prayer exactly in its developed form. Also of importance are the Coptic lives of St. Makarios (see E. Amélineau, *Histoire des monastères de la Basse-Égypte*, *Annales du Musée Guimet*, vol. xxv, Paris, 1894, pp. 142, 152–3, 160, 161, 163).

On the early history of the Jesus Prayer, see B. Krivocheine, 'Date du texte traditionnel de la "Prière de Jésus"', *Messager de l'Exarchat du Patriarche russe en Europe occidentale*, 7–8 (1951), pp. 55–59.

being termed 'Hesychasts'.[1] Since the sixth century, this living tradition of the Jesus Prayer has continued uninterrupted within the Orthodox Church. Transmitted by Greek missionaries to the Slavonic countries, and most notably to Russia, it has exercised an immense influence upon the spiritual development of the whole Orthodox world. There have been three periods when the practice of the Prayer was particularly intense: first, the golden age of Hesychasm in fourteenth-century Byzantium, with St. Gregory Palamas, the greatest theologian of the Hesychast movement; then the Hesychast renaissance in Greece during the late eighteenth century, with St. Nicodemus of the Holy Mountain and the *Philokalia*; and finally Russia during the nineteenth century, with St. Seraphim and St. John of Kronstadt, the *startsi* of the Optina Hermitage, and also Theophan the Recluse and Ignatii Brianchaninov. More recently still, during our own time, there has been a widespread practice of the Jesus Prayer in the Russian emigration, not least among lay people: no doubt the Russian publication of Father Chariton's anthology in 1936 played a part in this. Chiefly through contact with the Russian *diaspora*, many western people have also come to know and love the Jesus Prayer.[2]

Three things in the Jesus Prayer call for special comment, and help to account for its extraordinarily wide appeal. First, the Jesus Prayer brings together, in one short sentence, two essential 'moments' of Christian devotion: adoration and compunction. Adoration is expressed in the opening clause, 'Lord Jesus Christ, Son of God'; compunction, in the prayer for mercy that follows. The glory of God and the sin of man—both are vividly present in the Prayer; it is an act of thanksgiving for the salvation that Jesus brings, and an expression of sorrow for the weakness of

---

[1] From the Greek ἡσυχία, meaning 'quietness', 'repose'. Hesychasm strictly speaking embraces all forms of inner prayer, and not just the Jesus Prayer: but in practice most Hesychast teaching is concerned with the Jesus Prayer.

[2] Several great saints in the medieval west—St. Bernard of Clairvaux, for example, St. Francis of Assisi, and St. Bernardine of Siena—had a fervent devotion to the Holy Name of Jesus: but they do not seem to have known the Jesus Prayer in its Byzantine form.

our response. The Prayer is both penitential and full of joy and loving confidence.

In the second place, it is an intensely Christological prayer—a prayer addressed to Jesus, concentrated upon the Person of the Incarnate Lord, emphasizing at once both His life on earth—'Jesus Christ'—and His divinity—'Son of God'. Those who use this prayer are constantly reminded of the historical Person who stands at the heart of the Christian revelation, and so are saved from the false mysticism which allows no proper place to the fact of the Incarnation. But although Christological, the Jesus Prayer is not a form of meditation on particular episodes in the life of Christ: here too, as in other forms of prayer, the use of mental images and intellectual concepts is strongly discouraged. 'Standing with consciousness and attention in the heart,' Theophan teaches, 'cry out unceasingly: "Lord Jesus Christ, Son of God, have mercy upon me," *without having in your mind any visual concept or image*, believing that the Lord sees you and listens to you.'[1]

In the third place, the Invocation of the Name is a prayer of the utmost simplicity. It is a way of praying that anyone can adopt: no special knowledge is required, and no elaborate preparation. As a recent writer puts it, all we must do is 'simply begin': 'Before beginning to pronounce the Name of Jesus, establish peace and recollection within yourself and ask for the inspiration and guidance of the Holy Ghost. . . . Then simply begin. In order to walk one must take a first step; in order to swim one must throw oneself into the water. It is the same with the invocation of the Name. Begin to pronounce it with adoration and love. Cling to it. Repeat it. Do not think that you are invoking the Name; think only of Jesus Himself. Say His Name slowly, softly and quietly.'[2]

This element of simplicity is several times underlined by Theophan: 'The work of God is simple: it is prayer—children

[1] p. 96.
[2] 'A Monk of the Eastern Church', *On the Invocation of the Name of Jesus*, London, 1950, pp. 5–6.

talking to their Father, without any subtleties[1]. . . . The practice of the Jesus Prayer is simple[2]. . . . The practice of prayer is called an "art", and it is a very simple one. Standing with the consciousness and attention in the heart, cry out unceasingly: "Lord Jesus Christ, Son of God, have mercy upon me."[3]

The beginner, then, is advised to recite the Prayer 'slowly, softly, and quietly'. Each word should be said with recollection and without haste, yet at the same time without undue emphasis. The Prayer should not be laboured or forced, but should flow in a gentle and natural way. 'The Name of Jesus is not to be shouted, or fashioned with violence, even inwardly.'[4] We must pray always with inner attention and concentration, but at the same time there should be no sense of strain, no self-induced intensity or artificial emotion.

At the end of each Prayer, it is good to leave a short pause before beginning again, for this helps to keep the mind attentive. According to Bishop Ignatii, it should take about half an hour to say the Jesus Prayer a hundred times: some people, he adds, take even longer. Other texts suggest that the Prayer may also be said more quickly: in the anonymous *Way of a Pilgrim*—like Ignatii, from nineteenth-century Russia—the Pilgrim is told by his *staretz* to recite the Prayer at first 3,000 times daily, then 6,000 and finally 12,000 times, after which he stops counting.[5] Such high figures imply a quicker rhythm than that recommended by Brianchaninov.

In addition to these basic and very simple rules for reciting the Prayer, the Hesychasts also evolved—as an aid to concentration—a certain 'physical method'. A particular bodily posture was recommended—head bowed, chin resting on the chest, eyes fixed on the place of the heart; at the same time the breathing was to be carefully regulated, so as to keep time with the Prayer. These 'physical exercises' are first clearly described in a writing entitled *On the three methods of attention and prayer*, attributed to

[1] p. 106.   [2] p. 89.   [3] p. 96.
[4] 'A Monk of the Eastern Church', *op. cit.*, p. 6.
[5] *The Way of a Pilgrim*, translated by R. M. French, London, 1954, pp. 12–16.

St. Simeon the New Theologian (11th cent.) but almost certainly not by him: the author is probably St. Nikephoros the Solitary (14th cent.),[1] though he may be describing a practice already well established long before his own time.[2]

In a number of passages in *The Art of Prayer* Theophan and Ignatii refer to these breathing techniques. When they mention them, however, it is nearly always with disapproval, and they studiously refrain from any detailed descriptions. This reticence will doubtless disappoint a number of western readers, who see in Hesychasm a kind of Christian Yoga; what has attracted many non-Orthodox to the Jesus Prayer in recent years and has fascinated them most, has been precisely the bodily exercises. Such an approach to the inner prayer would certainly not have gained the approval of Ignatii and Theophan: any indiscriminate use of the breathing exercises they regarded as highly dangerous.

To appreciate the place of the physical method, three points must be kept clearly in mind:

First, the breathing exercises are nothing more than an accessory—an aid to recollection, useful to some but not obligatory upon all. They are in no sense an essential part of the Jesus Prayer, which can be practised in its fullness without them.

Secondly, these breathing exercises must be used with the utmost discretion, for they can prove exceedingly harmful if performed in the wrong way. In themselves they rest upon a perfectly sound theological principle—that man is a single and integrated whole, a unity of body and soul, and therefore the body has a positive rôle to play in the work of prayer. But at the same time such physical techniques, if misapplied, can gravely damage the health and even lead to insanity, as some have recently discovered to their cost. For this reason Orthodox writers normally insist that anyone practising the physical method should be under the close guidance of an experienced spiritual director. In the absence of such a *staretz*—and even in Orthodox countries

[1] See p. 104.

[2] Earlier writers—for example St. Hesychios (p. 103)—give such general advice as, 'Let the Jesus Prayer cleave to your breathing.' But there is no evidence that they knew the breathing exercises in their developed form.

there are few directors with the requisite knowledge—it is far better simply to practise the Prayer by itself, without troubling at all about elaborate physical techniques. To quote Bishop Ignatii: 'We advise our beloved brethren not to try to practise this mechanical technique unless it establishes itself in them of its own accord. . . . The mechanical method is fully replaced by an unhurried repetition of the Prayer, a brief pause after each Prayer, quiet and steady breathing, and enclosing the mind in the words of the Prayer.'[1]

In the third place, the practice of the Jesus Prayer (with or without the breathing technique) presupposes full and active membership of the Church. If the Prayer is sometimes described as an 'easy method' or 'quick way', such language must not be misunderstood: save in very exceptional cases, the Jesus Prayer does not dispense us from the normal obligations of the Christian life. Theophan and the other authors in *The Art of Prayer* take it for granted that their readers are practising Orthodox Christians, admitted to the Church through the sacrament of baptism, regularly attending the Liturgy, going frequently to confession and holy communion. If they say little about these things, this is not because they consider them unimportant, but because they assume that anyone proposing to use the Jesus Prayer is already properly instructed in the standard teaching of the Church.

But in the west today the situation is rather different. Some of those attracted to the Jesus Prayer are not practising Christians at all: indeed, what arouses their interest is precisely the fact that the Jesus Prayer appears as something fresh, exciting, and exotic, while the more familiar practices of ordinary Church life strike them as dull and uninspiring. But the Jesus Prayer is emphatically *not* a 'short cut' in this sense. A house cannot be built without foundations. Under normal conditions a balanced and regular sacramental life is a *sine qua non* for anyone practising the Prayer. 'The surest way to union with the Lord,' writes Bishop Justin, 'next to Communion of His Flesh and Blood, is the inner Jesus Prayer.'[2] Communion must come first, and then the Prayer;

the Invocation of the Name is not a substitute for the Eucharist, but an added enrichment.

Being so very short and simple, the Jesus Prayer can be recited at any time and in any place. It can be said in bus queues, when working in the garden or kitchen, when dressing or walking, when suffering from insomnia, at moments of distress or mental strain when other forms of prayer are impossible: from this point of view, it is a prayer particularly well adapted to the tensions of the modern world. It is a prayer specially recommended to the monk, who is given a rosary as part of the habit at his profession[1]; but it is equally a prayer for lay people, whatever their occupation in the world. It is a prayer for the hermit and recluse, but at the same time a prayer for those engaged in active social work, nursing, teaching, visiting in prisons. It is a prayer that fits every stage in the spiritual life, from the most elementary to the most advanced.

The Present Edition

The Art of Prayer appeared originally in Russian under the title УМНОЕ ДѢЛАНІЕ. О МОЛИТВѢ ІИСУСОВОЙ (The Mental Art. On the Jesus Prayer), published at the Monastery of Valamo in Finland, in 1936.

Four years after this Valamo was engulfed in the second world war. On 3 February 1940 it was heavily bombarded by Soviet troops, and on the following day the Igumen with seventy of the monks fled across the snow, taking refuge in the interior of Finland. At the end of the war the island of Valamo remained within the frontiers of the U.S.S.R., and no permission was given to resume the monastic life there: the monastery buildings are now used for a holiday camp. But after great hardships, the refugees in Finland managed to reestablish their community life, naming their fresh foundation 'New Valamo': today there are about twenty-five monks. The Superior of New Valamo, Igumen Nestor, has given his blessing to the English translators, so that

[1] See p. 39.

INTRODUCTION

this present edition may justly claim a spiritual continuity with the original 'Valamo anthology'.

As Father Chariton admits in his Foreword to the original edition, the work is far from systematic in arrangement, and is frequently repetitive. In the present edition the chapter divisions and the order of extracts have been modified, to render the book more easily intelligible to English readers, and some passages which make no fresh contribution have been omitted. But while there have been omissions, no additional texts have been inserted. Short titles have been put at the head of each extract; and all footnotes are due to the translators or editor of this English version. Extracts from Greek authors, wherever possible, are translated directly from the original Greek, not from Father Chariton's Russian text.

The translators and editor wish to express their sincere gratitude to all who have assisted them. In particular they offer their warmest thanks to an Anglican friend, Priscilla Napier, who devoted many hours to the revision of the English version; to Alexander Javoroncof, for help with the interpretation of the Russian text; to the Russian Orthodox Convent of the Mother of God of Lesna, Fourqueux, France; and to the Russian Orthodox Convent of the Annunciation, London.

This is the last piece of translation to be undertaken by Madame Kadloubovsky. She was working on the concluding chapters of *The Art of Prayer* during the last weeks of her life, and at the time of her death on 16 February 1965 she had just completed her share in the translation. May the Lord grant her rest with His saints.

HIEROMONK KALLISTOS
(Timothy Ware)
October 1965-May 1966

38

FOREWORD

When a monk takes monastic vows, he is given a rosary—which is termed his 'spiritual sword'—and he is instructed to practise the Jesus Prayer day and night.

On entering the monastery I was zealous to follow this instruction, and I was guided in this by my *staretz*, Father A., who continually solved the perplexities I encountered in the practice of this prayer. After the death of my *staretz*, to solve my difficulties I was forced to have recourse to the writings of wise Fathers. Drawing out of these writings all that was essential concerning the Jesus Prayer, I used to write it all down in my notebook, and so in the course of time collected an anthology on prayer.

The material of the anthology grew from year to year and this is why the subjects in it are not in a strict systematic order and sequence. Its purpose was to be of personal help to me as a book of reference.

Now the idea has come to me to publish this book of reference or anthology, in the hope that it may be of help to others also who look for guidance in perfecting their inner spiritual life. The wise counsels of the Holy Fathers and of ascetics of the present day, which are quoted here, may assist them in their good intentions.

If this book contains many repetitions of the same themes, this is because of my sincere desire to impress them deeply on the mind of the reader. After all, everything in it, representing as it does the deeply felt convictions of spiritual men, should be of the most vital interest. Their teaching is particularly needed in our times when one observes everywhere a severe dearth of effort in the domain of the spiritual life.

Thus our purpose in publishing this anthology is simply to explain, by all kinds of varied means and frequent repetitions, how the Jesus Prayer should be practised, and so to make clear how much all of us need this prayer and how necessary it is in our work of spiritually serving God. In a word, we seek to remind our contemporaries—both monks and all lay people striving for the salvation of their souls—of the instructions left by the Holy Fathers concerning inner work and struggle with the passions. We are all the more anxious to do this because, as Bishop Ignatii[1] says, people mostly have 'a very dim and confused idea of the Jesus Prayer. Some who regard themselves—and are regarded by others—as endowed with good spiritual judgement, fear this prayer as a kind of infection, giving as the reason for their fear the danger of illusion[2] which is supposed inevitably to accompany the practice of the Jesus Prayer. So they shun it themselves and advise others to do likewise.' Further on, Bishop Ignatii says: 'The original author of this theory is, in my opinion, the devil, who hates the Name of the Lord Jesus Christ since it robs him of all power. He trembles at this all-powerful Name and has therefore defamed it before many Christians, in order to make them reject this fiery weapon, fearsome to the enemy but a saving grace to men.'

For this reason the compiler felt a pressing need to collect all the necessary material for casting further light upon the perplexities of this spiritual task. The compiler, not daring even to presume that he has achieved Inner Prayer, has not ventured to contribute anything of his own, but has simply brought forth from the treasury of the works of the Holy Fathers their wise

---

[1] On Bishop Ignatii (Brianchaninov), see above, pp. 14–15.

[2] 'Illusion': Bishop Ignatii uses here a technical term in ascetic theology, *prelest* (прелесть), a translation of the Greek πλάνη. This means literally 'wandering' or 'going astray'. Elsewhere in his writings Bishop Ignatii defines *prelest* as the corruption of human nature through the acceptance by man of mirages mistaken for truth. To be in *prelest* is to be in a state of beguilement and illusion, accepting a delusion as reality.

counsels concerning unceasing prayer. These are as necessary to all who are zealous of their salvation as air is needful to breathing.

The present anthology concerning the task of Inner Prayer contains some 400 passages from Holy Fathers and from ascetics of the present day, with detailed instructions from wise men experienced in the work of prayer.

Valamo. 27 July 1936   Igumen Chariton

CHAPTER I

THE INNER CLOSET OF THE HEART
by St. Dimitri of Rostov[1]

Enter into thy closet and shut the door

There are many among you who have no knowledge of the inner
work required of the man who would hold God in remembrance.
Nor do such people even understand what remembrance of
God means, or know anything about spiritual prayer, for they
imagine that the only right way of praying is to use such prayers as
are to be found in Church books. As for secret communion with
God in the heart, they know nothing of this, nor of the profit that
comes from it, nor do they ever taste its spiritual sweetness.
Those who only hear about spiritual meditation and prayer and
have no direct knowledge of it are like men blind from birth,
who hear about the sunshine without ever knowing what it really
is. Through this ignorance they lose many spiritual blessings, and
are slow in arriving at the virtues which make for the fulfilment of
God's good pleasure. Therefore some idea of inner training and
spiritual prayer is given here for the instruction of beginners,
so that those who wish, with God's help, can start to learn the
rudiments.

Inner spiritual training begins with these words of Christ,
'When thou prayest, enter into thy closet, and when thou hast
shut thy door, pray to thy Father which is in secret' (Matt. vi. 6).

---

[1] St. Dimitri, Metropolitan of Rostov (1651–1709): one of the most celebrated preachers in the history of the Russian Church. His chief literary work
was a great collection of the Lives of the Saints.

The duality of man and the two kinds of prayer

Man is dual: exterior and interior, flesh and spirit. The outer man is visible, of the flesh; but the inner man is invisible, spiritual—or what the Apostle Peter terms ' . . . the hidden man of the heart, which is not corruptible, . . . a meek and quiet spirit' (1 Pet. iii. 4). And St. Paul refers to this duality when he says: 'But though our outward man perish, yet the inward is renewed' (2 Cor. iv. 16). Here the Apostle speaks clearly about the outer and inner man. The outer man is composed of many members, but the inner man comes to perfection through his mind—by attention to himself, by fear of the Lord, and by the grace of God. The works of the outer man are visible, but those of the inner man are invisible, according to the Psalmist: 'the inner man and the heart are very deep' (Ps. lxiii. 7: Septuagint).[1] And St. Paul the Apostle also says: 'For what man knoweth the things of a man, save the spirit of man which is in him?' (1 Cor. ii. 11). Only He who tests the innermost hearts and the inward parts knows all the secrets of the inner man.

Training, then, must also be twofold, outer and inner: outer in reading books, inner in thoughts of God; outer in love of wisdom, inner in love of God; outer in words, inner in prayer; outer in keenness of intellect, inner in warmth of spirit; outer in technique, inner in vision. The exterior mind is 'puffed up' (1 Cor. viii. 1), the inner humbles itself; the exterior is full of curiosity, desiring to know all, the inner pays attention to itself and desires nothing other than to know God, speaking to Him as David spoke when he said, 'My heart hath talked with thee: "Seek ye my face"; "Thy face Lord will I seek"' (Ps. xxvi. 8. Sept.).[2] And also 'Like as the hart desireth the water brooks, so longeth my soul after thee, O God' (Ps. xli. 2. Sept.).[3]

Prayer is likewise twofold, exterior and inner. There is

---

[1] Ps. lxiv. 6 in the Book of Common Prayer.
[2] xxvii. 9 (B.C.P.).   [3] xlii. 1 (B.C.P.).

prayer made openly, and there is secret prayer; prayer with others and solitary prayer; prayer undertaken as a duty and prayer voluntarily offered. Prayer as duty, performed openly according to the Church rules, in company with others, has its own times: the Midnight Office, Matins, the Hours, the Liturgy, Vespers and Compline. These prayers, to which people are called by bells, are a suitable tribute to the King of Heaven which must be paid every day. Voluntary prayer which is in secret, on the other hand, has no fixed time, being made whenever you wish, without bidding, simply when the spirit moves you. The first, in other words the prayer of the Church, has an established number of Psalms, troparia, canons,[1] and other hymns, together with rites performed by the priest: but the other kind of prayer—secret and voluntary—since it has no definite time, is also not limited to a definite number of prayers: everyone prays as he wishes, sometimes briefly, sometimes at length. The first kind is performed aloud by the lips and voice, the second only in spirit. The first is performed standing, the second, not only standing or walking, but also lying down, in a word, always—whenever you happen to raise your mind to God. The first, made in company with others, is performed in church, or on some special occasion in a house where several people are gathered together; but the second is performed when you are alone in the shut closet, according to the word of the Lord: 'When thou prayest, enter into thy closet, and when thou hast shut thy door, pray to thy Father which is in secret' (Matt. vi. 6).

The closet also is twofold, outer and inner, material and spiritual: the material place is of wood or stone, the spiritual closet is the heart or mind: St. Theophylact[2] interprets this

[1] A troparion (plural troparia) is a short piece of religious poetry—normally a stanza of about six lines—used in the services of the Orthodox Church. Sometimes these troparia occur singly, sometimes they are grouped together into odes. A canon consists normally in a series of nine such odes (in practice eight odes, as the second ode is usually omitted). A canon is read each day at Matins; canons are also appointed for Compline and the Midnight Office.

[2] St. Theophylact, Archbishop of Bulgaria (11th cent.): Byzantine theological writer, author of many commentaries on Holy Scripture.

phrase as meaning secret thought or inner vision. Therefore the material closet remains always fixed in the same place, but the spiritual one you carry about within you wherever you go. Wherever man is, his heart is always with him, and so, having collected his thoughts inside his heart, he can shut himself in and pray to God in secret, whether he be talking or listening, whether among few people or many. Inner prayer, if it comes to a man's spirit when he is with other people, demands no use of lips or of books, no movement of the tongue or sound of the voice: and the same is true even when you are alone. All that is necessary is to raise your mind to God, and descend deep into yourself, and this can be done everywhere.

The material closet of a man who is silent embraces only the man himself, but the inner spiritual closet also holds God and all the Kingdom of Heaven, according to the Gospel words of Christ Himself: 'The kingdom of God is within you' (Luke xvii. 21). Explaining this text, St. Makarios of Egypt[1] writes: 'The heart is a small vessel, but all things are contained in it; God is there, the angels are there, and there also is life and the Kingdom, the heavenly cities and the treasures of grace.'

Man needs to enclose himself in the inner closet of his heart more often than he need go to church: and collecting all his thoughts there, he must place his mind before God, praying to Him in secret with all warmth of spirit and with living faith. At the same time he must also learn to turn his thoughts to God in such a manner as to be able to grow into a perfect man.

Loving union with God

First of all it must be understood that it is the duty of all Christians—especially of those whose calling dedicates them to the spiritual life—to strive always and in every way to be united

---

[1] St. Makarios (?300–390), one of the greatest of early monastic leaders, founder of Scetis in the Egyptian Desert. The various writings traditionally attributed to him are now no longer considered to be his work: their exact origin remains obscure, but they seem to have been written in Egypt or Syria during the late 4th or early 5th century.

with God, their creator, lover, benefactor, and their supreme good, by whom and for whom they were created. This is because the centre and the final purpose of the soul, which God created, must be God Himself alone, and nothing else—God from whom the soul has received its life and its nature, and for whom it must eternally live. For all visible things on earth which are lovable and desirable—riches, glory, wife, children, in a word everything of this world that is beautiful, sweet, and attractive—belong not to the soul but only to the body, and being temporary, will pass away as quickly as a shadow. But the soul, being eternal by its nature, can attain eternal rest only in the Eternal God: He is its highest good, more perfect than all beauty, sweetness, and loveliness, and He is its natural home, whence it came and whither it must return. For as the flesh coming from the earth returns to the earth, so the soul coming from God returns to God and dwells with Him. For the soul was created by God in order to dwell with Him for ever; therefore in this temporary life we must diligently seek union with God, in order to be accounted worthy to be with Him and in Him eternally in the future life.

No unity with God is possible except by an exceedingly great love. This we can see from the story of the woman in the Gospel, who was a sinner: God in His great mercy granted her the forgiveness of her sins and a firm union with Him, 'for she loved much' (Luke vii. 47). He loves those who love Him, He cleaves to those who cleave to Him, gives Himself to those who seek Him, and abundantly grants fullness of joy to those who desire to enjoy His love.

To kindle in his heart such a divine love, to unite with God in an inseparable union of love, it is necessary for a man to pray often, raising the mind to Him. For as a flame increases when it is constantly fed, so prayer, made often, with the mind dwelling ever more deeply in God, arouses divine love in the heart. And the heart, set on fire, will warm all the inner man, will enlighten and teach him, revealing to him all its unknown and hidden wisdom, and making him like a flaming seraph, always standing before God within his spirit, always looking at Him within his mind, and drawing from this vision the sweetness of spiritual joy.

Prayer said by the lips without the attention of the mind is nothing

We should do well to apply to ourselves the words of St. Paul to the Corinthians. What use is it to you, O Corinthians (so he writes), if you pray only with the voice, while your mind pays no attention to the prayer but dreams about something else? What profit is there if the tongue says much but the mind does not think about what is said, even if you pronounce very many words? What profit is there if you should sing in full voice, and with all the strength of your lungs, while your mind does not stand before God and does not see Him, but wanders away in thought to some other place? Such a prayer will bring you no profit. It will not be heard by God but will remain fruitless. Well did St. Cyprian[1] judge when he said: 'How can you expect to be heard by God, when you do not hear yourself? How do you expect God to remember you when you pray, if you do not remember yourself?'

Prayer should be short, but often repeated

From those who have experience in raising their mind to God, I learned that, in the case of prayer made by the mind from the heart, a short prayer, often repeated, is warmer and more useful than a long one. Lengthy prayer is also very useful, but only for those who are reaching perfection, not for beginners. During lengthy prayer, the mind of the inexperienced cannot stand long before God, but is generally overcome by its own weakness and mutability, and drawn away by external things, so that warmth of the spirit quickly cools down. Such prayer is no longer prayer, but only disturbance of the mind, because of the thoughts wandering hither and thither: which happens both during prayers and psalms recited in church, and also during the rule of prayers for the cell,[2] which takes a long time. Short yet frequent prayer, on the other hand, has more stability, because

[1] St. Cyprian, Bishop of Carthage in North Africa, died as a martyr in 258.
[2] Besides the liturgical services held in church, an Orthodox monk is required by his rule to recite certain prayers daily in his own cell.

THE INNER CLOSET OF THE HEART

the mind, immersed for a short time in God, can perform it with greater warmth. Therefore the Lord also says: 'When ye pray, use not vain repetitions' (Matt vi. 7), for it is not for your prolixity that you will be heard. And St. John of the Ladder[1] also teaches: 'Do not try to use many words, lest your mind become distracted by the search for words. Because of one short sentence, the Publican received the mercy of God, and one brief affirmation of belief saved the Robber. An excessive multitude of words in prayer disperses the mind in dreams, while one word or a short sentence helps to collect the mind.'

But someone may ask: 'Why did the Apostle say in the Epistle to the Thessalonians, "Pray without ceasing"?' (1 Thess. v. 17).

Usually in the Holy Scriptures, the word 'always' is used in the sense of 'often', for instance, 'The priests went always into the first tabernacle, accomplishing the service for God' (Heb. ix. 6): this means that the priests went into the first tabernacle at certain fixed hours, not that they went there unceasingly by day and by night; they went often, but not uninterruptedly. Even if the priests were all the time in church, keeping alight the fire which came from heaven, and adding fuel to it so that it should not go out, they were not doing this all at the same time, but by turns, as we see from St. Zacharias: 'He executed the priest's office before God in the order of his course' (Luke i. 8). One should think in the same way about prayer, which the Apostle ordains to be done unceasingly, for it is impossible for man to remain in prayer day and night without interruption. After all, time is also needed for other things, for necessary cares in the administration of one's house; we need time for working, time for talking, time for eating and drinking, time for rest and sleep. How is it possible to pray unceasingly except by praying often? But oft-repeated prayer may be considered unceasing prayer.

Consequently do not let your oft-repeated but short prayer

[1] St. John of the Ladder, also known as John Climacus (?579–?649), of Mount Sinai, author of *The Ladder of Divine Ascent*, a classic work on the ascetic and spiritual life which is normally read each Lent in Orthodox monasteries: English translation by Archimandrite Lazarus Moore, London (Faber and Faber), 1959.

be expanded into too many words. This is what the Holy
Fathers also advise. In his commentary on the Gospel of St.
Matthew (vi. 7), St. Theophylact states, 'You should not make
long prayers, for it is better to pray little but often.' And St. John
Chrysostom,[1] in his commentary on St. Paul's Epistles, observes,
'Whoever says too much in prayer, does not pray, but indulges in
idle talk.' St. Theophylact also says in his interpretation of
Matthew vi. 6: 'Superfluous words are idle talk.' The Apostle
said well, 'I had rather speak five words with my understanding
. . . than ten thousand words in an unknown tongue' (1 Cor.
xiv. 19): that is, it is better for me to pray to God briefly but with
attention, than to pronounce innumerable words without attention, vainly filling the air with noise.

There is also another sense in which the Apostle's words must
be interpreted. 'Pray without ceasing' (1 Thess. v. 17) must be
taken in the sense of prayer performed by the mind: whatever a
man is doing, the mind can always be directed towards God,
and in this way it can pray to Him unceasingly.

Therefore begin now, O my soul, little by little, the course of
training set out for you, begin in the name of the Lord, according to the Apostle's instruction: 'And whatsoever ye do in word
or deed, do all in the name of the Lord Jesus' (Col. iii. 17). Do
all, he means, not primarily for your own profit, even spiritual,
but for the glory of God; and so in all your words, deeds and
thoughts, the Name of the Lord Jesus Christ, our Saviour, will be
glorified.

But before you start, explain to yourself briefly what prayer is.

Prayer is turning the mind and thoughts towards God. To
pray means to stand before God with the mind, mentally to gaze
unswervingly at Him, and to converse with Him in reverent fear
and hope.

And so collect all your thoughts: laying aside all outer worldly
cares, direct your mind towards God, concentrating it wholly
upon Him.

[1] St. John Chrysostom, Archbishop of Constantinople (?344–407), ascetic,
preacher, and writer. Of all the Greek Fathers he is perhaps the best loved in the
Orthodox Church, and the one whose works are most widely read.

CHAPTER II

WHAT IS PRAYER?
by Theophan the Recluse[1]

(i) THE TEST OF EVERYTHING

Ultimate questions[2]

What is prayer? What is its essence? How can we learn to pray? What does the spirit of the Christian experience as he prays in humility of heart?

All such questions should constantly occupy the mind and heart of the believer, for in prayer man converses with God, he enters, through grace, into communion with Him, and lives in God. And the Holy Fathers and teachers of the Church give answers to all these questions, based on the grace-given enlightenment which is acquired through the experience of practising prayer—experience equally accessible to the simple and to the wise.

The test of everything

Prayer is the test of everything; prayer is also the source of everything; prayer is the driving force of everything; prayer is also the director of everything. If prayer is right, everything is right. For prayer will not allow anything to go wrong.

---

[1] On Bishop Theophan, see above, pp. 11–14.
[2] The first extract is not from Theophan but from Bishop Nikon of Volodsk, Russian spiritual writer in the late 19th and early 20th century.

WHAT IS PRAYER?

Degrees of prayer

There are various degrees of prayer. The first degree is bodily prayer, consisting for the most part in reading, in standing, and in making prostrations. In all this there must needs be patience, labour, and sweat; for the attention runs away, the heart feels nothing and has no desire to pray. Yet in spite of this, give yourself a moderate rule and keep to it. Such is active prayer.

The second degree is prayer with attention: the mind becomes accustomed to collecting itself in the hour of prayer, and prays consciously throughout, without distraction. The mind is focused upon the written words to the point of speaking them as if they were its own.

The third degree is prayer of feeling: the heart is warmed by concentration so that what hitherto has only been thought now becomes feeling. Where first it was a contrite phrase now it is contrition itself; and what was once a petition in words is transformed into a sensation of entire necessity. Whoever has passed through action and thought to true feeling, will pray without words, for God is God of the heart. So that the end of apprenticeship in prayer can be said to come when in our prayer we move only from feeling to feeling. In this state reading may cease, as well as deliberate thought; let there be only a dwelling in feeling with specific marks of prayer.

When the feeling of prayer reaches the point where it becomes continuous, then spiritual prayer may be said to begin. This is the gift of the Holy Spirit praying for us, the last degree of prayer which our minds can grasp.

But there is, they say, yet another kind of prayer which cannot be comprehended by our mind, and which goes beyond the limits of consciousness: on this read St. Isaac the Syrian.[1]

---

[1] St. Isaac the Syrian (died c. 700), Nestorian Bishop of Nineveh and mystical author. His works, translated from Syriac into Greek during the ninth century, have long been widely read and honoured in the Orthodox Church.

The essence of prayer

Without inner spiritual prayer there is no prayer at all, for this alone is real prayer, pleasing to God. It is the soul within the words of prayer that matters, whether the prayer is at home or in church, and if inner prayer is absent, then the words have only the appearance and not the reality of prayer.

What then is prayer? Prayer is the raising of the mind and heart to God in praise and thanksgiving to Him and in supplication for the good things that we need, both spiritual and physical. The essence of prayer is therefore the spiritual lifting of the heart towards God. The mind in the heart stands consciously before the face of God, filled with due reverence, and begins to pour itself out before Him. This is spiritual prayer, and all prayer should be of this nature. External prayer, whether at home or in church, is only prayer's verbal expression and shape; the essence or the soul of prayer is within a man's mind and heart. All our Church order of prayer, all prayers composed for home use, are filled with spiritual turning to God. Anyone who prays with even the least part of attention cannot avoid this spiritual turning to God, unless he is completely inattentive to what he is doing.

Inner prayer is necessary for all

Nobody can dispense with inner prayer. We cannot live spiritually unless we raise ourselves in prayer to God. But the only way we can thus raise ourselves is through spiritual action: for God is spiritual. True, there is spiritual prayer linked with oral or exterior prayer, whether at home or in church, and there is also spiritual prayer, by itself, without any special outward form or bodily posture; but in both cases the essence of the thing is the same. Both forms are obligatory for the layman as well as the monk. The Saviour commanded us to enter into our closet and there pray to God the Father in secret. This closet, as interpreted by St. Dimitri of Rostov, means the heart. Consequently, to obey our Lord's commandment, we must pray secretly to God with the mind in the heart. This commandment

WHAT IS PRAYER?

embraces all Christians. The Apostle Paul also gives this direction
when he says, 'Praying always with all prayer and supplication in
the Spirit' (Eph. vi. 18). He means spiritual prayer of the mind,
and directs all Christians, without distinction, to pray thus.
He also directs all Christians to 'Pray without ceasing' (1 Thess.
v. 17). But unceasing prayer is only possible by praying with the
mind in the heart.

Rising in the morning, stand as firmly as possible before God in
your heart, as you offer your morning prayers; and then go to
the work apportioned to you by God, without withdrawing from
Him in your feelings and consciousness. In this way you will do
your work with the powers of your soul and body, but in your
mind and heart you will remain with God.

Outward prayer is not enough[1]

Outward prayer alone is not enough. God pays attention to the
mind, and they are no true monks who fail to unite exterior
prayer with inner prayer. Strictly defined, the word 'monk'
means a recluse, a solitary. Whoever has not withdrawn within
himself is not yet a recluse, he is not yet monk even though he
lives in the most isolated monastery. The mind of the ascetic
who is not withdrawn and enclosed within himself dwells necessarily amongst tumult and unquietness. Innumerable thoughts,
having free admission to his mind, bring this about; without
purpose or necessity his mind wanders painfully through the
world, bringing harm upon itself. The withdrawal of a man within
himself cannot be achieved without the help of concentrated
prayer, especially the attentive practice of the Jesus Prayer.

The achievement of passionlessness and sanctity—in other
words, of Christian perfection—is impossible without acquiring
inner prayer. All the Fathers are agreed on this.

The path of true prayer becomes incomparably more narrow
when the ascetic struggler begins to enter upon it through the
activity of the inner man. But when he enters this narrow path

[1] By Bishop Ignatii, not by Theophan.

54

and feels how right, saving, and necessary this way is, and when he comes to love his work in the inner cell, then he will also come to love the narrowness of his exterior life because it serves as a cloister and treasury of inner activity.

Oral prayer

'In psalms and hymns and spiritual songs, singing with grace in your hearts to the Lord . . .' (Col. iii. 16). The words 'in psalms and hymns and spiritual songs' describe oral prayer, prayer with words; but the words 'singing with grace in your hearts to the Lord' describe inner prayer, of the mind in the heart.

Psalms, canticles, hymns, odes, and so on, are different names for religious songs. It is difficult to indicate the difference between them, because their contents and form are very similar. All are expressions of the spirit of prayer. When moved to prayer, the spirit glorifies God, thanks Him and raises its petitions to Him. All these manifestations of the spirit of prayer are essentially indivisible, having no separate existence. When prayer begins to work, it passes from one of these manifestations to another, often more than once. Expressed in words, it is oral prayer, whether called a psalm, a hymn, or an ode. Therefore we will make no attempt to define the difference between their names. The Apostle intended, by this phrase, to embrace all kinds of prayer expressed in words. All prayers which are now in use come under this heading. Besides the Psalter, we use Church songs, stichera, troparia, canons, akathists,[1] and the various prayers which are contained in our prayer books. You will not go wrong if, when reading the Apostle's words about oral prayer, you understand this as the oral prayer which we use today. The power of prayer lies not in this or that oral prayer, but in the *way* in which we pray.

[1] On troparia and canons, see above, p. 45, n. 1. A *sticheron* is a stanza of religious poetry, similar to a troparion. An *akathist* is a composition in 24 stanzas, addressed to the Saviour, to the Mother of God, our Guardian Angel, or one of the Saints. The title means 'not sitting': an akathist must always be recited standing up.

In his use of the word 'spiritual' the Apostle shows us how we should pray orally. Prayers are spiritual because they are originally born in the spirit and ripen there, and are poured out from the spirit. Their spiritual nature is intensified because they are born and ripen by the grace of the Holy Spirit. Psalms and all other oral prayers were not oral at the very beginning. In their origin they were purely spiritual, and only afterwards came to be clothed in words and so assumed an oral form. But becoming oral did not deprive them of their spirituality: even now, they are oral only in their outer semblance, but in their power they are spiritual.

It follows from this that if you want to learn from the Apostle's words about oral prayer, you must act thus: enter into the spirit of the prayers which you hear and read, reproducing them in your heart; and in this way offer them up from your heart to God, as if they had been born in your own heart under the action of the grace of the Holy Spirit. Then, and then alone, is the prayer pleasing to God. How can we attain to such prayer? Ponder carefully on the prayers which you have to read in your prayer book; feel them deeply, even learn them by heart. And so when you pray you will express that which is already deeply felt in your heart.

The purpose of Church hymns

'Speaking to yourselves in psalms and hymns and spiritual songs, singing and making melody in your heart to the Lord' (Eph. v. 19).

How should we interpret these words? Do they mean that when you are filled with the Spirit, you should then sing with your mouth and your heart? Or that if you wish to be filled with the Holy Spirit, you should first sing? Is the singing with mouth and heart, mentioned by the Apostle, meant to be the consequence of being filled by the Spirit, or the means towards it?

The infusion of the Holy Spirit does not lie within our power. It comes as the Spirit Himself wishes. And when it comes, this infusion will so greatly animate the powers of our spirit that the song to God breaks out of itself. Freedom of choice lies only between leaving this song to be sung in the heart alone, or expressing it aloud for all to hear.

The words of the Apostle must be taken in the second sense rather than the first. Desire to be filled with the Spirit, and sing with that aim in mind. Singing will set alight the Spirit, or lead to a state of infusion by the Spirit, or show forth His action. According to Blessed Theodoret,[1] the Apostle refers to spiritual rapture when he says, 'Be filled with the Spirit' (Eph. v. 18), and he shows us how to attain this, namely by 'unceasingly singing praises to God, entering deeply into oneself, and always stimulating thought'. That is to say: by singing with the tongue and heart.

It is not difficult to understand that the most important part of this is not good harmony in the singing, but the content of what is sung. It has the same effect as a speech written with warm feeling, which animates whoever reads it. Feeling, expressed in words, is carried by words into the soul of those who hear or read them. The same can be said of Church songs. Psalms, hymns and Church songs are spiritually inspired outbursts of feeling towards God. The Spirit of God filled His elect, and they expressed the plenitude of their feelings in songs. He who sings them as they should be sung enters again into the feelings which the author experienced when he originally wrote them. Being filled by these feelings, he draws near to the state wherein he is able to receive the grace of the Spirit, and to adapt himself to it. The purpose of Church songs is precisely to make the spark of grace that is hidden within us burn brighter and with greater warmth. This spark is given by the sacraments. Psalms, hymns and spiritual odes are introduced, to fan the spark and transform it into flame. They act on the spark of grace as the wind acts on a spark hidden in firewood.

But let us remember that this effect is conditional on their use being accompanied by purification of the heart. St. John

[1] Theodoret, Bishop of Kyrrhos (c. 393–c. 458). Some of his writings were condemned at the fifth Ecumenical Council (Constantinople, 553), but his commentaries on Holy Scripture are for the most part excellent, and continue to be read and respected in the Orthodox Church.

Chrysostom enjoins this, guided by the teaching of St. Paul himself, and also says that the songs must primarily be spiritual, and sung not only by the tongue but also by the heart.

Therefore, in order that the singing of Church songs may lead us on to be filled by the Spirit, the Apostle is insistent that the songs should be spiritual. By this it should be understood that they must be not only spiritual in content but moved by the Spirit: they must themselves be the fruit of the Holy Spirit, and be poured forth by hearts that are filled with Him. Without this they will not lead to our possession by the Spirit. This is according to the law whereby the singer is given that which has been put into the song.

The second condition of the Apostle is that songs must be sung not by the tongue only, but by the heart. It is necessary not only to understand the song, but to be in sympathy with it, to accept the contents of the song in the heart, and to sing it as if it came from our own heart. A comparison of this text with others makes it evident that in the time of the Apostles only those who were in such a state used to sing; others entered into a similar mood and all the congregation sang and glorified God from the heart only. No wonder if, in consequence of this, the whole congregation was filled with the Spirit! What treasure is hidden in Church songs if they are performed properly!

St. John Chrysostom says: 'What is meant by "those who sing in their heart to the Lord"? It means: Undertake this work with attention, for those who are inattentive sing in vain, pronouncing only words, while their heart wanders elsewhere.' Blessed Theodoret adds to this: 'He sings in the heart, who not only moves his tongue, but incites his mind to understand what is said.' Other Holy Fathers, writing about prayer to God, believe that prayer is best achieved when offered by the mind established in the heart.

What the Apostle says here about gatherings in church, can also be applied to private psalmody. This everyone can perform alone at home. And the fruit of this will be the same, when it is done as it should be: that is, with attention, understanding and feeling, from the heart.

Let us note also that although the words of the Apostle refer to singing, his thought indicates turning in prayer to God. It is actually this that arouses the Spirit.

The prayer of the mind in the heart

Sometimes we pray by using the words of prayers already composed; at other times prayer is born directly in the heart, and from there rises to God. Such was the prayer of Moses before the Red Sea. The Apostle refers to it in the words, 'By grace, singing in your heart to the Lord'. Explaining this text, St. John Chrysostom writes: 'Sing from the grace of the Spirit, says Paul, not simply with the lips but with attention, standing with your thought before God in your heart. For this is what singing *to* God means: otherwise the song is in vain, and the words vanish into thin air. It is not sung to show off, for even if you are in the market place, you can turn to God within and sing, without being heard by anyone. It is good to pray in the heart even when travelling, and be lifted on high.' Only this kind of prayer is real prayer. Oral prayer is prayer only in so far as the mind and heart also pray.

This prayer is formed in the heart by the grace of the Holy Spirit. He who turns to God and is sanctified by the sacraments, immediately receives feeling towards God within himself, which from this moment begins to lay the foundation in his heart for the ascent on high. Provided he does not stifle it by something unworthy, this feeling will be kindled into flame, by time, perseverance, and labour. But if he stifles it by something unworthy, although the path of approach and reconciliation to God is not thereby closed to him, this feeling will no longer be given at once and gratis. Before him is the sweat and work of seeking and of gaining it by prayer. But no one is refused. Because all have grace, only one thing is necessary: to give this grace free scope to act. Grace receives free scope in so far as the ego is crushed and the passions uprooted. The more our heart is purified the more lively becomes our feeling towards God. And when the heart is fully purified, then this feeling of warmth towards God takes fire. Even in those who have ceased for a time to experience the working of grace, this warmth towards God revives long before they have arrived at a complete purification from passions. It is still only a seed or a spark, but when it is carefully tended, it glows and begins to flame. Yet it is not permanent, but blazes up and then dies down, and in its burning is not of even strength. But no matter how dimly or brightly it burns, this flame of love always ascends to the Lord and sings a song to Him. Grace builds up everything, because grace is always present in believers. Those who commit themselves irrevocably to grace, will pass under its guidance, and it shapes and forms them in a way known only to itself.

Feeling and words

Feeling towards God—even without words—is a prayer. Words support and sometimes deepen the feeling.

The gift of feeling

Guard this gift of feeling, given to you by the mercy of God. How? First and foremost by humility, ascribing everything to grace and nothing to yourself. As soon as you trust to yourself, grace will diminish in you; and if you do not come to your senses, it will cease to work completely. Then there will be much weeping and lamentation. Secondly, regarding yourself as dust and ashes, dwell in grace and do not turn your heart or thought to anything else except from necessity. Be all the time with the Lord. If the inner flame begins to die down a little, immediately hasten to restore its strength. The Lord is near. Turning to Him with contrition and fear, you will immediately receive His gifts.

Body, soul and spirit

The body is made of earth; yet it is not something dead but alive and endowed with a living soul. Into this soul is breathed a spirit—the spirit of God, intended to know God, to reverence Him, to seek and taste Him, and to have its joy in Him and nothing else.

Draw down the mind into the heart

Turn to the Lord, drawing down the attention of the mind into the heart, and calling upon Him there. With the mind firmly established in the heart, stand before the Lord with awe, reverence, and devotion. If we would fulfil this small rule unfailingly, then passionate desires and feelings would never arise, nor would any other thought.

The primary work of our life

Prayer is the primary work of the moral and religious life. The root of this life is a free and conscious relationship with God, which then directs everything. It is the practice of prayer that expresses this free and conscious attitude towards God, just as the social contacts of daily life express our moral attitude towards our neighbour, and our ascetic struggles and spiritual efforts express our moral attitude towards ourselves. Our prayer reflects our attitude to God, and our attitude to God is reflected in prayer. And since this attitude is not identical in different people, so the kind of prayer is not identical either. He who is careless of salvation has a different attitude to God from him who has abandoned sin and is zealous for virtue, but has not yet entered within himself, and works for the Lord only outwardly. Finally, he who has entered within and carries the Lord in himself, standing before Him, has yet another attitude. The first man is negligent in prayer just as he is negligent in life; and he prays in church and at home merely according to the established custom, without attention or feeling. The second man reads many prayers and goes often to church, trying at the same time to keep his attention from wandering and to experience feelings in accordance with the prayers which are read, although he is very seldom successful. The third man, wholly concentrated within, stands with his mind before God, and prays to Him in his heart without distraction, without long verbal prayers, even when standing for a long time at prayer in his home or in church. Take away oral prayer from the second, and you will take away all prayer from him; impose oral prayer on the third and you will extinguish prayer in him by the wind of many words. For every rank of person, and every degree of drawing near to God, has its own prayer and its own rules. How important it is to have experienced instruction here, and how very harmful it can be to guide and direct oneself!

Sounding and soundless prayer

'Which is better: to pray with the lips or with the mind?' The answer is that we must use both forms: pray sometimes in words, sometimes with the mind. But it is necessary to explain here that mental prayer also involves the use of words which in this case are not heard, but are only pronounced within the heart. It is better put in this way: Pray sometimes with sounding words, and sometimes inaudibly with words that are soundless. But it is necessary to take care that both sounding and soundless prayer should come from the heart.

The power is not in the words

To pray is quite straightforward. Stand with the mind in the heart before the face of the Lord and cry: 'Jesus Christ, Son of God, have mercy upon me', or just: 'Lord have mercy', 'Most merciful Lord, have mercy upon me, a sinner'—or with any other words. The power is not in the words, but in the thoughts and feelings.

A vigilant tension of the muscles

We shall not contradict the meaning of the Holy Fathers' instructions, if we say: Behave as you wish, so long as you learn to stand before God with the mind in the heart, for in this lies the essence of the matter.

Among bodily activities, however, there are some which seem to go hand in hand with inner prayer, and never leave it. Our aim must be to stand with the attention in the heart, and to hold the whole body in a vigilant tension of the muscles, and not to allow attention to be influenced and diverted by exterior impressions of the senses.

Prayer from the heart

Every prayer must come from the heart, and any other prayer is no prayer at all. Prayer-book prayers, your own prayers, and very short prayers, all must issue forth from the heart to God, seen before you. And still more must this be so with the Jesus Prayer.

The principal thing

The principal thing is to stand with the mind in the heart before God, and to go on standing before Him unceasingly day and night, until the end of life.

(ii) DEGREES OF PRAYER

Three degrees of prayer

We may distinguish three stages:

1. The habit of ordinary oral prayer in church and at home.
2. The union of prayerful thoughts and feelings with the mind and heart.
3. Unceasing prayer.

The Jesus Prayer may go with both of the first two, but its real place is with unceasing prayer. The principal condition for success in prayer is the purification of the heart from passions, and from every attachment to things sensual. Without this, prayer will remain all the time in the first or oral degree. The more the heart is purified, the more oral prayer will become prayer of the mind in the heart, and when the heart becomes quite pure, then unceasing prayer will be established. How can this be done? In church, follow the service and retain the thoughts and feelings which you experience there. At home, awake in yourself the thought and feeling of prayer, and maintain them in your soul with the help of the Jesus Prayer.

Further distinctions

Prayer has various degrees. At first it is only the prayer of the spoken word, but with this must go prayer of the mind and heart, warming it and maintaining it. Later, mind-in-heart prayer gains its independence: becoming sometimes active, stimulated by one's own efforts, and sometimes self-moving, bestowed as a gift. Prayer as a gift is the same as inward attraction towards God, and develops from it. Later on, when the state of the soul under the influence of this attraction becomes constant, mind-in-heart prayer will be active unceasingly. All earlier temporary attractions now become transformed into states of contemplation; and it is at this point that contemplative prayer begins. The state of contemplation is a captivity of the mind and of the entire vision by a spiritual object so overpowering that all outward things are forgotten, and wholly absent from the consciousness. The mind and consciousness become so completely immersed in the object contemplated that it is as though we no longer possess them.[1]

---

[1] Here Theophan apparently distinguishes five stages:
  (i) oral prayer
  (ii) mind-in-heart prayer, produced by our own efforts
  (iii) mind-in-heart prayer, bestowed as a gift
  (iv) unceasing mind-in-heart prayer
  (v) contemplative prayer (also described by Theophan as prayer of ravishment or ecstasy).
The last three stages are closely related, and cannot be sharply distinguished.

Prayer performed by man, prayer given by God, prayer of ecstasy

There is prayer which man himself makes; and there is prayer which God Himself gives to him who prays (1 Kings ii. 9: Sept.).[1] Who is there who does not know the first? And you must also know the second, at least in its inception. Anyone wishing to approach the Lord will first approach Him by prayer. He begins to go to church and to pray at home, with the help of a prayer book or without. But thoughts keep running away. He cannot manage to control them. All the same, the more he strives to pray, the more thoughts will quieten down, and the purer prayer will become. But the atmosphere of the soul is not purified until a small spiritual flame is kindled in the soul. This flame is the work of the grace of God; not a special grace, but one common to all. This flame appears when a man has attained a certain measure of purity in the general moral order of his life. When this small flame is kindled, or a permanent warmth is formed in the heart, the ferment of thoughts is stilled. The same thing happens in the soul as happened to the woman with an issue of blood: 'Her blood stanched' (Luke viii. 44). In this state, prayer more or less approaches permanency; and for this the Jesus Prayer serves as an intermediary. This is the limit to which prayer performed by man himself can rise. I think that this is very clear to you.

Further on in this state, another kind of prayer may be given, which comes to man instead of being performed by him. The spirit of prayer comes upon man and drives him into the depths of the heart, as if he were taken by the hand and forcibly led from one room to another. The soul is here taken captive by an invading force, and is kept willingly within, as long as this overwhelming power of prayer still holds sway over it. I know two degrees of such invasion. In the first, the soul sees everything and is conscious of itself and of its outer surroundings; it can reason and govern itself, it can even destroy this state if it so desires. This too, should be clear to you.

---

[1] 1 Samuel ii. 9 (Authorised Version). Here the text of the Septuagint differs from the Hebrew.

But the Holy Fathers, and especially St. Isaac the Syrian, mention a second degree of prayer which is given to or descends upon a man. Isaac considers that this prayer, which he calls ecstasy or ravishment, is higher than that described above. Here too, the spirit of prayer comes upon a man; but the soul, carried away by it, passes into such a state of contemplation that it forgets its outer surroundings, ceases to reason, and only contemplates; and it has no power to control itself or to break from this state. You remember how the Holy Fathers write of someone who began to pray before his evening meal and came to himself only next morning. This is the prayer of ravishment or contemplation. With some it has been accompanied by illumination of their faces, by light around them,[1] with others by levitation. St. Paul the Apostle was in this state when he was carried up into Paradise. And the Holy Prophets also were in the same state of ecstasy when the Spirit bore them away.

Gaze in wonder at the great mercy of God towards us sinners: a little effort and how great is the result. Rightly may we say to those who labour: Work on, for what you seek is of true value.

Three types of prayer: of the lips, of the mind, of the heart

You have probably heard such words as: oral prayer, mental prayer, prayer of the heart; you may also have heard discussions about each of them separately. What is the cause of this division of prayer into parts? Because it happens that sometimes through our negligence the tongue recites the holy words of prayer, but the mind wanders elsewhere: or the mind understands the words

---

1 A number of eastern saints have shared in the mystery of Our Lord's Transfiguration, their face or entire body being surrounded and illuminated with Divine Light, just as Christ's face and body were illuminated on Mount Tabor. A particularly impressive instance of this bodily transfiguration occurred in the life of a Russian saint, Seraphim of Sarov (1759–1833): see the eye-witness account by his friend Nicolas Motovilov, *Conversation of Saint Seraphim on the Aim of the Christian Life*, in *A Wonderful Revelation to the World*, Jordanville (N.Y.), 1953, pp. 23–5.

of the prayer, but the heart does not respond to them by feeling. In the first case prayer is only oral, and is not prayer at all, in the second, mental prayer joins the oral, but this prayer is still imperfect and incomplete. Complete and real prayer comes only when the prayer of word and thought is joined by prayer of feeling.

Spiritual or inner prayer comes when he who prays, after gathering his mind within his heart, from there directs his prayer to God in words no longer oral but silent: glorifying Him and giving thanks, confessing his sins with contrition before God, and asking from Him the spiritual and physical blessings that he needs. You must pray not only with words but with the mind, and not only with the mind but with the heart, so that the mind understands and sees clearly what is said in words, and the heart feels what the mind is thinking. All these combined together constitute real prayer, and if any of them are absent your prayer is either not perfect, or is not prayer at all.

The fire of prayer and Paradise in the soul

When inner prayer gains power, then it will control oral prayer, gaining dominion over external prayer and even absorbing it. As a result, the zeal of prayer will take fire, because then Paradise will be in the soul. If you content yourself with exterior prayer alone, you may cool in the work of prayer, even if you practise it with attention and understanding. The principal thing in prayer is a feeling heart.

Confine your mind within the words of prayer

I have already spoken more than once about how this work is to be done. You must not allow your thoughts to wander at random, but as soon as they run away, you must immediately bring them back, reproaching yourself, regretting and deploring this straying of the mind. St. John of the Ladder says of this, 'You must make a great effort to confine your mind within the words of prayer'.

WHAT IS PRAYER?

Prayer of the imagination, of the mind, of the heart

As we pass from without to within, we first encounter the powers of imagination and fantasy.[1] Many people stop here, not realizing that they must immediately pass beyond this first stage: for if we work chiefly through our imagination and fantasy, we are not yet praying in the correct way. This, then, is the first incorrect method of prayer. The second stage on the way within is represented by the reason, intellect, and mind, and in general by the rational and thinking power of the soul. Nor must we linger here, but pass on: and gathering this rational power together, we must descend into the heart. If we linger, we shall become involved in a second incorrect method of prayer, whose characteristic feature is that the mind remains in the head, wishing by itself to direct and govern everything in the soul. Nothing comes of these efforts: the mind pursues everything, but cannot dominate anything, and only undergoes defeats. This feebleness from which our mind suffers is described very fully by St. Simeon the New Theologian.[2] This second way of prayer can appropriately be termed 'mind-in-the-head', in contrast to the third way, which is 'mind-in-the-heart'. At this second stage, while this mental fermentation takes place in the head, the heart goes its own way; nobody watches over it, and so it is invaded by cares and passions, and only with great difficulty comes to itself again.

To this account of the second way of prayer, I would add a few words from the introduction to the writings of Gregory of Sinai,[3] written by the *staretz* Basil,[4] monk of the great

[1] On the meaning of 'imagination' here, see above, p. 25.

[2] St. Simeon the New Theologian (949–1022), Abbot of the Monastery of St. Mamas in Constantinople: probably the greatest of Byzantine mystical writers.

[3] St. Gregory of Sinai (late 13th cent.–1346), monk on Mount Athos, one of the leaders of the Hesychast Movement.

[4] *Staretz* Basil (died 1767), a Russian by birth, Igumen of several monasteries in Rumania. He wrote introductions to the works of various Greek authors who discuss the Jesus Prayer (see below, p. 106).

habit,[1] companion and friend of Paissy Velichkovsky.[2] Having quoted Simeon the New Theologian, *staretz* Basil adds: 'How can you hope to keep the mind intact merely by guarding your exterior sensations, when your thoughts by themselves stream in different directions and whirl towards material things? It is essential for the mind, in the hour of prayer, to withdraw as quickly as possible into the heart and to stand there, deaf and mute to all thoughts. Whoever withdraws only outwardly from seeing, hearing, and speaking, obtains little result. Enclose your mind in the inner cell of the heart, and then you will enjoy rest from evil thoughts; and you will experience the spiritual joy which is brought by inner prayer and attention of the heart.'

St. Hesychios[3] says: 'Our mind cannot defeat evil dreams by itself alone; and let it never hope to do so. Take heed, therefore, not to think highly of yourself like the old Israel, lest you also be delivered up to our invisible enemies. When the God of all creation delivered Israel from the Egyptians, the Israelites fashioned a molten image to be their helper. By the molten image you should understand our feeble mind: when it invokes Jesus Christ against the spirits of wickedness, it drives them away easily; but when in its folly it trusts wholly to itself, it experiences a sudden and grievous downfall.'

---

[1] Orthodox monks are divided into three grades: *rasophore* (one who wears the *rason* or cassock), monk of the little habit, and monk of the great habit (or *schema* monk). Only a few monks enter the third and highest of these grades, the great habit: in Russia a *schema* monk is normally expected to follow a life of strict seclusion and fasting (in Greek monasteries the rules for *schema* monks are often less rigorous).

[2] Paissy Velichkovsky (1722–94), Russian by origin, entered the monastic life on Mount Athos and later settled in Rumania, where he became Igumen of the monastery of Niamets. Editor of the Slavonic edition of the *Philokalia*. The spiritual and monastic renaissance in 19th century Russia was in large measure inspired by his disciples and followers.

[3] St. Hesychios of Batos was superior of a monastery on the Sinai peninsula during the 6th or 7th century.

WHAT IS PRAYER?

Desire and longing for God

What happens to the soul when we greatly desire to pray, or when we are drawn to prayer, and how should we behave?

Everyone experiences this desire in greater or lesser degree as they proceed on the path of the Christian life, once they have begun to seek God by personal effort, until they finally reach their goal of a living communion with Him. They also experience it after having attained to this goal. It is a state resembling that of a man plunged in deep thought, withdrawn within himself, concentrated in his soul, paying no attention to external surroundings, to people, things, and events. But when a man is plunged in thought it is the mind which is at work, whereas here it is the heart. When the longing for God comes, the soul is collected within itself, and stands before the face of God, and either pours out before Him its hopes and the sufferings of its heart, like Hannah, the mother of Samuel; or glorifies Him, like the most holy Virgin Mary; or stands before Him in wonder, as the Apostle Paul often stood. Here all personal actions, thoughts, and intentions cease; and everything external departs from the attention. The soul itself does not wish to be occupied with anything extraneous. This may happen in church or during the rule of prayer, or during reading or meditation, and even during some exterior occupations or in company. But in no case does it depend on your will. He who has once experienced this longing may remember it and desire its repetition, he may strive towards it, but he himself will never attract it by his own exertion: it comes of itself.

Only one thing depends on our free will—when this state of longing comes, do not allow yourself to destroy it, but take the utmost care, so as to give it full opportunity to remain within you as long as possible.

Two kinds of inner prayer

Inner prayer means standing with the mind in the heart before God, either simply living in His presence, or expressing

70

supplication, thanksgiving, and glorification. We must acquire the habit of always being in communion with God, without any image, any process of reasoning, any perceptible movement of thought. Such is the true expression of prayer. The essence of inner prayer, or standing before God with the mind in the heart, consists precisely in this.

Inner prayer consists of two states, one *strenuous*, when man himself strives for it, and the other *self-impelled*, when prayer exists and acts on its own. This last happens when we are drawn along involuntarily, but the first must be a constant object of endeavour. Although in itself such endeavour will not be successful because our thoughts are always being dispersed, yet as proof of our desire and effort to attain unceasing prayer, it will attract the mercy of the Lord; and because of this work God fills our heart from time to time with that compelling impulse through which spiritual prayer reveals itself in its true form.

'Self-moving' prayers

In the case of 'self-moving' prayers, when the spirit of prayer comes on a man, we have no power to choose which form of prayer shall be given to us; they are different streams of one and the same grace. But these 'self-moving' prayers are in fact of two kinds. In one kind the man has the power of obedience or of disobedience to this spirit; he can help it or can thwart it. In the other kind he has no power to do anything, but is driven into prayer and kept in it by a force outside himself, which leaves him no freedom to act differently. Thus complete absence of choice occurs only in this last kind of prayer. As regards all other kinds choice is possible.

Prayer of the Spirit

'But the Spirit itself maketh intercession for us with groanings which cannot be uttered' (Rom. viii. 26).

This will be easier to understand if we can relate it to something that happens in our own experience. The Spirit moves in us in the prayer which comes by itself. Usually we pray using either a prayer book or our own words. Prayer may be accompanied by feelings and sighings, but we cannot arouse them within ourselves deliberately. Besides these feelings and sighings, it sometimes happens that the very inspiration to pray comes by itself, forcing us to pray and giving no peace until prayer is completely poured out. This, or something similar, is what the Apostle describes. The content of such a prayer can seldom be clearly defined, but it is almost always inspired by surrender to the divine will, and by complete trust in the guidance of God, who knows better than we do what is good for our inner and outer being, who desires this for us more strongly than we do for ourselves, and who is ready to give us all that is good and to set all in order for us—as long as we ourselves do not put up a resistance. All prayers by the Holy Fathers which have come down to us are of this origin and are moved by the Spirit: that is why they remain so permanently effective.

The approach to contemplative prayer

In purely contemplative prayer, words and thoughts themselves disappear, not by our own wish, but of their own accord. Prayer of the mind changes into prayer of the heart, or rather into prayer of the mind in the heart: its appearance coincides with the birth of warmth in the heart. From now on in the usual course of spiritual life there is no other prayer. This prayer, taking deep root in the heart, may be without words or thought: it may consist only in a standing before God, in an opening of the heart to Him in reverence and love. It is a state of being irresistibly drawn within to stand before God in prayer; or it is the visitation of the spirit of prayer. But all this is not yet true contemplative prayer, which is prayer's highest state, appearing from time to time in God's elect.

Active and contemplative prayer

The action of prayer in the heart may be twofold. Sometimes

the mind reacts first, by cleaving to the Lord in unceasing remembrance of Him in the heart; sometimes it is the prayer itself that acts, when it is moved by the fire of joy and attracts the mind into the heart, holding it there in invocation of the Lord Jesus and in reverent standing before Him. The first kind of prayer requires effort, the second works by itself. In the first case, when the grip of passions is lessened, the action of the prayer begins to open out through fulfilment of commandments and warmth of heart, as a consequence of a strenuous invocation of the Lord Jesus. In the second case, the Spirit attracts the mind towards the heart and establishes it there in the depths, holding it from its usual wandering. In that case it is no longer like a prisoner who is taken away from Jerusalem into Assyria, but on the contrary it is a home-comer from Babylon to Zion, calling with the prophet: 'Thou, O God, art praised in Zion, and unto thee shall the vow be performed in Jerusalem' (Ps. lxiv. 2. Sept.).[1] Out of these two kinds of prayer there comes sometimes an active mind, sometimes a contemplative one. The active mind defeats the passions with the help of God. The contemplative mind sees God, in so far as this is possible for man.

The inner journey of the mind and heart

He who has repented travels towards the Lord. The way to God is an inner journey accomplished in the mind and heart. It is necessary so to attune the thoughts of the mind and the disposition of the heart that the spirit of man will always be with the Lord, as if joined with Him. He who is thus attuned is constantly enlightened by inner light, and receives in himself the rays of spiritual radiance (as Theodoret says), like Moses, whose face was glorified on the Mount because he was illumined by God. David refers to this, 'The light of thy countenance, O Lord, has been marked upon us' (Ps. iv. 7. Sept.). The means whereby this state can be achieved is prayer of the mind made in the heart. Only when this takes shape will the sight of the mind

[1] Ps. lxv. 1 (B.C.P.).

become clear,[1] and the spirit, beholding God clearly, will receive from Him the power to see and drive away everything which could put it to shame before God.

Yet there are many who expect to approach God merely by outer words and deeds. They live in expectation, but they never come near; for they do not follow the right way. To such we make this appeal: approach God with the mind and heart and you will be enlightened and will no longer be defeated by the enemy, who at present—despite all your external correctness—constantly overcomes you and puts you to shame in your thoughts and in the feelings of your heart. Drawing near to God in your mind and heart will give you power over all other movements of the soul, and power to put the enemy to shame whenever he attempts to shame you.

Pray as if beginning prayer for the first time

You must never regard any spiritual work as firmly established, and this is especially true of prayer; but always pray as if beginning for the first time. When we do a thing for the first time, we come to it fresh and with a new-born enthusiasm. If, when starting to pray, you always approach it as though you had never yet prayed properly, and only now for the first time wished to do so, you will always pray with a fresh and lively zeal. And all will go well.

If you are not successful in your prayer, do not expect success in anything. It is the root of all.

[1] Compare King Alfred's petition for 'clear eyes of the mind to see Thee'.

CHAPTER III

THE JESUS PRAYER

from various authors

(i) Secret Meditation[1]

The fruits of secret meditation

The wise man who is the owner of riches hides his treasures inside his house; for treasure which is on view excites the rapacity of robbers, and is coveted by the powerful ones of the earth. And in the same way the virtuous and humble monk hides his virtues as a rich man his treasures, and does not follow his own wishes. But he reproaches himself every hour and forcibly devotes his energies to secret meditation, following the words of Scripture: 'My heart grew hot within me, and a fire kindled in my meditation' (Ps. xxxviii. 4. Sept.).[2] What kind of fire? The fire of which Scripture speaks here is God: 'our God is a consuming fire' (Heb. xii. 29). Fire melts wax and dries up mud: in the same way secret meditation melts our evil thoughts and withers the passions of the soul; it enlightens our mind, makes the

---

[1] 'Secret meditation': in Greek, κρυπτὴ μελέτη; in Russian, тайное поучение. The term μελέτη (поучение) means literally 'practice', 'exercise', or 'study': in an ascetic and spiritual context, it embraces the ideas both of 'meditation' and of 'prayer'. According to Bishop Ignatii, 'Under the name of *meditation* (поучение) the Holy Fathers understand any short prayer or even any short spiritual thought, which they have acquired as a habit, and which they have endeavoured to assimilate with their mind and memory, in place of all other thoughts.' Thus the phrase 'secret meditation' can refer, among other things, to the practice of the Jesus Prayer, or to meditation upon some verse from the Psalms or other text in Scripture.

[2] Ps. xxxix. 4 (B.C.P.).

understanding radiant, and fills the heart with joy. Secret meditation wounds devils, and drives away thoughts of wickedness. He
who arms himself with this secret meditation, making his inner
man resplendent, is strengthened by God, fortified by the angels,
and glorified by men. Secret meditation and reading turn the soul
into an impregnable stronghold, an invincible fortress, a peaceful
haven, and they preserve it undisturbed and unshaken. The devils
are greatly disturbed and troubled when the monk arms himself
with this secret meditation and reading. Secret meditation is a
mirror for the mind and a light for the conscience; it tames lust,
calms fury, dispels wrath, drives away bitterness, puts irritability to flight, and banishes injustice. Secret meditation illumin-
ates the mind and expels laziness. From it is born the tenderness
that warms and melts the soul. Through it the fear of God enters
and dwells within you, touching you to tears. By secret meditation
a monk is given true humility of mind, untroubled prayer, a vigil
blessed by tenderness and warmth. Secret meditation disperses
evil thoughts, flogs the demons, sanctifies the body, teaches us
long-suffering and self-restraint, and keeps us mindful of Gehenna.
Secret meditation preserves the mind free of distractions and
helps it to reflect upon death. Secret meditation is full of every
kind of good work, adorned with every virtue; and it is far
removed from every evil deed.

ABBA ISAIAS[1]

Secret meditation and continual prayer

A certain brother by the name of John came from the coastal
country to the holy and great father Philemon,[2] and clasping his
feet, said to him: 'What must I do, Father, to be saved? I see
that my mind is distracted, and wanders hither and thither where
it should not.' After a short silence, Philemon said to him:
'This is a sickness suffered by those who are external, and it
remains in you because your love of God is not yet perfect;

[1] Abba Isaias, or St. Isaias the Hermit (died 488), lived as a monk first at
Scetis in Egypt, and then at Gaza in Palestine.

[2] Abba Philemon: an Egyptian hermit during the 6th–7th century.

up till now the warmth of the love and the knowledge of God has not yet arisen in you.' The brother asked him, 'What then shall I do?' 'Go,' answered the father, 'and for the time being practise secret meditation in your heart; this will cleanse your mind of its sickness.' The brother, not understanding what was told him, said to Philemon: 'What is this secret meditation, Father?' 'Go,' he answered, 'preserve sobriety in your heart, and in your mind repeat soberly, with fear and trembling, "Lord Jesus Christ, have mercy upon me." This is what the blessed Diadochos[1] prescribed for beginners.'

The brother left him, and by God's help and the prayers of the father he began to keep silence and to taste the sweetness of this secret meditation. But this lasted only for a short time. Since it suddenly departed from him and he could no longer maintain it or pray soberly, he came again to the father and told him what had happened. The father said: 'Now you have trod a little way on the path of silence and inner practice and tasted of its sweetness. Therefore keep it always in your heart. Whether you eat or drink, or talk to someone outside your cell or on the way somewhere, do not forget to recite this prayer with a sober and attentive mind, and to sing and meditate upon prayers and psalms. Even if you are satisfying some essential need, do not allow your mind to be idle, but let it meditate and pray in secret. All the time— when you drop off to sleep or wake up, when you eat or drink, or talk with someone—keep your heart at work secretly, sometimes meditating on a verse from the Psalms, and sometimes praying, "Lord Jesus Christ, Son of God, have mercy upon me."'

From the LIFE OF ABBA PHILEMON

Inner work must begin as soon as possible. This is extremely important

Gather yourself together in the heart, and there practise secret meditation. By this means, with the help of God's grace,

[1] St. Diadochos was Bishop of Photike in Epirus (North Greece) during the middle of the 5th century. His *Gnostic Chapters* are of particular importance in the historical development of the Jesus Prayer.

the spirit of zeal will be maintained in its true character—burning sometimes less and sometimes more brightly. Secret meditation sets our feet on the path of inner prayer, which is the most direct road to salvation. We may leave all else and turn only to this work, and all will be well. Conversely, if we fulfil all other duties and neglect this one task we shall bear no fruit.

He who does not turn within and look to this spiritual task, will make no progress. It would be true to say that this task is extremely difficult, especially at the beginning, but on the other hand it is direct and fruitful in result. A spiritual father should therefore introduce the practice of inner prayer among his children as early as possible, and confirm them in its use. It is even possible to start them in this before any exterior observances, or together with them; in any case it is essential not to leave it until too late. This is because the very seed of spiritual growth lies in this inner turning to God. All that is necessary is to make this clear, to emphasize its importance, and to explain the way to do it. When this pattern is woven into us then all exterior work will also be performed willingly, successfully and fruitfully: without it, outward activity will be like a rotten thread, always breaking. Note particularly that the practice must proceed step by step, slowly and with great restraint. Unless this way of life be adopted gradually it may lose its essential character and turn into nothing but an outward observance of rules. Therefore, although people do exist who proceed from outward rule to inner life, the unalterable principle must be this: to turn within as early as possible, and to kindle there the spirit of zeal.

It sounds on the face of it so simple, but unless you know about inner prayer you can sweat for a long while and produce no harvest. This is due to the nature of physical activity, which is easier and therefore attractive; inner activity is difficult and so it repels us. He who attaches himself to the first as essential, will himself gradually become material, and will accordingly cool down, his heart will be less moved, and he will go further and further away from inner work at the beginning, thinking to put it aside until the moment comes when he is ripe for it. Looking back later on he will realize that he has missed the moment. Instead of working gradually towards a full inner life he has all this while become incapable of so working. Not that we should abandon exterior work, which is, on the contrary, the support of that which goes on within: they should both be done together. Priority must go to inner worship, because one must serve God in spirit, must worship Him in spirit and truth. The two must be interdependent —bearing in mind their relative value. Let neither enforce claims upon the other, or be the cause of divided allegiance.

THEOPHAN THE RECLUSE

Dwell within and worship secretly

The most important thing that the Holy Fathers desired and recommended is the understanding of the spiritual state, and the art of maintaining it. There remains only one rule for whoever will attain this state: dwell within and worship secretly in the heart. Meditate on the thought of God, on the remembrance of death, and recollect your sins with self-reproach. Be conscious of these things and speak about them often to yourself—for example: Where am I going? or: I am a worm and no man. Secret meditation consists of pondering on such thoughts as these in our hearts, with due attention and feeling.

It is possible to sum up in this one short sentence the ways of warming and preserving the spirit of zeal: After waking, enter within yourself, stand enclosed in the heart, consider all the activity of the spiritual life, absorb yourself in a chosen part of it and there remain. Or, still more briefly: collect yourself and make secret prayer in your heart.

THEOPHAN THE RECLUSE

Avoiding numbness

Every day keep turning over in your mind some thought which has deeply impressed you and fallen into your heart. Unless you exercise your powers of thought, the soul becomes numb.

THEOPHAN THE RECLUSE

(ii) UNCEASING PRAYER

The way to unceasing prayer

Some godly thoughts come nearer the heart than others. Should this be so, after you have finished your prayers, continue to dwell on such a thought and remain feeding on it. This is the way to unceasing prayer.

THEOPHAN THE RECLUSE

Unceasing prayer without words

To raise up the mind towards the Lord, and to say with contrition: 'Lord, have mercy! Lord, grant Thy blessing! Lord, help!'—this is to cry out in prayer to God. But if feeling towards God is born and lives in your heart, then you will possess unceasing prayer, even though your lips recite no words and your body is not outwardly in a posture of prayer.

THEOPHAN THE RECLUSE

Pray at all times and in all places

'Praying always with all prayer and supplication in the spirit' (Eph. vi. 18).

Speaking of the necessity of prayer, the Apostle indicates here how we must pray in order to be heard. Pray, he says, 'with all prayer and supplication', in other words, very ardently, with pain in the heart and a burning striving towards God. And pray, he says, 'always', at any time; by this he urges us to pray persistently and indefatigably. Prayer must not be simply an occupation for a certain time, but a permanent state of the spirit. Make sure, says St. John Chrysostom, that you do not limit your prayer merely to a particular part of the day. Turn to prayer at any time, as the Apostle says in another place: 'Pray without ceasing' (1 Thess. v. 17). Thirdly, Paul tells us to pray 'in the spirit': in other words prayer must be not only outward, but also inner, an activity of the mind in the heart. In this lies the essence of prayer, which is the raising of the mind and heart towards God.

The Holy Fathers make a distinction, however, between prayer of the mind in the heart and prayer moved by the Spirit. The first is the conscious action of the praying màn, but the second comes to a man; and although he is aware of it, it works by itself independently of his efforts. This second kind of prayer, moved by the Spirit, is not something that we can recommend people to practise, because it does not lie in our power to achieve it. We can desire it, seek it, and receive it gratefully, but we cannot arrive at it whenever we want to. But in those who are purified, prayer is most generally moved by the Spirit. Therefore we must suppose that the Apostle refers to prayer of the mind in the heart when he says: 'Pray in the spirit.' One can add, pray with the mind in the heart with the desire of attaining to prayer moved by the Spirit. Such a prayer holds the soul consciously before the face of the ever-present God. Attracting the divine ray towards itself, and reflecting this same ray from itself, it disperses the enemies. One can say with certainty that no devils can draw near to the soul in such a state. Only in this way can we pray at any time, in any place.

THEOPHAN THE RECLUSE

The secret of unceasing prayer—love

'Pray without ceasing', St. Paul writes to the Thessalonians (1 Thess. v. 17). And in other epistles, he commands: 'Praying always with all supplication in the spirit' (Eph. vi. 18), 'continue in prayer and watch in the same' (Col. iv. 2), 'continuing instant in prayer' (Rom. xii. 12). Also the Saviour Himself teaches the need for constancy and persistency in prayer, in the parable about the importunate widow, who won over the unrighteous judge by the persistency of her appeals (Luke xviii. 1–8). It is clear from this that unceasing prayer is not an accidental prescription, but the essential characteristic of the Christian spirit. The life of a Christian, according to the Apostle, 'is hid with Christ in God' (Col. iii. 3). So the Christian must live in God continuously, with attention and feeling: to do this is to pray without ceasing. We are also taught that every Christian is 'the temple of God', in which 'dwelleth the Spirit of God' (1 Cor. iii. 16; vi. 19; Rom. viii. 9). It is this 'Spirit', always present and pleading in him, that prays within him 'with groanings that cannot be uttered' (Rom. viii. 26), and so teaches him how to pray without ceasing.

The very first action of God's grace in the turning of the sinner to God manifests itself by the bending of his mind and heart towards God. When later, after repentance and dedication of his life to God, the grace of God which acted from without descends on him and remains within him through the sacraments, then the turning of the mind and heart to God, which is the essence of prayer, will also become unchangeable and permanent in him. This turning is made evident in different degrees, and like any other gift, must be renewed. It is refreshed according to its kind: by the effort of prayer and especially by patient and attentive practice of Church prayers. Pray without ceasing, exert yourself in prayer, and you will achieve incessant prayer, which will act of itself in the heart without special effort.

It is clear to everyone that the advice of the Apostle is not carried out merely by the practice of established prayers at certain set hours, but requires a permanent walking before God, a dedication of all one's activities to Him who is all-seeing and omnipresent, an ever-fervent appeal to heaven with the mind in the heart. The whole of life, in all its manifestations, must be permeated by prayer. But its secret is love for the Lord. As the bride, loving the bridegroom, is not separated from him in remembrance and feeling, so the soul, united with God in love, remains in constancy with Him, directing warm appeals to Him from the heart. 'He that is joined unto the Lord is one spirit' (1 Cor. vi. 17).

THEOPHAN THE RECLUSE

UNCEASING PRAYER

The practice of the Apostles

I remember that St. Basil the Great[1] solved the question how the Apostles could pray without ceasing, in this way: in everything they did, he replied, they thought of God and lived in constant devotion to Him. This spiritual state was their unceasing prayer.

THEOPHAN THE RECLUSE

Unceasing prayer as an implicit attitude

You regret that the Jesus Prayer is not unceasing, that you do not recite it constantly. But constant repetition is not required. What is required is a constant aliveness to God—an aliveness present when you talk, read, watch, or examine something. But since you are already practising the Jesus Prayer in the correct manner, continue as you are doing now, and in due course the prayer will widen its scope.

THEOPHAN THE RECLUSE

Standing always before God with reverence

We can sometimes spend all the time set aside for prayer by the rule in reciting one psalm, composing our own prayer from each verse. Again, we can sometimes spend all the time allotted by the rule in reciting the Jesus Prayer with prostrations. We can also do a little of each of these things. What God asks for is the heart (Prov. xxiii. 26); and it is enough that it should stand before Him with reverence. Standing always before God with reverence is unceasing prayer: such is its exact description; and in this regard the rule of prayer is only fuel for the fire, or the throwing of wood into a stove.

THEOPHAN THE RECLUSE

[1] St. Basil the Great (c. 330–79), Archbishop of Caesarea in Cappadocia (Asia Minor). Friend of St. Gregory the Theologian (see p. 87, n. 1), and elder brother of St. Gregory of Nyssa: these three are known collectively as the Cappadocian Fathers, and their writings have exercised a formative influence upon Orthodox theology.

THE JESUS PRAYER

The fruits of unceasing prayer

Through unceasing prayer the ascetic attains true spiritual poverty: learning to ask unceasingly for God's help, he gradually loses trust in himself. If he does something successfully, he sees in it not his own success but God's mercy, for which he prays to God unceasingly. Unceasing prayer leads to the acquisition of faith, because he who prays unceasingly begins gradually to feel the presence of God. This feeling little by little grows and increases to such a degree that the spiritual eye sees God in His Providence more clearly than the physical eye sees material objects in the world; and then the heart knows by immediate experience the presence of God. He who has seen God in such a manner and has felt His presence thus, cannot fail to believe in Him with a living faith, which will be shown forth in deeds.

Unceasing prayer overcomes evil through hope in God, it leads a man into a holy simplicity, weaning his mind from its habit of diversity in thought, and from devising plans about himself and his neighbours, keeping him always in scantiness and humility of thoughts. This composes his training. He who prays ceaselessly gradually loses the habit of wandering thoughts, of distraction, of being filled with vain worries, and the more deeply this training in holiness and humility enters the soul and takes root in it, the more he loses these habits of mind. Finally he becomes as a child, as he is commanded in the Gospel, and is made a fool for Christ's sake, that is, he loses the false reason of the world, and receives from God a spiritual understanding.

By unceasing prayer curiosity, mistrustfulness and suspicion are destroyed, and because of this other people begin to seem good in our eyes. From such a mortgage of the heart in their favour, love of mankind is born. He who prays without ceasing dwells constantly in the Lord, knows the Lord as God, acquires fear of Him, by fear enters into purity, and by purity into divine love. The love of God fills him with the gifts of the Spirit, whose temple he is.

BISHOP IGNATII

84

I have set the Lord always before me

By the grace of God there comes a prayer of the heart alone, spiritual prayer, quickened in the heart by the Holy Spirit. He who prays is conscious of it, although it is not he who makes the prayer, for it goes on within him by itself. Such prayer is the attribute of the perfect. But the prayer which is accessible to everyone and which is required from all, is prayer in which thought and feeling are always united with the words.

There is also another kind of prayer, which is called standing before God, when he who prays is wholly concentrated within his heart and mentally contemplates God, present to him and within him. At the same time he experiences the feelings corresponding to such a state—fear of God and worshipful admiration of Him in all his greatness; faith and hope; love and surrender to His will; contrition and readiness for every sacrifice. Such a state comes to one deeply absorbed in ordinary prayer of word, mind, and heart. He who prays thus for a long time and in the proper way will enjoy such a state more and more frequently until it may finally become permanent: then it can be called walking before God, and it constitutes unceasing prayer. St. David was in this state when he testified of himself: 'I have set the Lord always before me; for he is on my right hand, therefore I shall not be shaken' (Ps. xv. 8. Sept.).[1]

THEOPHAN THE RECLUSE

Prayer that repeats itself

It often happens that no inner activity occupies a person during the fulfilment of outward duties, so that his life remains soulless. How can we avoid this ? Into every duty a God-fearing heart must be put, a heart constantly permeated by the thought of God; and this will be the door through which the soul will enter into active life. All endeavour must be directed towards the ceaseless thought of God, towards the constant awareness of His presence:

[1] Ps. xvi. 9 (B.C.P.).

'Seek the Lord . . . Seek his face constantly' (Ps. civ. 4. Sept.).[1]
It is on this basis that sobriety and inner prayer rest.

God is everywhere: see that your thoughts too are always with
God. How can this be done? Thoughts jostle one another like
swarming gnats, and emotions follow on the thoughts. In order
to make their thought hold to one thing, the Fathers used to
accustom themselves to the continual repetition of a short prayer,
and from this habit of constant repetition this small prayer clung
to the tongue in such a way that it repeated itself of its own accord. In this manner their thought clung to the prayer and,
through the prayer, to the constant remembrance of God. Once
this habit has been acquired, the prayer holds us in the remembrance of God, and the remembrance of God holds us in prayer;
they mutually support each other. Here, then, is a way of
walking before God.

Inner prayer begins when we establish our attention in the
heart, and from the heart offer prayer to God. Spiritual activity
starts when we stand with attention in the heart in recollection
of the Lord, rejecting every other thought that tries to enter in.

THEOPHAN THE RECLUSE

O my God, what severity is here

The principal monastic rule is to remain constantly with God in
mind and heart, that is, to pray unceasingly. To keep this endeavour alight and warm, definite prayers are laid down—the
cycle of daily services performed in church, and certain rules
of prayer for the cell. But the chief thing is to possess a constant
feeling for God. It is this feeling that gives us power in the spiritual
life, keeping our heart warm. It is this feeling that constitutes
our rule. So long as this feeling is there, all other rules are
replaced by it. If it is absent, no amount of strenuous reading
can take its place. Prayers are meant to feed this feeling, and if
they fail to do so they are no use: they are only labour that bears
no fruit—like an outer garment with no body inside or like a body

[1] Ps. cv. 4 (B.C.P.).

that has no soul. O my God, what severity is here! But one cannot describe things except as they are.

THEOPHAN THE RECLUSE

A command addressed to all

Let no-one think, my fellow Christians, that only priests and monks need to pray without ceasing, and not laymen. No, no: every Christian without exception ought to dwell always in prayer. Gregory the Theologian[1] teaches all Christians that the Name of God must be remembered in prayer as often as one draws breath.

When the Apostle commanded us to 'Pray without ceasing' (1 Thess. v. 17), he meant that we must pray inwardly with our mind: and this is something that we can do always. For when we are engaged in manual labour and when we walk or sit down, when we eat or when we drink, we can always pray inwardly and practise prayer of the mind, true prayer, pleasing to God. Let us work with our body and pray with our soul. Let our outer man perform physical work, and let the inner man be consecrated wholly and completely to the service of God and never flag in the spiritual work of inner prayer. This is also commanded by Jesus, the God-man, when He says in the Holy Gospel: 'But thou, when thou prayest, enter into thy closet, and when thou hast shut thy door, pray to thy Father which is in secret' (Matt. vi. 6). The closet of the soul is the body, the doors are the five bodily senses. The soul enters its closet when the mind does not wander hither and thither over worldly things, but remains within our heart. Our senses are closed and remain so, when we do not allow them to cling to outward and visible things; and

---

[1] St. Gregory the Theologian, usually known in the west as Gregory of Nazianzus (329–389): one of the three Cappadocian Fathers. As Bishop of Constantinople, he presided at the second Ecumenical Council, held in that city in 381. A brilliant orator, he is especially remembered for his sermons and homilies.

in this way our mind remains free from all worldly attachment, and by its secret and inward prayer is united with God our Father.

Attributed to ST. GREGORY PALAMAS[1]

(iii) THE JESUS PRAYER

For laymen as well as monks

Every Christian must always remember that he should unite with the Lord our Saviour with all his being, letting Him come and dwell in his mind and in his heart; and the surest way to achieve such a union with the Lord, next to Communion of His Flesh and Blood, is the inner Jesus Prayer.

Is the Jesus Prayer obligatory for laymen too, and not only for monks? Indeed it is obligatory, for, as we said, *every* Christian should be united with the Lord in his heart, and the best means to achieve such a union is precisely the Jesus Prayer.

BISHOP JUSTIN[2]

The power of the Name

What shall we say of this divine prayer, in invocation of the Saviour, 'Lord Jesus Christ, Son of God, have mercy upon me'?

It is a prayer and a vow and a confession of faith, conferring upon us the Holy Spirit and divine gifts, cleansing the heart, driving out devils. It is the indwelling presence of Jesus Christ within us, and a fountain of spiritual reflections and divine

[1] St. Gregory Palamas (1296–1359), Archbishop of Thessalonica: the greatest theologian in the Hesychast movement. His doctrine of prayer and teaching concerning the Divine Light were sharply attacked in his life-time, but were confirmed by two Councils (Constantinople: 1341, 1351) and so came to be accepted by the Orthodox Church as a whole.

[2] Justin (Polyansky), a celebrated spiritual writer in Russia during the late 19th and early 20th centuries, Bishop first of Tobolsk and later of Ryazan.

thoughts. It is remission of sins, healing of soul and body, and shining of divine illumination; it is a well of God's mercy, bestowing upon the humble revelations and initiation into the mysteries of God. It is our only salvation, for it contains within itself the saving Name of our God, the only Name upon which we call, the Name of Jesus Christ the Son of God. 'For there is none other name under heaven given among men, whereby we must be saved,' as the Apostle says (Acts iv. 12).

That is why all believers must continually confess this Name: both to preach the faith and as testimony to our love for the Lord Jesus Christ, from which nothing must ever separate us; and also because of the grace that comes to us from His name, and because of the remission of sins, the healing, sanctification, enlightenment, and, above all, the salvation which it confers. The Holy Gospel says: 'These are written, that ye might believe that Jesus is the Christ, the Son of God.' See, such is faith. And the Gospel adds, 'that believing ye might have life through his Name' (John xx. 31). See, such is salvation and life.

ST. SIMEON OF THESSALONICA[1]

The simplicity of the Jesus Prayer

The practice of the Jesus Prayer is simple. Stand before the Lord with the attention in the heart, and call to Him: 'Lord Jesus Christ, Son of God, have mercy on me!' The essential part of this is not in the words, but in faith, contrition, and self-surrender to the Lord. With these feelings one can stand before the Lord even without any words, and it will still be prayer.

THEOPHAN THE RECLUSE

Under God's eye

Work with the Jesus Prayer. May God bless you. But with the habit of reciting this prayer orally, unite remembrance of the

[1] St. Simeon, Archbishop of Thessalonica (died 1429): Byzantine theologian and liturgist.

Lord, accompanied by fear and piety. The principal thing is to walk before God, or under God's eye, aware that God is looking at you, searching your soul and your heart, seeing all that is there. This awareness is the most powerful lever in the mechanism of the inner spiritual life.

THEOPHAN THE RECLUSE

A refuge for the indolent

From experience in the spiritual life, it can fairly be concluded that he who has zeal to pray needs no teaching how to perfect himself in prayer. Patiently continued, the effort of prayer itself will lead us to prayer's very summit.

But what are weak and indolent people to do, and especially those who, before they have understood the true nature of prayer, have become hardened by outward routine, and cooled by their formal reading of the appointed prayers ? As a refuge and source of strength they can still use the technique for practising the Jesus Prayer. And is it not chiefly for them that this technique was invented, so as to graft true inner prayer into their hearts ?

THEOPHAN THE RECLUSE

A remedy against drowsiness

It is written in books, that when the Jesus Prayer gains force and establishes itself in the heart, then it fills us with energy and dispels drowsiness. But for it to become habitual to the tongue is one thing, and for it to be established in the heart is another.

THEOPHAN THE RECLUSE

Delve deeply

Delve deeply into the Jesus Prayer, with all the power that you possess. It will draw you together, giving you a sense of strength in the Lord, and will result in your being with Him constantly whether alone or with other people, when you do housework and when you read or pray. Only you must attribute the power of this prayer, not to the repetition of certain words, but to the turning of the mind and heart towards the Lord in these words—to the action accompanying the speech.

THEOPHAN THE RECLUSE

A song sung with understanding

As the Apostle said: 'I had rather speak five words with my understanding . . . than ten thousand words in an unknown tongue' (1 Cor. xiv. 19). Before everything else it is necessary to purify the mind and the heart with these few words, repeating them unceasingly in the depth of the heart: 'Lord Jesus Christ, have mercy upon me',[1] so that this prayer ascends as a song that is sung with understanding. Everyone who begins, filled though he may be with passions, can offer this prayer through the vigilance of his heart. It sings within him only when he is purified by spiritual prayer.

PAISSY VELICHKOVSKY

A lantern unto our feet

Learn to practise prayer of the mind in the heart; for the Jesus Prayer is a lantern unto our feet and a star leading us on the way to heaven, as the Holy Fathers teach in the *Philokalia*. The Jesus Prayer, shining ceaselessly in the mind and heart, is a sword against fleshly weakness and against the evil desires of gluttony and lust. After the opening words 'Lord Jesus Christ, Son of God,' you may continue thus, 'by the Mother of God have mercy upon me, a sinner.'

[1] In Slavonic, the phrase 'Lord Jesus Christ, have mercy upon me' contains exactly five words, not seven: hence the appropriateness of Paissy's quotation from 1 Cor.

Outward prayer alone is insufficient. God hearkens to the mind; and those monks who do not combine inner with exterior prayer are no monks, but are like firewood that is burnt out. The monk who does not know, or who has forgotten, the practice of the Jesus Prayer, has not the seal of Christ. Books cannot teach us inner prayer, they can only show us external methods for practising it. One must have persistence in performing it.

THEOPHAN THE RECLUSE

The hands at work, the mind and heart with God

You have read about the Jesus Prayer, have you not? And you know what it is from practical experience. Only with the help of this prayer can the necessary order of the soul be firmly maintained; only through this prayer can we preserve our inner order undisturbed even when distracted by household cares. This prayer alone makes it possible to fulfil the injunction of the Fathers: the hands at work, the mind and heart with God. When this prayer becomes grafted in our heart, then there are no inner interruptions and it continues always in the same, evenly flowing way.

The path to achievement of a systematic interior order is very hard, but it *is* possible to preserve this (or a similar) state of mind during the various and inevitable duties you have to perform; and what makes it possible is the Jesus Prayer when it is grafted in the heart. How can it be so grafted? Who knows? But it does happen. He who strives is increasingly conscious of this engrafting, without knowing how it has been achieved. To strive for this inner order, we must walk always in the presence of God, repeating the Jesus Prayer as frequently as possible. As soon as there is a free moment, begin again at once, and the engrafting will be achieved.

One of the means of renewing the Jesus Prayer and bringing it to life is by reading, but it is best to read mainly about prayer.

THEOPHAN THE RECLUSE

THE JESUS PRAYER

The Jesus Prayer, and the warmth which accompanies it

To pray is to stand spiritually before God in our heart in glorification, thanksgiving, supplication, and contrite penitence. Everything must be spiritual. The root of all prayer is devout fear of God; from this comes belief about God and faith in Him, submission of oneself to God, hope in God, and cleaving to Him with the feeling of love, in oblivion of all created things. When prayer is powerful, all these spiritual feelings and movements are present in the heart with corresponding vigour.

How does the Jesus Prayer help us in this?

Through the feeling of warmth which develops in and around the heart as the effect of this Prayer.

The habit of prayer is not formed suddenly, but requires long work and toil.

The Jesus Prayer, and the warmth which accompanies it, helps better than anything else in the formation of the habit of prayer.

Note that these are the means, and not the deed itself.

It is possible for both the Jesus Prayer and the feeling of warmth to be present without real prayer. This does indeed happen, however strange it may seem.

When we pray we must stand in our mind before God, and think of Him alone. Yet various thoughts keep jostling in the mind, and draw it away from God. In order to teach the mind to rest on one thing, the Holy Fathers used short prayers and acquired the habit of reciting them unceasingly. This unceasing repetition of a short prayer kept the mind on the thought of God and dispersed all irrelevant thoughts. They adopted various short prayers, but it is the Jesus Prayer which has become particularly established amongst us and is most generally employed: 'Lord Jesus Christ, Son of God, have mercy upon me, a sinner!'

So this is what the Jesus Prayer is. It is one among various short prayers, oral like all others. Its purpose is to keep the mind on the single thought of God.

Whoever has formed the habit of this Prayer and uses it properly, really does remember God incessantly.

93

Since the remembrance of God in a sincerely believing heart is naturally accompanied by a sense of piety, hope, thanksgiving, devotion to God's will, and by other spiritual feelings, the Jesus Prayer, which produces and preserves this remembrance of God, is called *spiritual* prayer. It is rightly so called only when it is accompanied by these spiritual feelings. But when not accompanied by them it remains oral like any other prayer of the same type.

This is how one should think of the Jesus Prayer. Now what is the meaning of this warmth which accompanies the practice of the Prayer?

In order to keep the mind on one thing by the use of a short prayer, it is necessary to preserve attention and so lead it into the heart: for so long as the mind remains in the head, where thoughts jostle one another, it has no time to concentrate on one thing. But when attention descends into the heart, it attracts all the powers of the soul and body into one point there. This concentration of all human life in one place is immediately reflected in the heart by a special sensation that is the beginning of future warmth. This sensation, faint at the beginning, becomes gradually stronger, firmer, deeper. At first only tepid, it grows into warm feeling and concentrates the attention upon itself. And so it comes about that, whereas in the initial stages the attention is kept in the heart by an effort of will, in due course this attention, by its own vigour, gives birth to warmth in the heart. This warmth then holds the attention without special effort. From this, the two go on supporting one another, and must remain inseparable; because dispersion of attention cools the warmth, and diminishing warmth weakens attention.

From this there follows a rule of the spiritual life: if you keep the heart alive towards God, you will always be in remembrance of God. This rule is laid down by St. John of the Ladder.

The question now arises whether this warmth is spiritual. No, it is *not* spiritual. It is ordinary physical warmth. But since it keeps the attention of the mind in the heart, and thus helps the development there of the spiritual movements described earlier, it is called spiritual—provided, however, that it is not accompanied by sensual pleasure, however slight, but keeps the soul and body in sober mood.

From this it follows that when the warmth accompanying the Jesus Prayer does not include spiritual feelings, it should not be called spiritual, but simply warm-blooded. There is nothing in itself bad about this warm-blooded feeling, unless it is connected with sensual pleasure, however slight. If it is so connected, it is bad and must be suppressed.

Things begin to go wrong when the warmth moves about in parts of the body lower than the heart. And matters become still worse when, in enjoyment of this warmth, we imagine it to be all that matters, without bothering about spiritual feelings or even about remembrance of God; and so we set our heart only on having this warmth. This wrong course is occasionally possible, though not for all people, nor at all times. It must be noticed and corrected, for otherwise only physical warmth will remain, and we must not consider this warmth as spiritual or due to grace. This warmth is spiritual only when it is accompanied by the spiritual impetus of prayer. Anyone who calls it spiritual without this movement is mistaken. And anyone who imagines it to be due to grace is still more in error.

Warmth which is filled with grace is of a special nature and it is only this which is truly spiritual. It is distinct from the warmth of the flesh, and does not produce any noticeable changes in the body, but manifests itself by a subtle feeling of sweetness.

Everyone can easily identify and distinguish spiritual warmth by this particular feeling. Each must do it for himself: this is no business for an outsider.

THEOPHAN THE RECLUSE

The easiest way to acquire unceasing prayer

To acquire the habit of the Jesus Prayer, so that it takes root in ourselves, is the easiest way of ascending into the region of unceasing prayer. Men of the greatest experience have found, through God's enlightenment, that this form of prayer is a simple yet most effective means of establishing and strengthening the whole of the spiritual and ascetic life; and in their rules for prayer they have left detailed instructions about it.

In all our efforts and ascetic struggles, what we seek is purification of the heart and restoration of the spirit. There are two ways to this: the active way, the practice of the ascetic labours; and the contemplative way, the turning of the mind to God. By the first way the soul becomes purified and so receives God; by the second way the God of whom the soul becomes aware Himself burns away every impurity and thus comes to dwell in the purified soul. The whole of this second way is summed up in the one Jesus Prayer, as St. Gregory of Sinai says[1]: 'God is gained either by activity and work, or by the art of invoking the Name of Jesus.' He adds that the first way is longer than the second, the second being quicker and more effective. For this reason some of the Holy Fathers have given prime importance, among all the different kinds of spiritual exercise, to the Jesus Prayer. It enlightens, strengthens, and animates; it defeats all enemies visible and invisible, and leads directly to God. See how powerful and effective it is! The Name of the Lord Jesus is the treasury of all good things, the treasury of strength and of life in the spirit.

It follows from this that we should from the very first give full instructions on the practice of the Jesus Prayer to everyone who repents or begins to seek the Lord. Only following on from this should we introduce the beginner into other practices, because it is in this way that he can most quickly become steadfast and spiritually aware, and achieve inner peace. Many people, not knowing this, may be said to waste their time and labour in going no further than the formal and external activities of the soul and body.

The practice of prayer is called an 'art', and it is a very simple one. Standing with consciousness and attention in the heart, cry out unceasingly: 'Lord Jesus Christ, Son of God, have mercy upon me,' without having in your mind any visual concept or image, believing that the Lord sees you and listens to you.

It is important to keep your consciousness in the heart, and

[1] See pp. 114–15.

as you do so to control your breathing a little so as to keep time with the words of the prayer. But the most important thing is to believe that God is near and hears. Say the prayer for God's ear alone.

At the beginning this prayer remains for a long time only an activity like any other, but in time it passes into the mind and finally takes root in the heart.

There are deviations from this right way of praying; therefore we must learn it from someone who knows all about it. Mistakes occur chiefly from the attention being in the head and not in the heart. He who keeps his attention in the heart is safe. Safer still is he who at all times clings to God in contrition, and prays to be delivered from illusion.

THEOPHAN THE RECLUSE

One thought, or the thought of One only

This short prayer to Jesus has a higher purpose—to deepen your remembrance of God and your feeling towards Him. These callings out of the soul to God are all too easily disrupted by the first incoming impression; and besides, in spite of these callings, thoughts continue to jostle in your head like mosquitoes. To stop this jostling, you must bind the mind with one thought, or the thought of One only. An aid to this is a short prayer, which helps the mind to become simple and united: it develops feeling towards God and is engrafted with it. When this feeling arises within us, the consciousness of the soul becomes established in God, and the soul begins to do everything according to His will. Together with the short prayer, you must keep your thought and attention turned towards God. But if you limit your prayer to words only, you are as 'sounding brass'.

THEOPHAN THE RECLUSE

'Techniques' and 'methods' do not matter: one thing alone is essential

The prayer, 'Lord Jesus Christ, Son of God, have mercy upon me' is an oral prayer like any other. There is nothing special about it in itself, but it receives all its power from the state of mind in which it is made.

The various methods described by the Fathers (sitting down, making prostrations, and the other techniques used when performing this prayer) are not suitable for everyone: indeed without a personal director they are actually dangerous. It is better not to try them. There is just one method which is obligatory for all: *to stand with the attention in the heart*. All other things are beside the point, and do not lead to the crux of the matter.

It is said of the fruit of this prayer, that there is nothing higher in the world. This is wrong. As if it were some talisman! Nothing in the words of the prayer and their uttering can alone bring forth its fruit. All fruit can be received without this prayer, and even without any oral prayer, but merely by directing the mind and heart towards God.

The essence of the whole thing is *to be established in the remembrance of God, and to walk in His presence*. You can say to anyone: 'Follow whatever methods you like—recite the Jesus Prayer, perform bows and prostrations,[1] go to Church: do what you wish, only strive to be always in constant remembrance of God.' I remember meeting a man in Kiev who said: 'I did not use any methods at all, I did not know the Jesus Prayer, yet by God's mercy I walk always in His presence. But how this has come to pass, I myself do not know. God gave!'

It is most important to realize that prayer is always God-given: otherwise we may confuse the gift of grace with some achievement of our own.

People say: attain the Jesus Prayer, for that is inner prayer. This is not correct. The Jesus Prayer is a good means to arrive at inner prayer, but in itself it is not inner but outer prayer. Those who attain the habit of the Jesus Prayer do very well.

---

[1] In Orthodox practice it is common to bow or prostrate oneself after making the sign of the Cross. This bowing or prostration takes two main forms:

(i) a profound bow from the waist, touching the ground with fingers of the right hand

(ii) a full prostration, touching the ground with the forehead.

But if they stop only at this and go no further, they stop half way.

Even though we are reciting the Jesus Prayer, it is still necessary for us to keep the thought of God: otherwise the Prayer is dry food. It is good that the Name of Jesus should cleave to your tongue. But with this it is still possible not to remember God at all and even to harbour thoughts which are opposed to Him. Consequently everything depends on conscious and free turning to God, and on a balanced effort to hold oneself in this.

THEOPHAN THE RECLUSE

Why the Jesus Prayer is stronger than other prayers

The Jesus Prayer is like any other prayer. It is stronger than all other prayers only in virtue of the all-powerful Name of Jesus, Our Lord and Saviour. But it is necessary to invoke His Name with a full and unwavering faith—with a deep certainty that He is near, sees and hears, pays whole-hearted attention to our petition, and is ready to fulfil it and to grant what we seek. There is nothing to be ashamed of in such a hope. If fulfilment is sometimes delayed, this may be because the petitioner is still not yet ready to receive what he asks.

THEOPHAN THE RECLUSE

Not a talisman

The Jesus Prayer is not some talisman. Its power comes from faith in the Lord, and from a deep union of the mind and heart with Him. With such a disposition, the invocation of the Lord's Name becomes very effective in many ways. But a mere repetition of the words does not signify anything.

THEOPHAN THE RECLUSE

Mechanical repetition leads to nothing

Do not forget that you must not limit yourself to a mechanical repetition of the words of the Jesus Prayer. This will lead to nothing except a habit of repeating the prayer automatically with the tongue, without even thinking about it. There is of course nothing wrong in this, but it constitutes only the extreme outer limit of the work.

The essential thing is to stand consciously in the presence of the Lord, with fear, faith and love.

THEOPHAN THE RECLUSE

Oral and inner prayer

One can recite the Jesus Prayer with the mind in the heart without movement of the tongue. This is better than oral prayer. Use oral prayer as a support to inner prayer. Sometimes it is required in order to strengthen inner prayer.

THEOPHAN THE RECLUSE

Avoid visual concepts

Hold no intermediate image between the mind and the Lord when practising the Jesus Prayer. The words pronounced are merely a help, and are not essential. The principal thing is to stand before the Lord with the mind in the heart. This, and not the words, is inner spiritual prayer. The words here are as much or as little the essential part of the prayer as the words of any other prayer. The essential part is to dwell in God, and this walking before God means that you live with the conviction ever before your consciousness that God is in you, as He is in everything: you live in the firm assurance that He sees all that is within you, knowing you better than you know yourself. This awareness of the eye of God looking at your inner being must not be accompanied by any visual concept, but must be confined to a simple conviction or feeling. A man in a warm room feels how the warmth envelops and penetrates him. The same must be the effect on our spiritual nature of the all-encompassing presence of God, who is the fire in the room of our being.

The words 'Lord Jesus Christ, Son of God, have mercy upon

me' are only the instrument and not the essence of the work; but they are an instrument which is very strong and effective, for the Name of the Lord Jesus is fearful to the enemies of our salvation and a blessing to all who seek Him. Do not forget that this practice is simple, and must not have anything fanciful about it. Pray about everything to the Lord, to our most pure Lady, to your Guardian Angel; and they will teach you everything, either directly or through others.

THEOPHAN THE RECLUSE

Images and illusion

In order not to fall into illusion[1] while practising inner prayer, do not permit yourself any concepts, images, or visions. For vivid imaginings, darting to and fro, and flights of fancy do not cease even when the mind stands in the heart and recites prayer: and no one is able to rule over them, except those who have attained perfection by the grace of the Holy Spirit, and who have acquired stability of mind through Jesus Christ.

ST. NIL SORSKI[2]

Dispel all images from your mind

You ask about prayer. I find in the writings of the Holy Fathers, that when you pray you must dispel all images from your mind. That is what I also try to do, forcing myself to realize that God is everywhere—and so (among other places) here, where my thoughts and feelings are. I cannot succeed in freeing myself entirely from images, but gradually they evaporate more and more. There comes a point when they disappear completely.

THEOPHAN THE RECLUSE

[1] The word used here in Russian is *prelest* (see p. 40, n. 2).
[2] St. Nil Sorski (Nilus of Sora, ?1433–1508), Russian ascetic writer; monk at a remote hermitage in the forest beyond the Volga, and leader of the 'Non-Possessors' (a movement in 15th and 16th century Russia which protested against the monastic ownership of land).

THE JESUS PRAYER

Cry out unceasingly: Lord Jesus Christ

A monk, whether he eats or drinks, whether he sits or serves, travels, or does anything else, must cry out unceasingly: 'Lord Jesus Christ, Son of God, have mercy upon me.' In this way the Name of the Lord Jesus, descending into the depths of the heart, will tame the dragon that guards the pastures of the heart, and will save the soul and quicken it. Dwell unceasingly with the Name of the Lord Jesus, so that your heart may absorb the Lord, and the Lord absorb your heart, and the two be one. Do not sever your heart from God, but dwell with Him. Always guard your heart with the remembrance of our Lord Jesus Christ, until the Name of the Lord is deeply rooted there and you cease to think of anything else: and so Christ will be glorified in you.

KALLISTOS AND IGNATIOS XANTHOPOULOS[1]

If Jesus Christ is in us, all things are possible

Our illustrious guides and teachers, having the Holy Spirit dwelling within them, in their wisdom impart instruction to all of us, and especially to those who wish to cast themselves into the world of heaven-made silence and to consecrate their whole being to God, tearing themselves away from the world and wisely practising silence. They teach us to prefer prayer in the Lord above all other good works or activities, imploring His mercy with an undoubting trust, and having as our task and continual occupation the invocation of His most holy and sweet Name. We must bear it always in the heart and in the mind and on our lips, we must compel ourselves to breathe and live, to sleep and wake, to walk, eat and drink, and in general to do everything with Him and in Him. If He is absent, all that is harmful rushes towards us, leaving no room for anything that is profitable to us; but if He is present within us, all that opposes Him is driven

[1] Kallistos and Ignatios Xanthopoulos: Byzantine spiritual writers at the end of the 14th and beginning of the 15th century. Kallistos was Patriarch of Constantinople in 1397.

away. Then is there no lack of anything blessed, and nothing remains impossible, as our Lord Himself says: 'He that abideth in me, and I in him, the same bringeth forth much fruit: for without me ye can do nothing' (John xv. 5).

KALLISTOS AND IGNATIOS XANTHOPOULOS

Let the Jesus Prayer cling to your breathing

If you truly wish to put your thoughts to shame, to be serenely silent, and to live in the effortless enjoyment of a sober and quiet heart, let the Jesus Prayer cleave to your breathing, and in a few days you will see all this realized.

ST. HESYCHIOS

A rosary or rhythmic breathing

There is a technique suggested by one of the early Fathers, rhythmic breathing in time with the Jesus Prayer in place of the use of a rosary.[1]

THEOPHAN THE RECLUSE

Breathing techniques, illusion and lust

To practise the Jesus Prayer, as we are all gaining the habit of doing, is an excellent thing. In monasteries it is being set as a task. Would they set it as a task if it were dangerous? What is dangerous is only the mechanical techniques which were added later and adjusted to fit the recitation of the prayer: and these are dangerous because they sometimes plunge us into a dream world of illusion, and sometimes—strange to say—into a constant state of lust. For this reason we should advise against such techniques and forbid them. But to call on the most sweet Name of the Lord in simplicity of heart is something we can suggest and recommend to anyone.

THEOPHAN THE RECLUSE

[1] On the 'breathing technique' in the Jesus Prayer and the many dangers by which it is accompanied, see the Introduction, pp. 35–36.

THE JESUS PRAYER

The place of breathing techniques (i)

In the treatise of Simeon the New Theologian about the three forms of prayer, in the works of Nikephoros the Monk,[1] and in the Century of Kallistos and Ignatios Xanthopoulos—all contained in the *Philokalia*—the reader will find instructions about the technique whereby the mind can be introduced into the heart with the aid of physical breathing—in other words, a mechanical method designed to help us achieve inner prayer. This teaching of the Fathers has created and continues to create many perplexities for its readers, although in fact there is really nothing difficult about it. We advise our beloved brethren not to try to practise this mechanical technique unless it establishes itself in them of its own accord. Many who have attempted to learn it by practical experience have damaged their lungs and achieved nothing. The essential thing is for the mind to unite with the heart at prayer, and this is accomplished by divine grace, in its own time, determined by God. The mechanical method described in these writings is fully replaced by an unhurried repetition of the prayer, a brief pause after each prayer, quiet and steady breathing, and enclosing the mind in the words of the prayer. With the aid of such means we can easily achieve a certain degree of attention. Before long the heart begins to be in sympathy with the attention of the mind as it prays. Little by little the sympathy of the heart with the mind begins to change into a union of mind and heart; and then the mechanical technique suggested by the Fathers will appear by itself. All the mechanical methods of a material character are suggested by the Fathers solely as aids for a quicker and easier attainment of attention during prayer, and not as something essential. The essential, indispensable element in prayer is attention. Without attention there is no prayer. True

[1] Nikephoros the Solitary, monk of Mount Athos in the early 14th century, spiritual father of St. Gregory Palamas. He is the earliest ascetic author to describe in detail the physical exercises associated with the recitation of the Jesus Prayer. The treatise on the three methods of prayer, to which Bishop Ignatii refers here, is almost certainly by Nikephoros, not by Simeon the New Theologian.

attention, given by grace, comes when we make our heart dead to the world. Aids always remain no more than aids. The union of the mind with the heart is a union of the spiritual thoughts of the mind with the spiritual feelings of the heart.

BISHOP IGNATII

The place of breathing techniques (ii)

St. Simeon[1] and other writers in the *Philokalia* suggest physical methods to be used in conjunction with the Jesus Prayer. Some people are so much absorbed in these external methods that they forget about the proper work of prayer; in others, prayer itself is distorted because of using these methods. Since, then, for lack of instructors these physical techniques may be accompanied by harmful effects, we do not describe them. In any case they are nothing but an external aid to inner work and are in no way essential. What is essential is this: to acquire the habit of standing with the mind in the heart—of being within this physical heart of ours, although not physically.

It is necessary to bring the mind down from the head into the heart and to establish it there, or, as one of the Fathers put it, to join the mind with the heart. But how can this be achieved?

Seek and you will find. The easiest way to achieve it is by walking before God, and by the work of prayer, especially by going to church.

But we must remember that ours is only the labour; the object itself, that is, the union of mind and heart, is a gift of grace, which the Lord grants to us as and when He chooses. The best example is Maximos of Kapsokalyvia.[2]

THEOPHAN THE RECLUSE

[1] i.e. Nikephoros of Mount Athos.

[2] St. Maximos of Kapsokalyvia, monk of Mount Athos in the middle of the 14th century, contemporary and friend of St. Gregory of Sinai. For a long time he prayed to the Holy Virgin that he might be granted the gift of unceasing prayer: then one day, as he stood in fervent prayer before the icon of the Mother of God, he suddenly felt a particular warmth in his heart—what Theophan elsewhere terms the 'spark' of grace (p. 108)—and from that moment unceasing prayer never left him.

THE JESUS PRAYER

Children talking to their Father

Do not be led astray by external methods when practising the inner Jesus Prayer. For some people they are necessary, but not for you. In your case, the time for such methods has already passed. You must already know by experience the place of the heart about which they speak: do not bother about the rest. The work of God is simple: it is prayer—children talking to their Father, without any subtleties. May the Lord give you wisdom for your salvation.

For someone who has not yet found the way to enter within himself, pilgrimages to holy places are a help. But for him who has found it they are a dissipation of energy, for they force him to come out from the innermost part of himself. It is time for you now to learn more perfectly how to remain within. You should abandon your external plans.

THEOPHAN THE RECLUSE

Growth in prayer has no end

You read the *Philokalia*? Good. Do not let yourself be confused by the writings of Ignatios and Kallistos Xanthopoulos, Gregory of Sinai, and Nikephoros. Try to find whether someone has the life of the *staretz* Paissy Velichkovsky. It contains prefaces to certain texts in the *Philokalia*, composed by the *staretz* Basil, and these prefaces explain about the place of mechanical techniques when reciting the Jesus Prayer. They will help you, too, to understand everything correctly. I have already told you that in your case these mechanical techniques are not necessary. What they would produce you already possessed from the moment you felt the call to practise the Prayer. But do not come to the wrong conclusion that your journey on the path of prayer is already completed. Growth in prayer has no end. If this growth ceases it means that life ceases. May the Lord save you and have mercy on you! It is possible to lose the right state, and to accept the mere memory of it as being the state itself. God forbid that this should happen to you!

THE JESUS PRAYER

You feel that you suffer from wandering thoughts. Take care: this is very dangerous. The enemy wants to drive you into some thicket and kill you there. Thoughts begin to wander when the fear of God decreases and the heart grows cool. The cooling down of the heart is caused by many things—chiefly by smugness and conceit. These are very close to your nature. Beware of them, and make haste to restore the fear of God and a feeling of warmth to your soul.

THEOPHAN THE RECLUSE

Spiritual reading. Russian authors are easier than Greek

All the writings of the Greek Fathers are worthy of the deepest respect because of the wealth of grace and spiritual wisdom living in them and breathing from them. But the writings of Russian Fathers are more accessible to us than those of the Greek authorities, owing to their particular clarity and simplicity of exposition, and also because they are closer to us in time. The writings of the *staretz* Basil are the first book which should be consulted by anyone wishing to practise the Jesus Prayer successfully. Indeed, the *staretz* wrote them specially with this purpose in mind. He termed them 'introductions' or 'preliminary studies', which prepare the reader for the Greek Fathers.

BISHOP IGNATII

How to plan our reading

In the question of reading we should bear in mind the principal aim of our life and choose those things which accord with it. Then something will result that is integrated, coherent, and therefore strong. This solidity of knowledge and conviction will give strength also to our character as a whole.

THEOPHAN THE RECLUSE

THE JESUS PRAYER

It is not the words that matter, but your love for God

If your heart grows warm through reading ordinary prayers, then kindle its inner warmth towards God in this way.

The Jesus Prayer, if said mechanically, is valueless: it is no more help than any other prayer spoken by the tongue and lips. As you recite the Jesus Prayer, try at the same time to quicken your realization that our Lord Himself is near, that He stands in your soul and listens to what is happening within it. Awaken in your soul the thirst for salvation, and the assurance that our Lord alone can bring it. And then cry out to Him whom in your thoughts you see before you: 'Lord Jesus Christ, Son of God, have mercy upon me,' or: 'O merciful Lord, save me by the way that Thou knowest.' It is not the words that matter, but your feelings towards the Lord.

The spiritual burning of the heart for God springs from our love towards Him. It kindles from the Lord's touch on the heart. Because He is entirely love, His touch on the heart immediately kindles love for Him; and from love comes burning of the heart towards Him. It is this which must be the object of your search.

Let the Jesus Prayer be on your tongue; let God's presence be before your mind; and in your heart let there be the thirst for God, for communion with the Lord. When all this becomes permanent, then the Lord, seeing how you exert yourself, will give you what you ask.

THEOPHAN THE RECLUSE

God's spark

What do we seek through the Jesus Prayer? We seek for the fire of grace to appear in our heart, and we seek for the beginning of unceasing prayer which manifests a state of grace. When God's spark falls into the heart, the Jesus Prayer fans it into flame. The prayer does not of itself produce the spark, but helps us to receive it. How does it help? By collecting our thoughts, by enabling the soul to stand before the Lord and to walk in His presence. This is the most important part—to stand and walk before God, to call on Him out of our heart. This was what Maximos of Kapsokalyvia[1] did: and all those who seek the fire of grace should do the same. They should not worry about words and positions of the body, for God looks upon the heart.

I am telling you this because some people altogether forget about calling from the heart. Their whole concern is with the words and with the position of the body, and having recited the Jesus Prayer a certain number of times in their chosen position, with prostrations, they rest satisfied with this, not without self-esteem, not without criticism of those who go to church for the usual order of prayer. Some people live out their lives in this way and are devoid of grace.

If anyone should ask me how to carry out the task of prayer, I would say to him: Accustom yourself to walk in the presence of God, keep remembrance of Him, and be reverent. To preserve this remembrance, choose a few short prayers, or simply take the twenty-four short prayers of St. John Chrysostom,[2] and repeat them often with appropriate thoughts and feelings. As you accustom yourself to this, remembrance of God will bring light to your mind and warmth to your heart. And when you attain this state, God's spark, the ray of grace, will fall at last into your heart. There is no way in which you yourself can produce it: it comes forth direct from God. When it comes, dwell in the Jesus Prayer alone, and with this prayer blow the spark of grace into flame. This is the most direct way.

THEOPHAN THE RECLUSE

A small spark

Later, when you notice that someone begins to go more deeply into prayer, you can suggest to him that he should use the Jesus Prayer unceasingly, always preserving the remembrance of God

[1] On Maximos of Kapsokalyvia and the 'spark' of grace, see p.105 , n. 2.
[2] These twenty-four prayers of St. John Chrysostom occur among the daily prayers prescribed for use each evening by all Orthodox, whether clergy, monks, or laity. They are mainly penitential in character.

with fear and reverence. Prayer is the great essential. What we must chiefly seek in prayer is the reception of a small spark, such as was given to Maximos of Kapsokalyvia. This spark is not to be attracted by any artifice, but is given freely by the grace of God. For this the unwearied effort of prayer is necessary, as St. Makarios says: 'If you wish to acquire true prayer, persevere steadfastly in praying, and God, seeing how strenuously you seek, will give it to you.'

THEOPHAN THE RECLUSE

A murmuring stream

You ask what is needful in praying the Jesus Prayer. What you did was correct. Remember how you did it, and continue in the same way. I will remind you of only one thing: one must descend with the mind into the heart, and there stand before the face of the Lord, ever-present, all-seeing, within you. The prayer takes a firm and steadfast hold when a small fire begins to burn in the heart.

Try not to quench this fire, and it will become established in such a way that the prayer repeats itself: and then you will have within you a small murmuring stream, to use the expression of the *staretz* Parthenii of the Kiev Lavra.[1] And one of the early Fathers said: 'When thieves approach a house in order to creep up to it and steal, and hear someone inside talking, they do not dare to climb in; in the same way, when our enemies try to steal into the soul and take possession of it, they creep all round but fear to enter when they hear that short prayer welling out.'

THEOPHAN THE RECLUSE

[1] *Staretz* Parthenii (1790–1855), monk of the great habit, member of Pechersky Lavra at Kiev: spiritual father to a very wide circle, both monks and people in the world. He practised the Jesus Prayer and recommended its use to others. Theophan, while a student at the Kiev Academy (1837–41), used to visit *staretz* Parthenii, and was deeply influenced by him in his spiritual development. During the last seventeen years of his life, Father Parthenii celebrated the Liturgy daily; during the last year of all, although having no longer the strength to perform the Liturgy, he still received holy communion each day.

THE JESUS PRAYER

Human efforts and the grace of God

There are only a few words in the Jesus Prayer, but they contain everything. From of old it was recognized that this prayer, once acquired as a habit, could take the place of all other oral prayers. Is anyone who strives for salvation ignorant of this method? If used in the way described by the Holy Fathers, this prayer has great power; but among those who acquire the habit of reciting it, not all discover its power, not all taste of its fruits. Why should this be so? It is because they wish to grasp for themselves that which is a gift of God, coming only by His grace.

We do not need any special help from God in order to begin the work of repeating this prayer in the morning, in the evening, walking, sitting, lying down, working, or at leisure. By being always active in this way we can of ourselves train the tongue to repeat the Prayer even without conscious effort. A certain easement of thought may follow from this, even a kind of warmth of heart. But all of this, says the monk Nikephoros in the *Philokalia*, is only the action and fruit of our own efforts. To stop at this point is to remain satisfied merely with a parrot-like facility in reciting the words *Lord, have mercy*: it is to imagine that we have achieved something when in reality we have achieved nothing at all. This is what happens when we fall into the habit of repeating the words of this prayer mechanically without understanding what prayer really is. As a result we rest satisfied with the natural beginnings of its action, and cease to look any further. But whoever has truly understood the nature of prayer will continue to search. Realizing that no matter how diligently he follows the instructions of the elders the true rewards of prayer still elude him, he will cease to expect them from his own efforts and will lay all his hope on God. From this moment grace can flow into him; and at a moment known only to itself it will graft the prayer into his heart. Everything, as the elders teach us, will be outwardly the same: the difference will lie in our inner power.

What is true of this prayer is true of all forms of spiritual growth. A hot-tempered man may be filled with the desire to stamp out irritability and acquire meekness. In the books on asceticism there are instructions how to discipline oneself into achieving this. A man can read these instructions and follow them; but how far will he get by his own efforts? No farther than outward silence during bouts of anger, with only such quelling of the rage itself as self-control can afford him. He will never himself attain the complete extinction of his anger and the establishment of meekness in his heart. This only happens when grace invades the heart and itself places meekness there.

This is true of every spiritual quality. Whatever you may be seeking, seek it with all your strength, but do not expect your own search and efforts to bear fruit of themselves. Put your trust in the Lord, ascribing nothing to yourself, and He will give you your heart's desire (Ps. xxxvi. 3–4 Sept.).[1]

Pray thus: 'I desire and seek, quicken Thou me by Thy righteousness.' The Lord has said 'Without me ye can do nothing' (John xv. 5), and this law is fulfilled with exactitude in the spiritual life; it does not swerve by a hair's breadth. When people ask 'What must I do to acquire this or that virtue?' there is only one answer: 'Turn to the Lord and He will give it to you. There is no other way to find what you seek.'

THEOPHAN THE RECLUSE

A brook that murmurs in the heart

As you begin to accustom yourself to praying as you should with prayers written by others, your own prayers and cries to God will well up in you. Never neglect these aspirations to God that manifest themselves in your soul. Every time that they arise, be still, and pray with your own words; nor think that in so praying you do harm to prayer itself. No: it is just in this way that you pray as you should, and this prayer ascends more quickly to God than any other. For this reason there is a rule applying to everyone: whether in church or at home, if your soul wishes to pray in its own and not in other men's words, give it freedom;

[1] Ps. xxxvii. 3–4 (B.C.P.).

let it pray, even if it prays thus during the whole service, or leaves undone its own rule of prayer at home and has not time to fulfil it.

Both forms of prayer are pleasing to God—prayer recited attentively from prayer books and accompanied by suitable holy thoughts and feelings; and prayer without books and in your own words. Only perfunctory prayer is displeasing to Him, when someone reads the prayers at home or stands in church at the service without attending to the meaning of the words: the tongue reads or the ear listens, but the thoughts wander who knows where. There is no prayer here. But while both forms are pleasing to God, the prayer that is not read, but is your own, is nearer to the heart of the matter and much more fruitful.

It is not enough, however, just to wait for the desire to pray. To achieve spontaneous prayer, we must force ourselves to pray in a particular way—with the Jesus Prayer—not only during the church service and during prayer at home, but at all times. Men experienced in prayer have chosen this one prayer, addressed to the Lord and Saviour, and have established rules for its performance, so that with its help we can acquire the habit of self-impelled or spontaneous prayer. These rules are simple. Stand with the mind in the heart before the Lord and pray to Him: 'Lord Jesus Christ, Son of God, have mercy upon me.' Do so at home before beginning prayers, in the intervals between prayers, and at the end of praying; do so in church, and all day long, so as to fill every moment of the day with prayer.

At first this saving prayer is usually a matter of strenuous effort and hard work. But if one concentrates on it with zeal, it will begin to flow of its own accord, like a brook that murmurs in the heart. This is a great blessing, and it is worth working hard to obtain it.

Those who with long endeavour have achieved success in this prayer prescribe a not very difficult exercise which will quickly enable us to master it. Before or after your rule of prayer, night and morning or during the day, consecrate a fixed period of time for the performance of this one prayer. Do it in this way. Sit down, or—better still—stand in a prayerful position, concentrate your attention in the heart before the Lord, in complete certainty that He is there and is listening to you, and call out to Him: 'Lord Jesus Christ, Son of God, have mercy upon me.' If you wish, accompany this with bows from the waist, or else with prostrations. Do this for a quarter or half hour—or more, or less—as it suits you. The more zealous your efforts, the more quickly will the prayer be grafted in your heart. It is best to begin this work with zeal, and not to cease until you have achieved what you wish, and this prayer starts to move of itself in your heart. After that you have only to maintain it in its course.

The warmth of heart or glow of spirit, about which we spoke before, is achieved in just this way. The more the Jesus Prayer penetrates into the heart, the warmer the heart becomes, and the more self-impelled becomes the prayer, so that the fire of spiritual life is kindled in the heart, and its burning becomes unceasing. At the same time the Jesus Prayer will fill the whole heart, and will never cease to move within it. That is why those in whom the perfect inner life is being brought to birth will pray almost exclusively with this prayer alone, making it comprise their entire rule of prayer.

THEOPHAN THE RECLUSE

The buried treasure of baptismal grace

The gift which we have received from Jesus Christ in holy baptism is not destroyed, but is only buried as a treasure in the ground. And both common sense and gratitude demand that we should take good care to unearth this treasure and bring it to light. This can be done in two ways. The gift of baptism is revealed first of all by a painstaking fulfilment of the commandments; the more we carry these out, the more clearly the gift shines upon us in its true splendour and brilliance. Secondly, it comes to light and is revealed through the continual invocation of the Lord Jesus, or by unceasing remembrance of God, which is one and the same thing. The first method is powerful but the second is more so; so much so that even fidelity to the commandments receives its full strength from prayer. For this reason, if we truly desire to bring to flower the seed of grace that is hidden within us, we should hasten to acquire the habit of this exercise of the heart, and always practise this prayer within it, without any image or form, until it warms our mind and inflames our soul with an inexpressible love towards God and men.

ST. GREGORY OF SINAI

Act always in great humility. The need for a spiritual director

This prayer is called the Jesus Prayer because it is addressed to the Lord Jesus, and like every other short prayer, in its outward form it is verbal. It becomes inner prayer, and must be so called, when it is offered not only in words but with the mind and heart, with feeling and with awareness of its content; and especially when through long and attentive practice, it is so fused with the movements of the spirit that these last alone are apparent and the words seem to vanish. Every short prayer may rise to this level. Preference belongs to the Jesus Prayer because it unites the soul with the Lord Jesus: and He is the only door to communion with God, which is the aim of all prayer. He himself said: 'No man cometh unto the Father but by me' (John xiv. 6). Whoever, therefore, has acquired this prayer wins for himself the whole riches of the divine husbandry of the Incarnation, wherein lies our salvation. Hearing this, you will not be astonished at those who in their zeal for salvation spared no effort to gain the habit of this prayer, and made its strength their own. Follow their example.

The habit of the Jesus Prayer is outwardly mastered when the words begin by themselves to move incessantly on the tongue. Its inward achievement involves the undivided attention of the mind in the heart and constant standing of the whole being before God, accompanied by varying degrees of warmth of heart, by the casting off of all other thoughts, and above all by contrite and humble cleaving to the Lord and Saviour. This spiritual state is achieved by repeating the Prayer as frequently as possible, with our attention firmly established in the heart. By persevering in this continual repetition we unify the mind so that it stands in wholeness before God. The establishment of such an order within ourselves is accompanied by the warming of the heart, and it is followed by the driving away of all thoughts, ordinary and harmless as well as passionate. When the flame of our longing for God begins to burn unceasingly in the heart, it will be joined by a sense of inward peace in the soul, as the mind draws near to the Lord in humility and contrition.

Our own efforts (supported by God's grace) reach only thus far: any prayer higher than this will be the gift of grace alone. The Holy Fathers mention this with the sole purpose of showing those who have reached the stage I have just described, that they should not think that they have nothing more to wish for, nor imagine that they stand on the very summit of prayerful or spiritual perfection.

Do not rush one prayer after another, but say them with orderly deliberation, as one would normally address a great person from whom one asked a favour. Yet do not just pay attention to the words, but rather let the mind be in the heart, standing before the Lord in full awareness of His presence, in full consciousness of His greatness and grace and justice.

For the avoidance of errors, have someone to advise you—a spiritual father or confessor, a brother of like mind; and make known to him all that happens to you in the work of prayer. For yourself, act always in great humility and with the utmost simplicity, not ascribing any success to yourself. Know that true success is achieved within, unconsciously, and happens as imperceptibly as the growth of the human body. Therefore when you hear an inner voice saying 'Ah! Here it is!' you should realize that this is the voice of the enemy, showing you a mirage rather than the reality. This is the beginning of self-deception. Stifle this voice immediately, otherwise it will resound in you like a trumpet, inflating your self-esteem.

THEOPHAN THE RECLUSE

No progress without suffering

It must be realized that the true sign of spiritual endeavour and the price of success in it is suffering. He who proceeds without suffering will bear no fruit. Pain of the heart and physical striving bring to light the gift of the Holy Spirit, bestowed in holy baptism upon every believer, buried in passions through our negligence in fulfilling the commandments, and brought once more to life by repentance, through the ineffable mercy of God. Do not, because of the suffering that accompanies them, cease to make painstaking efforts, lest you be condemned for fruitlessness and hear the words, 'Take the talent from him' (Matt. xxv. 28).

Every struggle in the soul's training, whether physical or mental, that is not accompanied by suffering, that does not require the utmost effort, will bear no fruit. 'The kingdom of heaven suffereth violence, and the violent take it by force' (Matt. xi. 12). Many people have worked and continue to work without pain, but because of its absence they are strangers to purity and out of communion with the Holy Spirit, because they have turned aside from the severity of suffering. Those who work feebly and carelessly may go through the movements of making great efforts, but they harvest no fruit, because they undergo no suffering. According to the prophet, unless our loins are broken, weakened by the labour of fasting, unless we undergo an agony of contrition, unless we suffer like a woman in travail, we shall not succeed in bringing to birth the spirit of salvation in the ground of our heart.

THEOPHAN THE RECLUSE

The other side of Jordan

The practice of the Jesus Prayer culminates in the attainment of pure prayer, which is crowned by passionlessness or Christian perfection—a gift of God, which He grants to such spiritual wrestlers as it pleases Him to choose.

St. Isaac the Syrian says: 'Not many are granted the gift of pure prayer, but only the few. From one generation to another, there is scarcely a single person who attains to the mystery fulfilled in pure prayer and who, by the grace and love of God, reaches the other side of Jordan.'

BISHOP IGNATII

(iv) REMEMBRANCE OF GOD

Remembrance in the heart and in the head

When remembrance of God lives in the heart and there maintains the fear of Him, then all goes well; but when this remembrance grows weak or is kept only in the head, then all goes astray.

THEOPHAN THE RECLUSE

Be still and silent

I have often reminded you, my dear sister, about the remembrance of God, and now I tell you again: unless you work and sweat to impress on your heart and mind this awe-inspiring Name, you keep silence in vain, you sing in vain, you fast in vain, you watch in vain. In short, all a nun's work will be useless without this activity, without recollection of God. This is the beginning of silence for the Lord's sake, and it is also the end. This most desirable Name is the soul of stillness and silence. By calling it to mind we gain joy and gladness, forgiveness of sins and a wealth of virtues. Few have been able to find this most glorious Name, save only in stillness and silence. Man can attain it in no other way, even with great effort. Therefore, knowing the power of this advice, I entreat you for the love of Christ always to be still and silent, since these virtues enrich remembrance of God within us.

THEOPHAN THE RECLUSE

REMEMBRANCE OF GOD

Secret converse with the Lord

Everywhere and always God is with us, near to us and in us. But we are not always with Him, since we do not remember Him; and because we do not remember Him we allow ourselves many things which we would not permit if we did remember. Take upon yourself this task—to make a habit of such recollection.

Make yourself a rule always to be with the Lord, keeping your mind in your heart, and do not let your thoughts wander; as often as they stray, turn them back again and keep them at home in the closet of your heart, and delight in converse with the Lord.

THEOPHAN THE RECLUSE

Become a real man

The more firmly you are established in the recollection of God —in mentally standing before God in your heart—the more quiet will your thoughts become and the less will they wander. Inner order and success in prayer go together.

In this way our spirit is restored to its just rights. When it is so re-established, there will begin an active and vital transformation of soul and body, and of outer relationships, until they are finally cleansed. And you will become a real man.

THEOPHAN THE RECLUSE

A swift entry to Paradise

When you establish yourself in the inner man by the remembrance of God, then Christ the Lord will enter and dwell within you. The two things go together.

And here is a sign for you, by which you can be certain that this glorious work has begun within you: you will experience a certain feeling of warmth towards the Lord. If you fulfil everything prescribed, then this feeling will soon begin to appear more and more often, and in time will become continuous. This feeling is sweet and beatific, and from its first appearance it stimulates us to desire and seek it, lest it leave the heart: for in it is Paradise.

THE JESUS PRAYER

Do you wish to enter this Paradise as quickly as possible? Here, then, is what you must do. When you pray, do not end your prayer without having aroused in your heart some feeling towards God, whether it be reverence, or devotion, or thanksgiving, or glorification, or humility and contrition, or hope and trust. Also when after prayer you begin to read, do not finish reading without having felt in your heart the truth of what you read. These two feelings—the one inspired by prayer, the other by reading—mutually warm one another; and if you pay attention to yourself, they will keep you under their influence during the whole day. Take pains to practise these two methods exactly and you will see for yourself what will happen.

THEOPHAN THE RECLUSE

Unceasing remembrance is a gift from God

Remembrance of God is something that God Himself grafts upon the soul. But the soul must also force itself to persevere and to toil. Work, making every effort to attain the unceasing remembrance of God. And God, seeing how fervently you desire it, will give you this constant recollection of Himself.

THEOPHAN THE RECLUSE

Frequent prostrations

All the time from waking to sleeping, walk in the remembrance of the omnipresence of God, having always in mind that the Lord sees you and assesses every movement of your thoughts and heart. For this purpose pray with the Jesus Prayer unceasingly, and, frequently approaching the icons, bow down or prostrate yourself according to the movement and demands of your heart. Thus during the whole day your time will be frequently interrupted by these prostrations, and will be passed in the unceasing thought of God and in performance of the Jesus Prayer, during every kind of occupation.

THEOPHAN THE RECLUSE

REMEMBRANCE OF GOD

The thought of God and the Jesus Prayer

It is possible to replace the thought of God by the Jesus Prayer, but where is the necessity for this when they are one and the same? The thought of God is the keeping in mind—without any deliberately imposed concept—of some truth such as the Incarnation, the death on the Cross, the Resurrection, God's omnipresence, or others.

THEOPHAN THE RECLUSE

God's nearness and presence in the heart

Seek and ye shall find. But what is one to seek? A conscious and living communion with the Lord. This is given by the grace of God, but it is also essential that we ourselves should work, that we ourselves should come to meet Him. How? By always remembering God, who is near the heart and even present within it. To succeed in this remembrance it is advisable to accustom oneself to the continual repetition of the Jesus Prayer, 'Lord Jesus Christ, Son of God, have mercy upon me', holding in mind the thought of God's nearness, His presence in the heart. But it must also be understood that in itself the Jesus Prayer is only an outer oral prayer; inner prayer is to stand before the Lord, continually crying out to Him without words.

By this means remembrance of God will be established in the mind, and the countenance of God will be in your soul like the sun. If you put something cold in the sun it begins to grow warm, and in the same way your soul will be warmed by the remembrance of God, who is the spiritual sun. What follows on from this will presently appear.

Your first task is to acquire the habit of repeating the Jesus Prayer unceasingly. So begin: and continually repeat and repeat, but all the time keep before you the thought of our Lord. And herein lies everything.

THEOPHAN THE RECLUSE

THE JESUS PRAYER

Cast your care upon the Lord

Our whole object is to acquire the habit of keeping our attention always on the Lord, who is omnipresent and sees everything, who desires the salvation of all of us and is ready to help us towards it.

This habit will not allow you to grieve, whether your sorrow be within or without; for it fills the soul with a sense of perfect contentment, which leaves no room for any feeling of scarcity or need. It makes us entrust ourselves and all we have into the Lord's hands, and so gives birth to a sense of His permanent protection and help.

THEOPHAN THE RECLUSE

The perils of forgetfulness

To pray does not only mean to stand in prayer. To keep the mind and heart turned towards God and directed to Him—this is already prayer, whatever the position in which one may be. Prayer according to the rule is one thing, and this state of prayer is another. The way to it is to attain the habit of constant remembrance of God, of the last hour and the judgement that follows it. Accustom yourself to this, and all will go well. Every step you take will be inwardly consecrated to God. You must direct your steps according to the commandments; and you know what the commandments are. That is all. It is possible to apply these commandments to every event, and to consecrate all your activities inwardly to God; and then all your life will be dedicated to Him. What more is necessary? Nothing. You see how simple it is.

You have zeal for salvation. When you have this zeal, it shows itself in a fervent care for salvation. It is absolutely necessary to avoid lukewarmness. This is how lukewarmness arises: it begins with forgetfulness. God's gifts are forgotten, and so are God Himself, and our salvation in Him, and the danger of being without God; and the remembrance of death disappears—in a word, the whole spiritual realm is closed to us. This is due to the enemy, or to the dispersion of thoughts by business cares and excessive social contacts. When all is forgotten the heart grows cool, and its sensitivity to spiritual things is interrupted: and so we fall into a state of indifference, and then into negligence and carelessness. As a result, spiritual occupations are postponed for a time, and afterwards abandoned completely. And then we begin again our old way of life, careless and negligent, forgetful of God, seeking only our own pleasure. Even if there is nothing disorderly in it, do not look for anything divine. It will be an empty life.

If you do not want to fall into this abyss, beware of the first step—that is, forgetfulness. Therefore walk always in godly recollections—in remembrance of God and divine things. This will keep you sensitive to such things, and these two together—recollection and sensitivity—will set you on fire with zeal. And here will be life indeed.

THEOPHAN THE RECLUSE

Fall down as dust before the face of God

With regard to spiritual prayer, take one precaution. Beware lest in ceaselessly remembering God you forget also to kindle fear, and awe, and the desire to fall down as dust before the face of God—our most merciful Father, but also our dread Judge. Frequent recollection of God without reverence blunts the feeling of the fear of God, and thereby deprives us of the saving influence which this sense of fear—and it alone—can produce in our spiritual life.

THEOPHAN THE RECLUSE

CHAPTER IV

THE FRUITS OF PRAYER
by Theophan the Recluse

(i) ATTENTION AND THE FEAR OF GOD

The first-fruits of prayer—attention and a warm tenderness of heart[1]

Any rule of prayer that is properly followed will produce as its first-fruits attention and a warm tenderness of heart[2]; but especially will these things come from the practice of the Jesus Prayer, which stands on a higher level than psalmody and other forms of prayer. Attention gives birth to warm tenderness of heart, which in its turn increases attention. They grow in strength together, supporting each other. They give depth to prayer, gradually quickening the heart: banishing distraction and wandering thoughts, they bestow on prayer its purity. True prayer is a gift of God; so also are attention and warm tenderness of heart.

Prayer of the heart never comes prematurely

You should know that attention must never leave the heart. Work in the heart, however, is sometimes only mental,

[1] This first paragraph is by Bishop Ignatii, not by Theophan.

[2] 'Warm tenderness of heart': in Russian, умиленіе. ' ... *umilenie*, a word which resists translation. It could perhaps be rendered as "a sudden softening of the heart", or "a flood of deep emotion in the heart". It is a sudden and unexpected impulse that takes hold of a man, a feeling of inexplicable tenderness which seizes the hardest of hearts ... it is the thrill of love and forgiveness, the tears of repentance and joy, and the gift of self offered in joy' (Nicholas Arseniev, *Russian Piety*, London, 1964, pp. 75–76).

performed by the mind, whereas sometimes it is not only *in* but *of* the heart, in other words, it is begun and continued with warm feeling. This law applies not just to hermits but to all Christians, to all who would stand before God in purity of heart and work before His Face. If the mind becomes exhausted by saying the words of the prayer, then pray without words, bowing down before the Lord inwardly in your heart and giving yourself to Him. This is true prayer. Words are only prayer's expression and are always weaker in God's eyes than prayer itself.

Prayer of the heart never comes prematurely. With its advent God begins to work within us; as it becomes increasingly established in the heart this work is brought more and more to its fullness. This prayer must be sought with no scant effort; then God, seeing our travail, will give us what we seek. True prayer will not be achieved by human efforts; it is a gift of God. Seek and you will find.

It is no loss that you have prayed without using artificial techniques to engraft the prayer; for such techniques are not indispensable. What is important is not the position of the body but the inner state. Our whole aim is *to stand with attention in the heart, and look towards God, and cry out to Him.*

I have never in fact met anyone who approved of the artificial techniques. Neither Bishop Ignatii nor Father Makarii of Optina[1] approve of them.

Natural fruits and the fruit of grace

Our task is the art of the Jesus Prayer. We must try to perform it quite simply, with our attention in the heart, always preserving the remembrance of God. This brings by itself its own natural fruit—collectedness of mind, devoutness and fear of God, recollection of death, stillness of thought, and a certain warmth of heart. All these are natural fruits of prayer in the

---

[1] Father Makarii (1788–1860), *staretz* at the Optina Hermitage in Russia. Highly educated, a Patristic scholar, he was in close contact with the intellectual movements of his day, and influenced a number of writers, such as Gogol, Khomiakov, and Dostoevsky.

heart, and are not the fruit of grace. This fact must be kept well in mind, lest we boast to ourselves and to others and become proud.

Our prayer begins to be of value only when grace comes. As long as we have only the natural fruits of prayer, what we achieve is valueless, both in itself and in the judgement of God. For the coming of grace is the sign that God has looked on us in mercy.

I cannot tell you just how this action of grace will be made manifest, but it is certain that grace cannot come before these natural fruits of inner prayer have made their appearance.

The natural fruits are accessible to all

The fruit of prayer is the concentration of attention in the heart accompanied by a feeling of warmth. This is the natural effect. Everyone can achieve it. And everyone, not only monks but laymen as well, can perform prayer of such a kind.

This sort of work is simple, and not on a high level. The Jesus Prayer is not in itself miraculous, but like any other short prayer it is oral and consequently external. Yet it can become the prayer of mind-in-heart in a wholly natural way. As for what comes from grace, on the other hand, this we must simply await; no kind of technique can lay hold on it by force.

When concerned with high contemplative prayer, it is necessary in the first place to be cleansed of passions. But here we are concerned with simple prayer, although this may lead to higher prayer.

If the practice of prayer is to proceed successfully, it is always essential at the outset to lay everything else aside, so that the heart is completely free of distraction. Nothing should obtrude on the mind: neither face, nor activity, nor object. At such a time all is to be driven out. Keep to this rule and there will be no need to desist from such prayer, which is to be said at any time. As soon as you are free, return to it immediately.

During the service attention must be paid to the office, but when something is read or sung indistinctly, repeat the Jesus Prayer.

ATTENTION AND THE FEAR OF GOD

The dangers of distraction

As a special favour, you have allowed yourself a little distraction and have not taken enough care to keep watch over your eyes, your tongue, and your thoughts. So warmth has gone from you, and you are left empty. This is bad. Hasten to re-establish the proper inner order, or to receive it again in answer to your prayers. Shut yourself in, and do nothing but pray and read about prayer until your attention unites with God in the heart, and a spirit of contrition and warm tenderness is established there: this spirit will make it clear to you whether you are in the right state or have turned aside from it. You seem to regard attention as an excessive austerity, whereas in fact it is the root of all our inner spiritual life. This is why the enemy so particularly takes up arms against it, and uses every means to build up attractive images before the eyes of the soul, and suggests thoughts about special favours and distractions.

Soreness in the heart

Whether it be the Jesus Prayer or any other short prayer, it is good if it is always in the mouth. Only take care that the attention is in the heart and not in the head, and hold to this not only when standing in prayer but at all other times as well. Try to acquire a kind of soreness in your heart. Constant effort will achieve this quickly. There is nothing peculiar in this: the appearance of this pain is a natural effect. It will help you to collect yourself better. But the chief thing is that the Lord, who sees your effort, will give you help and grace in prayer. A different order will then be established in the heart.

Inner reintegration begins

Continue to practise this rule, and your thoughts will gradually quieten down more and more, while the debility you have noticed will be cured. If you persevere in the right way, it will create a soreness in your heart, and this pain will make your thoughts cleave to God alone; and so the wandering of your thoughts will cease. From that moment, if our Lord grants it, the reintegration of all our inner being commences and we never cease to walk before Him.

Falling in love with spiritual sweetness

You say that you are afraid of falling in love with spiritual sweetness. But you surely cannot think of doing any such thing. It is not for its sweetness that prayer is practised, but because it is our duty to serve God in this way, although sweetness goes of necessity with true service. The most important thing in prayer is to stand before God in reverence and fear, with the mind in the heart; for this sobers and disperses every folly and plants contrition before God in the heart. These feelings of fear and sorrow in the sight of God, the broken and contrite heart, are the principal features of true inner prayer, and the test of every prayer, by which we can tell whether or not our prayer is performed as it should be. If they are present, prayer is in order. When they are absent, prayer is not in its true course and must be brought back to its proper condition. If we lack this sense of sorrow and contrition, then sweetness and warmth may breed self-conceit; and that is spiritual pride, and will lead to pernicious illusion. Then the sweetness and warmth will vanish, leaving only their memory, but the soul will still imagine that it has them. Of this you should be afraid, and so you must increasingly kindle in your heart the fear of God, lowliness, and contrite prostration before Him, walking always in His presence. This is the heart of the matter.

The instability of inner sweetness[1]

Do not become attracted by inner sweetness: without the Cross it is unstable and dangerous.

[1] By the Nun Magdalina (1827-69), a member of the Convent of Our Lady of the Sign in Yeletsk, Russia.

ATTENTION AND THE FEAR OF GOD

Consider every one to be better than yourself. Without this thought even a worker of miracles is far from God.

Sobriety of mind and warmth of heart

Fulfilling the rule zealously, preserve sobriety of mind and warmth of heart. If the latter begins to diminish, hasten to warm it, being convinced that its disappearance will mean that you have withdrawn more than half way from God. The fear of God is the guardian and quickener of interior warmth, but humility is also necessary, and patience, and fidelity to rules, and above all, sobriety. Watch yourself closely, for the sake of God. Wake yourself if you have grown drowsy, rouse yourself up in every way so as not to fall asleep.

Sobriety and discernment

The warriors of Christ should keep watchful guard over two things in particular: sobriety and discernment. The first is directed within, the second outward. With sobriety we observe movements which come out of the heart itself; with discernment we foresee movements which are about to be roused in it under the impulse of external influences. The rule for sobriety is: after every thought has been banished from the soul by the memory of God's presence, stand at the door of the heart and watch carefully everything that enters or goes out from there. Especially do not let your actions be prejudiced by emotion and desire, for all evil comes thence.

Be sober, be vigilant

To be sober means not to let the heart cling to anything except God. Cleaving to other things makes the soul drunk, and it begins to do quite unaccountable things. To be vigilant means to watch carefully, lest something evil springs up in the heart.

THE FRUITS OF PRAYER

Humility and warmth of heart

Have you still preserved your state of spiritual warmth? It should be preserved. Its basis is humility. As soon as humility decreases, coolness enters. For when the soul begins to regard itself as something important, the Lord at once withdraws; and, left by itself, the soul grows cold. It is not just with the tongue that we should keep saying 'I am nothing', but we should feel our nothingness in the heart. Then the Lord will always be there, He who creates and has created everything out of nothing. The Lord will give warmth, but we must do our own part as well.

What, then, can we contribute to this work? Humility and attention, and a suffering submission to God in the depths of the heart, which should continue unceasingly whatever we may be doing or saying, whether we are sitting down or moving about, whether at home or in church. May the Lord grant you wisdom. Read holy writings, reflect upon them, and absorb all that is useful, applying it to your life and to your soul.

Spiritual reading. The fear of God

You have a book? Then read it, reflect on what it says, and apply the words to yourself. To apply the content to oneself is the purpose and fruit of reading. If you read without applying what is read to yourself, nothing good will come of it, and even harm may result. Theories will accumulate in the head, leading you to criticise others instead of improving your own life. So have ears and hear. If you already have the *Philokalia*, look up Hesychios and read what he says on sobriety. He gives exact directions how to control and set in order one's thoughts. Read his words attentively, take them in with your heart, and then act as suggested.

We should always hold fast to the fear of God. It is the root of all spiritual knowledge and all right action. When the fear of God rules in the soul everything goes well both within and without. Try to kindle this sense of fear in your heart every morning before you do anything else. Then it will go on working by itself as a kind of pendulum.

ATTENTION AND THE FEAR OF GOD

The principal fruit of prayer

The principal fruit of prayer is not warmth and sweetness, but fear of God and contrition.

The root of inner order

The root of good inner order is the fear of God. Preserve this fear within you constantly: it will hold everything taut, and will allow no slackness either in physical members or thoughts, creating a vigilant heart and a sober mind, and allowing no bodily torpor or blurring of thought.

But one must always remember that success in any aspect of the spiritual life is the fruit of the grace of God. Spiritual life comes entirely from His most holy Spirit. We have our own spirit but it is void of power. It begins to gain strength only when the grace of God flows into it.

Feelings of ecstasy

What you must seek in prayer is to establish in the heart a quiet but warm and constant feeling towards God, not expecting ecstasy or any extraordinary state. But when God does send such special feelings in prayer, you must be grateful for them and not imagine that they are due to yourself, nor regret their disappearance as if it were a great loss; but always descend from these heights to humility and quietness of feeling towards the Lord.

Human efforts and the fruits of the Spirit[1]

Unless we are adorned with simplicity and goodness, the outward semblance and attitude of prayer will profit us nothing. This is true not only of prayer, but of any labour or endeavour, such as virginity or fasting, or any kind of work whatever done for the sake of virtue. If we do not see abundantly present in

[1] By St. Makarios of Egypt.

ourselves the fruits of love, peace, joy and meekness, of humility, simplicity and sincerity, of faith and long-suffering, then we have laboured without profit and in vain: for the whole purpose of our labour and toil was to gain these fruits. If the fruits of love and peace are not in us, then our entire labour has been useless and in vain. Those who toil in such a way, on the day of judgement will prove to be like the five foolish virgins who were called foolish because they did not yet have in the vessels of their hearts the spiritual oil, that is, the virtues which we mentioned; and so they were shut out from the marriage feast, gaining no profit from their virginity. Husbandmen who work in a vineyard undergo all their labour and care in the hope of obtaining fruit, and if there is no fruit all their work proves to no purpose; and in the same way, if we do not see in ourselves, through the action of the Spirit, the fruits of love, peace, joy, humility, and all the other virtues enumerated by the Apostle (Gal. v. 22), if we do not feel in full assurance and spiritual perception that they are present within us, then all the labour of chastity, prayer, psalmody, fasting, and vigil will prove in vain and profitless. For these labours of soul and body must be practised in the hope of gaining spiritual fruits; and the fruit of the Spirit that the virtues bear is spiritual enjoyment of an uncorrupted delight, conferred by the Spirit upon the hearts of the faithful. Therefore efforts and endeavours should simply be regarded—for such they are in truth—as efforts and endeavours and no more, and the fruit as fruit. But if, because of insufficient knowledge, anyone comes to regard his effort and endeavour as the fruit of the Spirit, he deceives himself utterly; and by this false opinion deprives himself of the real fruits of the Spirit, which are incomparably great.

(ii) DIVINE GRACE AND HUMAN EFFORT

The call of grace and man's free choice

At the first call and beckoning of grace, at the first entering within, the spiritual realm opens up before us, and we are granted the vision of another world, independently of whether we desire it or not. But afterwards this vision, together with the power to dwell constantly within, are left to man's free choice and we must work to attain them.

Nothing comes without effort

May the Lord give you the blessing of a strong desire to stand inwardly before God. Seek and you will find. *Seek God*: such is the unalterable rule for all spiritual advancement. Nothing comes without effort. The help of God is always ready and always near, but is only given to those who seek and work, and only to those seekers who, after putting all their own powers to the test, then cry out with all their heart: Lord, help us. So long as you hold on to even a little hope of achieving something by your own powers, the Lord does not interfere. It is as though He says: 'You hope to succeed by yourself—Very well, go on trying! But however long you try you will achieve nothing.' May the Lord give you a contrite spirit, a humble and a contrite heart.

The tree of life

The essential mood of the penitent is this: 'In the way Thou knowest, O Lord, save me. For my part I will labour without hypocrisy, without deviation and misinterpretation, but according to a pure conscience, doing everything that I understand and that lies in my power.' Whoever can truly feel this in his heart, is accepted by the Lord, who then comes to rule as king within him.

God is his teacher, God it is who prays in him, God it is who wills and acts in him, God it is who bears fruit in him. God is his ruler. Such a state is the seed and the heart of the heavenly tree of life within him.

THE FRUITS OF PRAYER

Dependence on the grace of God

The first seed of the new life lies in the combination of freedom and grace; and growth and ripening come from the development of the same elements. When making a vow to live according to the will of God, for His glory, the penitent should say, 'Only do Thou strengthen and confirm my resolve'; and from then on he must, as it were, place himself every minute in the hand of God, with the prayer, 'Do Thou Thyself perform within me what is pleasing to Thy will'. In this way, alike in consciousness and will and in actual fact, it is God who will be acting in us, both in what we desire and in what we do according to His good pleasure.

But as soon as man himself expects to achieve something in virtue of his own power and self-mastery, then immediately true spiritual life, full of grace, is extinguished. In this state, in spite of immeasurable efforts, true fruit cannot come into being.

Complete serenity

Complete serenity of mind is a gift of God; but this serenity is not given without our own intense effort. You will achieve nothing by your own efforts alone; yet God will not give you anything, unless you work with all your strength. This is an unbreakable law.

The union of freedom with grace

St. Makarios of Egypt says (*First Treatise on Guarding of the Heart*, Chap. xii) that the grace which comes to man 'does not bind his will by force of necessity, nor does it make him unchangeably good willy-nilly. On the contrary, the power of God which exists in the man gives way before his free will, in order to reveal whether the man's will is in accordance with grace or not.' From this moment the union of freedom with grace begins. At first grace stands outside, and acts from the outside. Then it enters within and begins to take possession of parts of the spirit: but it only does this when man by his own desire opens the door for it, or opens his mouth to receive it. Grace is ready to help, if man desires. By himself man cannot do or establish within himself that which is good, but he longs and strives for it. Because of this longing, grace consolidates within him the good for which he yearns. And so it goes on, until man acquires final mastery over himself, and thus is able to fulfil that which is good and pleasing to God.

Human endeavours and grace-given prayer[1]

In response to his asking, a man is sometimes granted grace-given prayer, together with a partial repose and joy in the Spirit, even though in his own lack of prayer he has forced himself to pray with this end only in view, and without acquiring meekness, humility, and love, or fulfilling the other commandments of the Lord. But in character he will remain as he was before. For he has not meekness, since he has made no effort to gain this virtue and has not prepared himself to receive it. He has no humility, because he has not asked for it nor forced himself to be humble. He has no love for mankind, for he has not made this his concern nor has he strenuously prayed to be granted this love. For each man who compels and forces himself to pray, even against his own heart's desire, has also to compel himself to love, to be humble, meek, innocent, and generous. So also must he force himself to self-belittlement, regarding himself as poor and the lowest of all men; he must refrain from idle talk, always studying the words of the Lord and keeping them on his lips and in his heart. He should also force himself to avoid irritation and angry speech, as it is written: 'Let all bitterness, and wrath, and anger, and clamour, and evil speaking, be put away from you, with all malice' (Ephes. iv. 31).

In response to all this the Lord, who thus sees the man's eagerness and purpose, will give him the power to achieve without toil or coercion all the things which previously he found

[1] By St. Makarios of Egypt.

difficulty in preserving, even with strong coercion, because of the sin dwelling in him. And all these virtuous practices will become second nature within him, for at last the Lord comes to the man and dwells in him, and he in the Lord; and the Lord Himself effortlessly works His own commandments within him, filling him with the fruit of the Spirit.

Poor, naked, blind, and worthless

There is no need to be afraid of illusion.[1] It overtakes those who become vain, who begin to think that as soon as warmth has come into the heart they are already at the summit of perfection. In fact this warmth is only the beginning and may not prove stable. For this warmth and peace in the heart may just be something natural—the fruit of concentrated attention. We have to labour and labour, to wait and wait, until the natural is replaced by the grace-given. It is best never to think of yourself as having attained anything, but always to see yourself as poor, naked, blind, and worthless.

Fellow-workers with God

The Lord sees your need and your efforts, and will give you a helping hand. He will support and establish you as a soldier, fully armed and ready to go into battle. No support can be better than His. The greatest danger lies in the soul thinking that it can find this help within itself; then it will lose everything. Evil will dominate it again, eclipsing the light that as yet flickers but weakly in the soul, and it will extinguish the small flame which is still scarcely burning. The soul should realize how powerless it is alone; therefore, expecting nothing of itself, let it fall down in humility before God, and in its own heart recognize itself to be nothing. Then grace—which is all-powerful—will, out of this nothing, create in it everything. He who in total humility puts himself in the hand of the merciful God, attracts the Lord to himself, and becomes strong in His strength.

[1] In Russian, *prelest* (see p. 40, n. 2).

DIVINE GRACE AND HUMAN EFFORT

Although expecting everything from God and nothing from ourselves, we must nevertheless force ourselves to action, exerting all our strength, so as to create something to which the divine help may come, and which the divine power may encompass. Grace is already present within us, but it will only act after man has himself acted, filling his powerlessness with its own power. Establish yourself, therefore, firmly in the humble sacrifice of your will to God, and then take action without any irresolution or half-heartedness.

The spirit of grace and the spirit of a Pharisee

When you undertake some special endeavour, do not concentrate your attention and heart on it, but look upon it as something secondary; and by entire surrender to God open yourself up to God's grace, like a vessel laid out ready to receive it. Whoever finds grace finds it by means of faith and zeal, says St. Gregory of Sinai, and not by zeal alone. However painstaking our work, so long as we omit to surrender ourselves to God while performing it, we fail to attract God's grace, and our efforts build up within us not so much a true spirit of grace but the spirit of a Pharisee. Grace is the soul of the struggle. Our efforts will be rightly directed so long as we preserve self-abasement, contrition, fear of God, devotion to Him, and the realisation of our dependence on divine help. If we are self-satisfied and contented with our efforts, it is a sign that they are not performed in the right way, or that we lack wisdom.

True Christian life is the life of grace

Life is the strength to act. Spiritual life is the strength to act spiritually, according to the will of God. Man has lost this strength; therefore until it is restored to him, he cannot live spiritually, no matter how much he intends to. That is why the flow of grace into the soul of a believer is essential for a true Christian life. True Christian life is the life of grace. A man makes some religious resolution: but in order to be able to act according to it, it is necessary that grace be united with his spirit. When this union is present, moral strength, hitherto evident only temporarily in his first enthusiasm, is impressed on his spirit and remains there always. This re-establishment of the moral strength of the spirit is effected by the regenerating action of baptism, through which man is granted justification and the strength to act 'after God in righteousness and true holiness' (Eph. iv. 24).

Truths which the finger of God inscribes

You write that at times, during prayer, a solution to some problem that perplexes you in your spiritual life comes of itself from an unknown source. This is good. It is the true Christian way of being taught God's truth. Here the promise is fulfilled, 'And they shall be taught of God' (John vi. 45). So indeed it is. Truths are inscribed in the heart by the finger of God, and remain there firm and indelible. Do not neglect these truths which God inscribes, but write them down.

Purifying the source

In order to purify and heal man, divine grace begins first of all by entrusting the source and fountain-head of all human activities to God. In other words, grace turns man's consciousness and power of free will towards Him, so that, using this as its starting point, it may in due course effect healing of all man's powers by means of their own activity: the source has been healed and sanctified, and so all the faculties dependent on that source are gradually purified from this same fountain-head.

Progress in the life of grace

Here is some account of the practices which help to strengthen the powers of man's soul and body in goodness, and which enable the life of grace within the spirit to burn more and more brightly. According to the zeal and efforts of the man who gives himself to God, grace will enter and penetrate him increasingly with its power, sanctifying him and making him its own. But one cannot and should not stop at this stage. This is still only a seed, a starting point. It is necèssary that this light of life should go further, and permeating the entire substance of the soul and body should in this way sanctify them, claiming them for itself; uprooting the alien and unnatural passionateness which now dominates us, it should raise the soul and body to their pure and natural state. The light should not remain enclosed within itself but should spread over our whole being with all its powers.

But since these powers are all infected with what is unnatural, the pure spirit of grace, coming into the heart, is unable to enter directly and immediately into them, being barred out by their impurity.

Therefore we must establish some channel between the spirit of grace living within us and our own powers, so that the spirit may flow into them and heal them, just as dressings heal the sore places to which they are applied.

It is evident that, to act effectively as a channel, all these means must on the one hand bear the character and qualities of a divine and heavenly origin, and on the other be perfectly adapted to our own powers in their natural arrangement and purpose. Otherwise they will not act as an effective channel of grace, nor will our powers be enabled to draw healing from them. Such, then, must necessarily be the origin and inner qualities of these means of healing. As to their outward form, they cannot be anything other than activities, exercises, labour; for they are applied to human powers and faculties whose distinctive quality is action.

These, then, are the activities and exercises which are the means of healing our powers and bringing them back to their lost purity and wholeness: fasting, labour, vigil, solitude, withdrawal from the world, control of the senses, reading of the scriptures and the Holy Fathers, attendance at church, frequent confession and communion.

The two movements of free will

When we are quickened by grace, it is impossible not to be conscious of the fact, but it *is* possible not to pay due attention to it; and so, after living in this quickened state for a while, we descend again into the usual round of activities of the soul and body. The quickening does not complete the act of the sinner's conversion, but only begins it, and there still remains work on oneself; and this work is very complicated. But all that relates to this work may be accomplished in two movements of free will—the turning from the outside world to one's inner self, and the subsequent turning from self towards God. In the first movement, man regains the power over himself which he had lost, and in the second he brings himself as an offering to God—the free will offering of burnt sacrifice. In the first he decides to abandon sin, and in the second, drawing near to God, he vows to belong to Him alone all the days of his life.

The grace of God cleaves a man in two

God's grace, coming first at a man's initial awakening, and afterwards visiting him during the whole period of his conversion, cleaves him in two. It makes him aware of a duality within himself, and enables him to distinguish between what is unnatural and what should be natural; and thus it makes him resolve to sift or winnow all that is unnatural, so that his God-like nature should be brought fully to light. But obviously such a decision is only the beginning of the undertaking. At this stage it is only with his will and intention that he has left the domain of alien unnaturalness, rejecting it, and aiming at the naturalness which he expects and desires. But in fact his whole structure remains as before—that is, saturated with sin; and passions dominate his soul in all its faculties and his body in all its functions, just as they did before—with only this difference, that formerly he chose and embraced all this with desire and pleasure, but now it is not desired or chosen, but is hated, trampled on, rejected. In this state a man has emerged from himself as from a putrefying corpse: he sees how the reek of passion flows from different parts of himself against his will, and sometimes he experiences the stench given off by himself so strongly that it stifles his mind.

Thus the true life of grace in man is in its beginning only a seed, a spark; but a seed sown amongst tares, a spark constantly smothered by ashes. It is still only a feeble candle glimmering in the densest fog. Man by his consciousness and will has attached himself to God, and God has accepted him, has united with him in this self-awareness and point of free choice, within his mind— what is termed the spirit, in St. Antony of Egypt[1] and St. Makarios the Great. And this is the only part of him which is healthy, agreeable to God, and saved. All the other parts are still held prisoner and do not want and cannot be obedient to the demands of the new life: the mind as a whole does not yet know how to think in the new way but thinks as before; the will does not yet know how to desire in the new way, but desires as before; the heart does not know how to feel in the new way, but feels as before. It is the same in the body in all its functions. Consequently man is as yet wholly impure except at one point which is the conscious power of free choice within his mind—what we termed the spirit. God, being wholly pure, enters into union only with this one part; but all the other parts, being impure, remain outside Him and estranged from Him. He is ready to fill the entire man, but does not do so because man is impure. Afterwards, as soon as he is cleansed, God makes known His full dwelling in him.

The all-embracing action of grace

Before the birth of inner life—before the palpable manifestation of the action of grace and union with God—it frequently happens that a man still acts on his own initiative, up to the limit

---

[1] St. Antony of Egypt (251–356), the father of Christian monasticism, lived the greater part of his life as a hermit. The earliest and most celebrated of the monastic *starts*, he became (as his biographer, St. Athanasius of Alexandria, put it) 'a physician to all Egypt'. He was without education, and was never ordained priest. A few of his Letters survive.

of his powers. But when he is exhausted by the failure of his efforts he at last casts aside his own activity, and whole-heartedly gives himself up to the all-embracing action of grace. Then the Lord visits him with His mercy, and kindles the fire of inner spiritual life in him, and he knows from experience that it is not his own former efforts which have effected this great transformation. Afterwards, the more or less frequent withdrawals of divine grace teach him by experience that the sustaining of this fire of life is likewise not dependent on his own efforts.

The frequent appearance of good thoughts and intentions, his frequent infusion by the spirit of prayer—coming he knows not whence or how—similarly convince him by experience that all this good is possible for him only through the action of divine grace, which is always present in him, by the mercy of the Lord, who saves all who are striving for salvation. He gives himself to the Lord, and the Lord alone acts in him. Experience shows that he only succeeds in everything when he entrusts himself wholly to God. So he never turns back, but guards this grace in every way possible.

Theorists are greatly occupied by the question of the relationship between grace and free will. For anyone who has grace within him, this question is resolved by practical experience. He who bears grace in his heart, surrenders himself wholly to the action of grace, and it is grace that acts in him. For him this truth is more evident, not only than any mathematical truth, but even than any experience of his exterior life, because he has already ceased to live outside himself and is wholly concentrated within. He has now only one care, always to be faithful to the grace present within him. Unfaithfulness offends grace, causing it either to retreat, or to reduce its action. Man testifies his faithfulness to grace or to the Lord, by not permitting—either in thoughts, feelings, actions, or words—anything which he knows to be contrary to the will of the Lord. Conversely, he does not leave undone any work or undertaking, as soon as he knows that it is God's will that it should be done, judging from the run of circumstances, and from the indications provided by his inner longings and impulses. This sometimes requires much work, painful self-coercion, and resistance to self, but he is glad to sacrifice everything to the Lord, because after every such sacrifice, he receives inner rewards: peace, joy, and a special boldness in prayer.

These acts of faithful devotion to grace, combined with prayer (which at this stage is already continual) cause the gift of grace to increase in fervour and warmth. When a fire is kindled, movement of air is necessary to keep the flame alight and to strengthen it: in exactly the same way, when the fire of grace is kindled in the heart, prayer is necessary, for it acts as a kind of current of spiritual air in the heart. What is this prayer? It is the mind's ceaseless turning to the Lord in the heart, it is the continual standing before God with the mind in the heart, accompanied or not by appeals to Him, but with feelings only of devotion and contrite surrender to Him in the heart. In this activity, or rather in this frame of mind, lies the principal means of sustaining inner warmth and the whole of the inner order, of dispersing evil or empty thoughts, and of confirming good thoughts and undertakings. Good thoughts and intentions come; man goes deeper into prayer, and according to whether they become stronger during prayer or disappear, he knows whether these thoughts and enterprises are pleasing to God or not. When evil thoughts come, or something begins to trouble the soul, he again goes deeper into prayer without paying attention to what is happening within, and the troublous thoughts vanish. In this way, inner prayer is established in him as the principal driving force and ruler of his spiritual life. No wonder then, that all instructions in the writings of the Fathers are directed pre-eminently towards teaching us how to pray inwardly to the Lord in the right way.

Two stages of prayer. Inward martyrdom[1]

To begin with, during the first stage on the path of prayer, we are left to pray solely by our own efforts. Without doubt, the grace of God helps anyone who prays in sincerity, but it does

[1] By Bishop Ignatii.

not reveal its presence. During this period, passions hidden in the heart come into play, and lead the man who prays to a martyrdom in which defeats and victories alternate ceaselessly, and man's free will and weakness are clearly exposed.

During the second period, the grace of God makes its presence and action felt tangibly, uniting the mind with the heart, and making it possible to pray without dreaming or distraction, but with a heart that weeps and has warmth. At this point sinful thoughts lose their power to overcome the mind.

The first state in the life of prayer can be likened to the bare trees during winter; the second, to the same trees covered with leaves and blossoms brought out by the spring warmth. In both states repentance must be the soul and aim of the prayer. As a reward for the repentance which a man offers while still proceeding by his own endeavours, God grants, in His own good time, a repentance that comes full of grace; and the Holy Spirit, having entered the man, 'maketh intercession' for him 'with groanings which cannot be uttered . . . He maketh intercession for the saints according to the will of God', which He alone knows (Rom. viii. 26–27).

It is thus quite clear that the beginner's search for the place of the heart, that is, his untimely and premature attempts to kindle the manifest action of grace, is a most mistaken undertaking, perverting the due order and system of the science of prayer. Such an undertaking is one of pride and foolishness. In the same way it is not right for a beginner to use the practices recommended by the Holy Fathers for advanced monks and hesychasts.

The quickening power of grace

Work, exert yourself, seek and you shall find; knock, and it shall be opened unto you. Do not relax and do not despair. But at the same time remember that these efforts are no more than attempts on our part to attract grace; they are not grace itself, which we still have to go on seeking. The principal thing we lack is the quickening power of grace. It is very noticeable that when we reason, or pray, or do something else of this nature, it is as though we are forcing into our heart something foreign from outside. This is what sometimes happens: our thoughts or prayers make an impression on us, and their effects descend into the heart to a certain depth, depending on the strength of the efforts which we make; but then, after a while, this impression is cast out again—as a stick which is thrust vertically into water is forced up once more—because of a kind of resistance in the heart which is disobedient and unaccustomed to such things. Immediately following this, coolness and coarseness begin again to take hold of the soul: a sure sign that it was not the action of grace that we experienced there, but only the effects of our own work and effort. Therefore do not be content with these efforts alone; do not rest on them as if they were what you have to find. This is a dangerous illusion. It is equally dangerous to think that in these labours there is merit, which grace is bound to reward. Not at all: these efforts are only the preparation for receiving grace; but the gift itself depends entirely on the will of the Giver. Therefore, with careful use of all the means already mentioned, he who seeks must still walk in the expectation of divine visitation, which gives no warning of its coming, and arrives from whence no one knows.

Only when this quickening power of grace comes will the inner work of the transformation of our life and character really begin Without it, we cannot expect success; there will only be unsuccessful attempts. Blessed Augustine[1] testifies to this, for he worked on himself long and hard, but mastered himself only when he was filled with grace. Work, with confident expectation. Grace will come and set everything in order.

Grace draws all things into unity

So long as the strivings of the spirit burst through spasmodically, first one and then the other, now on this side and now on that, there is no life in them. But when the higher power of divine

[1] St. Augustine (354–430), Bishop of Hippo in North Africa: author of the *Confessions* and the *City of God.*

grace, flowing into the spirit, draws all these strands of effort in one and holds them in unity, then comes the fire of spiritual life.

Serpents and dark clouds

When grace does not dwell in man, demons curl like serpents in the depths of his heart, completely preventing the soul from desiring good; but when grace enters the soul, then these demons are blown about like dark clouds from one part of the heart to another, transforming themselves into sinful passions or distractions, in order to eclipse the remembrance of God and draw the mind away from discourse with grace.

The illusions of the devil and the grace of God: how they are distinguished[1]

Let no one, hearing great tidings about the action of the Spirit from the lips of a sinner, hesitate in unbelief and be troubled in thought, considering that the action he hears about is the work of devils and an illusion. He must cast aside any such blasphemous thought. No! No! Not such is the action of illusion, nor its attributes. Tell me: is it possible for the devil, the enemy and murderer of man, to become his physician? Is it possible for the devil to unite in one the parts and powers of man which were severed by sin, to liberate them from the domination of sin, to lead them out from the state of contradiction and civil war into the state of holy peace in the Lord? Is it possible for the devil to deliver a man from the deep abyss of his ignorance of God, and to give him living knowledge of God, based on experience, which no longer needs any proofs from outside? Is it possible for the devil to preach and explain in detail about the Saviour— to preach and explain how we can draw near to Him through repentance? Is it possible for the devil to restore the lost image in man, to set the distorted likeness in order? Is it possible for him to impart the savour of spiritual poverty, and along with it,

[1] By Bishop Ignatii.

the savour of resurrection, of renewal and union with God ? Is it possible for the devil to raise man to the height of communion with God, a communion in which man becomes as nothing, without thoughts, without desires, entirely immersed in wondrous silence ? This silence is the absorption of all the powers of a human being: they are all drawn towards God, and as it were disappear before His endless majesty.

Illusion acts in one way, and God in another—God the illimitable Master of man, who was and is now their Creator. He who created and re-creates, does He not remain always the Creator ? Therefore, beloved brother, listen how the action of illusion differs from divine action. Illusion, when it approaches man in thought or in dream, in some subtle idea, by some apparition which can be seen with the physical eyes, or by a voice from on high heard by the physical ears, never approaches as an absolute master, but comes as a charmer who seeks acceptance by man, and from his acceptance gains power over him. The action of illusion inside or outside man is always action from without; it is open to man to repel it. Illusion is always met at first by a certain doubt in the heart: only those whom it has conquered decisively accept it without question. Illusion never unites a man who is divided by sin, it does not stop the upsurge of blood, does not lead the ascetic to repentance, does not make him small in his own eyes; on the contrary it fires his imagination, encourages the rush of blood, brings him a certain tasteless, poisonous enjoyment, and flatters him insidiously, inspiring him with self-conceit and establishing in his soul an idol—'I'.

The union of mind and heart and their immersion in God[1]

Divine action is not something material: it is invisible, inaudible, unexpected, unimaginable, and inexplicable by any analogy taken from this world. Its advent and its working within us are a mystery. First it shows man his sin, magnifying it in his eyes, and keeping the horror of sin constantly before his sight.

[1] By Bishop Ignatii.

Leading his soul to self-condemnation, divine action shows him our Fall—this terrible, dark, deep abyss of destruction into which man fell through the sin of our first father. Afterwards, little by little, divine action grants to man increased attention and contrition of the heart in prayer. Having prepared the vessel in this manner, it touches the severed parts suddenly, unexpectedly, immaterially, and they become united in one. Who touched it? I cannot explain: I see nothing, I hear nothing; but I know and feel a sudden change in myself, due to an all-powerful action. The Creator has acted now in renewal, as He acted once in creation. Tell me: could Adam's body, formed of dust, still lying before the Creator and not yet animated by the soul, have any conception of life or any sensation of it? When it was suddenly quickened by the breath of life, could it have considered whether to accept or reject it? The created Adam felt himself suddenly alive, thinking, desiring. Re-creation is accomplished with the same suddenness. The Creator was and is the absolute Ruler: He acts autocratically, in a supernatural manner, far above any thought or conception, with infinite subtlety. He acts spiritually, and not materially.

By the touch of His hand on my entire being, my mind, heart, and body were united, composing a single and unified whole. They became immersed in God, and in God they remain as long as the invisible, incomprehensible, all-powerful Hand holds them there.

Three kinds of desire: mental, compassionate, active

He who has sought the help of grace and now feels its presence must be firmly resolved, not only to correct himself but also to begin to do this *at once*. This desire to correct himself has already directed him in all his previous efforts, but there is still something to be added to its composition or to its perfecting. For there are various kinds of desire. There is mental desire: the mind demands something and the man makes the effort; such a desire directs the preparatory labour. There is compassionate desire: this is born under the influence of the affections and feelings induced by grace. Finally, there is active desire: consent of the will to begin at once in the task of rising from one's fallen state. Supported by God's grace, you should start now.

(iii) THE BURNING OF THE SPIRIT

Quench not the Spirit

'Quench not the Spirit . . . ' (1 Thess. v. 19). Man usually lives careless and unconcerned about the worship of the Church and his own salvation. Then grace awakes the sleeping sinner and calls him to salvation. Listening to this call with a sense of repentance, he resolves to devote the rest of his life to works that are pleasing to God, and by so doing to achieve salvation. This resolution shows itself in eagerness and zeal: and these in their turn become effective when strengthened by divine grace through the holy sacraments. From this moment the Christian begins to burn in spirit—that is, he begins to be unremittingly zealous to fulfil all that his conscience shows him to be the will of God.

It is possible either to sustain and strengthen this burning of the spirit, or to quench it. It is warmed above all by acts of love towards God and our neighbour—this, indeed, is the essence of the spiritual life—by a general fidelity to all God's commandments, with a quiet conscience, by deeds that are pitiless to our own soul and body, and by prayer and thoughts of God. The spirit is quenched by distraction of the attention from God and God's works, by excessive anxiety about worldly matters, by indulgence in sensual pleasure, by pandering to carnal desires, and by infatuation with material things. If this spirit is quenched, then the Christian life will be quenched too.

St. John Chrysostom discusses this burning of the spirit at some length. Here in brief is what he says. 'A thick mist, darkness and clouds are spread over the earth. Referring to this the Apostle said: "For ye were sometimes darkness" (Eph. v. 8). We are surrounded by night, with no moonlight to help us, and it is through this night that we must walk. But God gave us a bright lamp when He kindled the grace of the Holy Spirit in our souls. But of those who have received this light, some have made it brighter and clearer, such as Paul, Peter, and all the saints; but others have quenched it, such as the five foolish virgins or those who suffered shipwreck in the faith, the Corinthian fornicator or the fallen Galatians. And so Paul says, "Quench not the Spirit", that is the gift, for he usually speaks of the "gift" of the Holy Spirit. And what quenches it is an impure life. For if anyone pours water or throws earth upon the light of a lamp, it goes out, and this also happens if they simply pour the oil out of it: in the same manner the gift of grace is extinguished. If you have filled your mind with earthly things, if you have given yourself up to the cares of daily business, you have already quenched the Spirit. The flame also goes out when there is not enough oil, that is, when we do not show charity. The Spirit came to you by God's mercy; and so if it does not find corresponding fruits of mercy in you, it will flee away from you. For the Spirit does not make its dwelling in the unmerciful soul.

'Let us, then, take care not to quench the Spirit. All evil actions extinguish this light: slander, offences and the like. The nature of fire is such that everything foreign to it destroys it, and everything akin to it gives it further strength. This light of the Spirit reacts in the same manner.'

This is the way in which the spirit of grace manifests itself in Christians. Through repentance and faith it descends into the soul of each man in the sacrament of baptism, or else is restored to him in the sacrament of repentance. The fire of zeal is its essence. But it can take different directions according to the individual. The spirit of grace leads one man to concentrate entirely on his own sanctification by severe ascetic feats, another it guides pre-eminently to works of charity, another it inspires to devote his life to the good organization of Christian society, and again another it directs to spread the Gospel by preaching: as for example Apollos, who, burning in spirit, spoke and taught about our Lord (Acts xviii. 25).

THE BURNING OF THE SPIRIT

The signs of the burning of the spirit

'Rejoicing in hope; patient in tribulation; continuing instant in prayer' (Rom. xii. 12).

Here are the signs of the burning of the spirit. 'He who burns in spirit works zealously for the Master, waiting to delight in the good things for which he hopes, and he overcomes the temptations which he encounters, meeting their attacks with patience, and calling unceasingly for help from divine grace' (Blessed Theodoret). 'All these things serve to maintain this fire, the burning of the Spirit' (St. John Chrysostom).

'Rejoicing in hope.' From the first moment of the awakening of the spirit by grace, man's consciousness and yearning pass from the creation to the Creator, from the earthly to the heavenly, from the temporary to the eternal. In this realm lies his treasure, and there is his heart. He does not expect anything here, all his hopes are in the world beyond. His heart withdraws from whatever belongs to this world, nothing in it attracts him, he does not set his expectation on anything here and does not look for present joy. It is in the good things to come that he rejoices, it is these that he firmly hopes to possess. This transplanting of a man's treasure and the hopes of his heart is an essential feature of the awakened and burning spirit. It makes man essentially a pilgrim on earth, seeking his fatherland, the heavenly Jerusalem. Such must be the character of all Christians who have received grace. Therefore the Apostle prescribes also in another place: 'If ye then be risen with Christ (that is, if you are quickened in spirit by the grace of Christ), seek those things which are above, where Christ sitteth on the right hand of God. Set your affection on things above, not on things on the earth. For ye are dead (that is, you have died to all that is earthly, created, temporary), and your life is hid with Christ in God' (Col. iii. 1–3).

Why we fail to burn in spirit

'Burning in spirit . . . ' We all received grace in baptism and chrismation. Therefore we should burn in our spirit, which is

151

animated by the grace of the Holy Spirit. Why is it, then, that we do not burn in the spirit? Because we are occupied largely or even exclusively with our own personal affairs, with worldly business and public life, so that the spirit, although it still makes itself felt, is choked. In order to kindle the spirit, we must be aware of the unsatisfactory direction of our activities, especially their orientation towards earthly and worldly things; and we must enter deeply into the contemplation of what is divine, holy, heavenly, and eternal. The most important thing is to begin to act in a manner that is truly spiritual. And then the spirit will start to burn: for as a result of all this, the gift of grace which lives within us will begin to grow in warmth.

This is the teaching of the Holy Fathers and our spiritual guides. St. John Chrysostom, after describing the different ways of act-ing with firmness and decision, then continues: 'If you fulfil all this, you will attract the Spirit. And if the Spirit dwells in you, then He will make you fervent in all that I have spoken of. And when you become enflamed by the Spirit and by love, then everything will become easy for you. Have you never seen how terrible the bull is when fire is alight on his back? In the same way, you will become unbearable to the devil if you take hold of these two flaming torches'—by which he means the grace of the Spirit and love. Blessed Theodoret speaks of this in fuller detail: 'The Apostle calls the Spirit a gift (that is to say, a gift of grace, animating our spirit) and he commands us to feed this gift with our zeal as a fire is fed with wood: and this means meditation on divine things and spiritual deeds. He says the same in another place: "Quench not the Spirit" (1 Thess. v. 19). The spirit is quenched by those who are unworthy of grace, because they have not kept the eye of their mind pure, and so they do not perceive the rays of grace. In the same way, light is darkness for the physi-cally blind, and in daylight they work in darkness. Therefore the Apostle commands us to burn in spirit, and to have a burning love for things divine.'

THE BURNING OF THE SPIRIT

Solitude, prayer, meditation

Cast aside everything that might extinguish this small flame which is beginning to burn within you, and surround yourself with everything which can feed and fan it into a strong fire. Isolate yourself, pray, think over for yourself what you should do. The order of life, of occupation and work, which you forced yourself to adopt when you were seeking for grace, is also the most helpful in prolonging within you the action of grace which has now begun. What you need most in your present position is solitude, prayer, and meditation. Your solitude must become more collected, your prayer deeper, and your meditation more forceful.

A burning heart

How did our ascetics, fathers, and teachers warm the spirit of prayer inwardly, and establish themselves firmly in prayer? Their great object was to make the heart burn unceasingly towards the Lord alone. God claims the heart because within it lies the source of life. Where the heart is, there is consciousness, attention, mind; there is the whole soul. When the heart is in God, then the whole soul is in God, and man remains in unceasing worship of Him in spirit and in truth.

To some this essential achievement came quickly and easily: such is the mercy of God. How deeply the fear of God shook them, how swiftly was their conscience quickened in all its strength, how rapidly was zeal kindled, sending them on their way pure and blameless before the Lord, how quickly their eagerness in pleasing God fanned the small spark into flames! These are seraphic souls, burning, quick of movement, very active.

But with others everything lags. Perhaps they are indolent by nature, or God's intention for them is different, but their heart does not warm itself quickly. They have all the habits of piety and their life appears outwardly righteous; but all is not well, for their heart is empty of what should be there. This happens not only in the case of laymen but with people living in monasteries and even with hermits.

How to kindle a constant flame of fire in the heart

I will now tell you the way to kindle a constant flame of warmth in your heart. Remember how we come by warmth in the physical world: we rub wood against wood and warmth comes, followed by fire; or we leave a thing in the sun and it becomes warm, and if more rays are concentrated on it, it bursts into flame. The method of bringing spiritual warmth to birth is just the same. The necessary friction is the struggle and tension of ascetic life; inner prayer to God is the exposure to the sun's rays.

Fire in the heart may be kindled by ascetic striving, but such effort alone will not quickly kindle it into flame. There are many obstacles on the path. Therefore from ancient times those who were zealous for salvation and experienced in the spiritual life—through God's inspiration and without relinquishing their ascetic struggle—discovered another way to warm the heart, which they have handed on for the use of others. This appears simpler and easier, but is in fact no less difficult to carry out. This short cut to the achievement of our aim is the whole-hearted practice of inner prayer to our Lord and Saviour. This is how it should be performed: stand with your mind and attention in the heart, being very sure that the Lord is near and listening, and call to Him with fervour: 'Lord Jesus Christ, Son of God, have mercy upon me a sinner'. Do this constantly in church and at home, travelling, working, at table, and in bed: in a word, from the time that you open your eyes till the time that you shut them. This will be exactly like holding an object in the sun, because this is to hold yourself before the face of the Lord, who is the Sun of the spiritual world. At the beginning you must give up an allotted part of your time, night and morning, exclusively to this prayer. Then you will find that the prayer begins to bear fruit, as it lays hold of the heart and becomes deeply rooted in it.

When all this is performed with zeal, without laziness or omission, the Lord will look mercifully upon you and kindle a flame in your heart; and this flame is a sure testimony to the quickening of spiritual life in the innermost parts of your being, to the enthronement of the Lord within.

The distinctive feature of this state when the Kingdom of God is revealed within us, or (which is the same thing) when the unceasing spiritual fire is kindled in the heart, is that our being comes to be centred upon its inner life. The whole of our consciousness is gathered into the heart and stands before the face of the Lord: we pour out before Him all our feelings, falling down before Him in humble repentance, ready to devote all of our life to the service of Him alone. Such a pattern in the soul is established every day from the moment of waking from sleep; it continues amongst all our various activities and occupations, and does not leave us until sleep once again closes our eyes. With the formation of such an order, the misrule which prevailed in the soul until this moment comes to an end.

The sense of incompleteness and dissatisfaction that troubled us before the spiritual fire was kindled in our hearts, the unrestrainable wanderings of thought from which we suffered: all cease now. The atmosphere of the soul becomes clear and cloudless: there remains only one thought and only one remembrance, which is of God. There is clarity within and throughout, and in this clearness every movement is noticed and is valued according to its merits in the spiritual light that flows from the Lord whom we contemplate. Every evil thought and feeling assailing the heart meets with opposition as soon as it approaches and is driven away. If something contrary slips in despite our will, it is at once humbly confessed to the Lord, and cleansed either by inner repentance or outward confession, so that the conscience is always kept clean before the Lord. As a reward for all this inner struggle, we are granted boldness of approach to God in prayer which unceasingly glows in the heart. An unwavering warmth of prayer is the true breath of this life, so that progress in our spiritual journey ends when this warmth is extinguished, just as the life of the body ends with the cessation of our natural breath.

THE FRUITS OF PRAYER

The transfiguration of soul and body by divine fire

I do not say that all is accomplished at once as soon as we attain the state of conscious communion with God. This is only the foundation laid for the next stage, for a new chapter in our Christian life. From now on the transfiguration or spiritualization of soul and body will begin as we share increasingly in the spirit of life that is in Jesus Christ. Having mastered himself, man will begin to instil into himself all that is true, holy, and pure, and to drive out all that is false, sinful, and corporeal. Until now he made strenuous efforts to do this, but was robbed of the fruits of his efforts every moment of the day; so that whatever he succeeded in achieving was at once all but destroyed. Now the case is different. He stands firmly on his feet, not yielding at all before difficulties, and conducts himself according to the aim of his life.

According to St. Barsanouphios,[1] when we receive in our heart the fire which the Lord came to send on earth (Luke xii. 49), all our human faculties begin to burn within. When by long friction fire is ignited and logs begin to burn with it, the logs thus kindled will crackle and smoke until they are properly alight. But when they are properly alight they appear to be permeated with fire, and produce a pleasing light and warmth without smoke and crackling. So it happens within men. They receive the fire and begin to burn—and how much smoke and crackling there is only those who have experienced it can know. But when the fire is properly alight the smoke and crackling cease, and within reigns only light. This condition is a state of purity; the way to it is long, but the Lord is most merciful and all powerful. Thus it is clear that when a man has received the fire of conscious communion with God, what lies before him is not peace but great labour. But from this point onwards he will find the labour sweet and full of fruit, whereas before the work was bitter and bore little fruit or none.

[1] St. Barsanouphios (died c. 540), monk of a monastery near Gaza in Palestine, celebrated as a spiritual guide and director. Together with another monk of the same monastery, John (died c. 530), he is the author of a large collection of more than 800 letters addressed both to monks and lay people.

THE BURNING OF THE SPIRIT

Inner disorder and inner light

The problem which concerns the seeker more than anything is the inner disorder in his thoughts and desires; all his eagerness is bent on finding some way to eliminate this disorder. There is only one way to achieve this—acquire spiritual feeling or warmth of heart, together with the remembrance of God.

As soon as this warmth is kindled, your thoughts will settle, the inner atmosphere will become clear, the first emergence of both good and bad movements in the soul will become plainly apparent to you, and you will acquire power to drive away the bad. This inner light also extends to outside things and makes clear the distinction between right and wrong, giving you the strength to establish yourself in what is right, despite any kind of obstacles. In a word, you now begin true, active spiritual life, for which hitherto you were still searching; and if it appeared, it appeared in you only fitfully.

Those longings for God of which I spoke earlier will also bring warmth, but it is a temporary warmth, ceasing when the longings cease. But the warmth now conceived in the heart remains permanently within, and holds the attention of the mind always fixed upon it.

When the mind is in the heart, this is in fact that union of mind and heart which represents the reintegration of our spiritual organism.

Ceaseless burning within, and the Lord's advent in the heart

The Lord will come to shed His light on your understanding, to purify your emotions, to guide your actions. You will feel in yourself forces which until now were unknown to you. This light will come: not apparent to the sight and senses, but arriving invisibly and spiritually—yet none the less effectively. The symptom of its advent is the engendering at this point of a constant burning of the heart: as the mind stands in the heart, this ceaseless burning infuses it with the remembrance of God, you acquire the power to dwell inwardly, and consequently all your inner potentialities are realized. You accept what is pleasing to God, while all that is sinful you reject. All your actions are conducted with a precise awareness of God's will regarding them; strength is given you to govern the whole course of your life, both within and without, and you acquire mastery over yourself. In this state man is usually more acted upon than active. When the coming of God is consciously experienced in his heart, he achieves freedom of action. Then is fulfilled the promise, 'If the Son therefore shall make you free, ye shall be free indeed' (John viii. 36). It is this and not something wholly unknown that the Lord brings to you.

Do not try to measure your progress

Warmth of heart, about which you write, is a good condition, which should be guarded and maintained. When it weakens, you must continue to kindle it, gathering yourself together inwardly with all your strength and calling upon God. To prevent it leaving you, you must avoid distraction of thought and impressions coming through the senses, which are incompatible with this state. Avoid the attachment of your heart to anything visible, or the absorption of your attention by any wordly care. Let your attention toward God be unwavering, and the tautness of your body unslackened, like a bowstring, or a soldier on parade. But the most important thing is to pray to God and ask Him to prolong this mercy of warmth in the heart.

When the query arises 'Is this it?', make it your rule once and for all mercilessly to drive away all such questions as soon as they appear. They originate from the enemy. If you linger over this question the enemy will pronounce the decision without delay, 'Oh yes, certainly it is—you have done very well!' From then on you stand on stilts and begin to harbour illusions about yourself and to think that others are good for nothing. Grace will vanish: but the enemy will make you think that grace is still with you. This will mean that you think you possess something, when really you have nothing at all. The Holy Fathers wrote, 'Do not measure yourself.' If you think you can decide any question about your progress, it means that you are beginning to measure yourself to see how much you have grown. Please avoid this as you would avoid fire.

The two kinds of warmth

Real warmth is a gift of God; but there is also natural warmth which is the fruit of your own efforts and passing moods. The two are as far apart as heaven and earth. It is not clear in the early stages which kind of warmth you have; later on it will be revealed.

You say that your thoughts tire you out, that they do not allow you to stand firmly before God. This is a sign that your warmth comes not from God but from yourself. The first-fruit of the warmth of God is the gathering of thoughts into one, and their ceaseless concentration upon God. Think of the woman whose issue of blood suddenly dried up. In the same way, when we receive warmth from God, the flux of thoughts is halted.

What then is necessary? Keep your natural warmth but set no value on it, and consider it only as a kind of preparation for God's warmth. And then, grieved over the faintness of the echo of God's warmth in your heart, pray to Him unceasingly and with suffering: 'Be merciful! Turn not Thy face from me! Let Thy face shine on me!' Along with this, increase bodily privations in food, sleep, work and so on. And place everything in the hands of God.

Physical warmth, lustful warmth, spiritual warmth

According to Speransky,[1] those zealous in the spiritual life begin with 'Lord have mercy', but soon they pass beyond this stage. Such has also been our own experience. The flame, once kindled, burns by itself and no one knows how it is fed. Herein

---

[1] It is not clear whom Theophan has in mind here: Count Michael Speransky (1772–1839), the celebrated Russian statesman, or possibly some other Speransky, less well known.

lies the mystery. Only at the moment of coming to ourselves do we find 'Lord have mercy' again in our thoughts.

The words of this prayer are 'Lord Jesus Christ, Son of God, have mercy upon me' or 'Jesus, Son of God, have mercy upon me'. The flame of which we spoke does not kindle immediately, but only after visible labours, when there arises in the heart a certain warmth, constantly increasing and burning ever more brightly during inner prayer. Prayer to the Lord, offered from the depths of our being, arouses spiritual warmth. Experienced Fathers make a strict distinction between the three kinds of warmth: physical warmth, which is straightforward and comes as a result of concentrating our powers in the region of the heart by attention and exertion; lustful bodily warmth, which is sometimes produced in us by the enemy; and spiritual warmth, which is sober and pure. This last is of two kinds: natural— the result of combining the mind with the heart—and grace-given. Experience teaches how to distinguish each kind. This warmth is full of sweetness and so we long to keep it, both for the sake of the sweetness itself, and because it brings right harmony to everything within. But whoever strives to maintain and increase this warmth for the sake of its sweetness alone, will develop in himself a kind of spiritual hedonism. Therefore those who practise sobriety pay no attention to this sweetness, but try simply to stand firmly rooted before the Lord in complete surrender to Him, giving themselves up into His hands. They do not lean on the sweetness coming from this warmth, nor fasten their attention upon it. It is possible, on the other hand, to attach our whole attention to this feeling of sweetness and warmth, taking pleasure in it as in a warm room or garment, and to stop at this point, without trying to climb any higher. Some mystics go no further than this, but regard such a state as the highest that man can attain: it immerses them in a kind of nothingness, in a complete suspension of all thought. This is the 'state of contemplation' attained by some mystics.

THE BURNING OF THE SPIRIT

Inwardness and warmth of heart

The spiritual world is open to him who lives within himself. By remaining within and gazing upon this vision of the other world, we arouse a sense of warmth in our spiritual feelings: and conversely, this same sense of spiritual warmth enables us to dwell within, and awakens our awareness of the inner spiritual realm. The spiritual life matures by the mutual action of both these things—inwardness and warmth. He who lives in spiritual feeling and warmth of heart has his spirit bound and tied, but the spirit of a man who lacks this warmth will wander. Therefore, so as to further constant inwardness, strive after warmth of heart; but strive also, through intense effort, to enter and remain within. That is why he who seeks to remain collected only in the mind— without warmth of heart—strives in vain: in a moment everything is dispersed. And so it is no wonder that, in spite of all their education, scientists constantly miss the truth—it is because they work only with their head.

Inward warmth and dwelling in the heart

To experience some feeling of warmth is very important in the spiritual life. He who has such feeling is already within himself and within his heart. Our attention is always held by the part of us that is active, and if the heart is active—making itself manifest by this feeling of warmth—then we are in the heart.

Preserving warmth and recollection

As soon as you wake up in the morning take care to collect yourself inwardly, and to kindle a feeling of warmth within. Consider this as your normal condition. As soon as it ceases to be so, you may be sure that your inner self is not in order. When, in the morning, you have brought yourself to a warm and collected condition, you must fulfil all your obligations in such a way as not to destroy your inner order, and, when you have the choice, do what supports this condition. In no circumstance do anything that destroys it, for this would mean being your own enemy. Only make it a rule to maintain collectedness and warmth, standing in your mind before God. This in itself will then show you what you must do, and what you should deny yourself.

The all-powerful help in this is the Jesus Prayer. Its practice should become so habitual that it is repeated unceasingly in the innermost heart. This habit will not be established without persistent labour. If it is not already habitual with you, you must begin to do it *now*. It seemed to me that you practised it only when fulfilling your rule of prayer. It has its place there, but you must also practise it unceasingly—sitting or walking, at food and at work. If the Jesus Prayer is not firmly rooted in your heart, leave everything else and practise it alone, until it is established there. This task is simple.

Stand or sit before the icons in an attitude of prayer, and bring your attention down to the place where your heart is: then, without hurrying, practise the Jesus Prayer there, always keeping in remembrance the presence of God. Do this for half an hour, an hour, or more. It is hard at the beginning, but when the habit is once acquired, it will be accomplished as naturally as breathing.

When you have established this order within, spiritual life (or spiritual works as they are called) will begin in you. Here the first demand is purity of conscience, its irreproachability—not only before God, but before men and before yourself, even before inanimate objects. If something minute slips into your thoughts or words which disturbs your conscience, you must immediately repent inwardly before God, who sees everything and will give peace to your conscience.

There remains the struggle with thoughts which will often continue to buzz like importunate mosquitoes. You must learn for yourself how to overcome them: experience will teach you. Of one thing I will warn you. It is normal for thoughts to whirl round the head, and these are of no importance: but watch the ones which pierce your heart like an arrow, leaving their mark as an arrow might leave a scar. Set to work immediately and erase this mark with prayer, restoring the opposite feeling in its place. But when warmth is preserved, such cases are rare and slight.

All is in the hands of God

Where there is zeal, the grace of the Holy Spirit, like a flame, will also be present. A flame is kept ablaze by fuel, and spiritual fuel is prayer. As soon as grace touches the heart, the seed of prayer is sown there, and there straightway follows the turning of mind and heart towards God. Thoughts of God then follow in due course.

The grace of God turns the attention of the mind and heart towards God, and keeps them fixed upon Him. Since the mind is never without activity, when it is turned towards God it will think about Him. That is why the remembrance of God is the constant companion of the state of grace. Remembrance of God is never idle but invariably leads us to meditate on the perfection of God and on His goodness, truth, creation, providence, redemption, judgement, and reward. All these together comprise God's universe or the realm of the spirit. He who is zealous lives always in this realm. Conversely, dwelling in this realm supports and animates zeal. If you want to remain zealous, keep yourself in the state described above. Each part of this realm is as it were a log of spiritual fuel. Always have such fuel within reach, and as soon as you notice that the fire of zeal is waning, take a log from your spiritual woodpile and renew the fire, and all will go well. Out of the sum of all these spiritual movements there will emerge the fear of God, the standing in awe before God in the heart. This fear is the guardian and defender of the state of grace. Steep yourself in this godly fear, reflect deeply upon it, and impress it firmly upon your conscience and heart. Revivify it constantly within yourself, and in its turn it will fill you with life.

Your garret is exactly like a cell in the desert. It is possible for you not to see or hear anything. You can read a little and think; you can pray a little and again think. And that is all. If only God would give us warmth of heart and establish it in us! Pure conscience and unceasing turning to God in prayer will normally produce this warmth. But all is in the hands of God.

CHAPTER V

THE KINGDOM OF THE HEART

from various authors

(i) THE KINGDOM WITHIN US

The ladder to the Kingdom

Enter eagerly into the treasure-house that lies within you, and so you will see the treasure-house of heaven: for the two are the same, and there is but one single entry to them both. The ladder that leads to the Kingdom is hidden within you, and is found in your own soul. Dive into yourself and in your soul you will discover the rungs by which to ascend.

ST. ISAAC THE SYRIAN

The essence of Christian life

People concern themselves with Christian upbringing but leave it incomplete: they neglect the most essential and most difficult side of the Christian life, and dwell on what is easiest, the visible and external.

This imperfect or misdirected upbringing produces people who observe with the utmost correctness all the formal and outward rules for devout conduct, but who pay little or no attention to the inward movements of the heart and to true improvement of the inner spiritual life. They are strangers to mortal sins, but they do not heed the play of thoughts in the heart. Accordingly they sometimes pass judgements, give way to boastfulness or pride, sometimes get angry (as if this feeling were justified by the rightness of their cause), are sometimes distracted by beauty and pleasure, sometimes even offend others in fits of irritation, are sometimes too lazy to pray, or lose themselves in useless thoughts while at prayer. They are not upset about doing these things, but regard them as without significance. They have been to church, or prayed at home according to the established rule, and carried out their usual business, and so they are quite content and at peace. But they have little concern for what is happening in the heart. In the meantime it may be forging evil, thereby taking away the whole value of their correct and pious life.

Let us now take the case of one who has been falling somewhat short in the work of salvation; he becomes aware of this incompleteness, and sees the incorrectness of his way of life and the instability of his efforts. And so he turns from outward to inward piety. He is led into this either by reading books about spiritual life, or by talking with those who know what the essence of Christian life is, or by dissatisfaction with his own efforts, by a certain intuition that something is lacking, and that all is not going as it should.

Despite all his correctness he has no inner peace; he lacks what was promised to true Christians, 'peace and joy in the Holy Spirit' (Rom. xiv. 17). Once this troubling thought is born in him, then by talking with people who have knowledge he will come to realize what the matter is, or he may read about it in a book. Either of these things will enable him to see the essential defect in the order of his life, namely his lack of attention to the movements within himself, and his lack of self-mastery.

He understands then that the essence of the Christian life consists in establishing himself with the mind in the heart before God, in the Lord Jesus Christ, by the grace of the Holy Spirit: in this way he is enabled to control all inward movements and all outward actions, so as to transform everything in himself, whether great or small, into the service of God the Trinity, consciously and freely offering himself wholly to God.

THEOPHAN THE RECLUSE

Mind, heart, and feeling

Once a man has become conscious of what the essence of the Christian life is, and has found that it is something that he does not yet possess, he sets to work with his mind in order to achieve it. He reads, thinks, and talks. And so he comes to realise that the Christian life depends on union with the Lord. But though he reflects on this truth with his mind, it still remains far from his heart, and still is not felt. And so it bears no fruit.

THEOPHAN THE RECLUSE

Look inward: what do you find?

At this point the zealous man looks inward, and what do you think he finds there? Ceaseless wandering of thoughts, constant onslaughts from the passions, hardness and coldness of heart, obstinacy and disobedience, desire to do everything according to his own will. In a word, he finds everything within himself in a very bad state. And seeing this, his zeal is inflamed, and he now directs strenuous efforts to the development of his inner life, to controlling his thoughts and the dispositions of his heart.

From directions on inner spiritual life he discovers the necessity of paying attention to oneself, of watching over the movements of the heart. In order not to admit anything bad, it is necessary to preserve the remembrance of God.

And so he sets to work to achieve this remembrance. But his thoughts can no more be arrested than the wind; his bad feelings and worthless impulses can no more be evaded than the stench of a corpse; his mind, like a wet and frozen bird, cannot rise to the remembrance of God.

What is to be done? Be patient, they say, and go on working. Patience and labour are exercised, but all within remains the same. At last someone of experience is found who explains that all is inwardly in disorder because the forces within are divided: mind and heart each go their own way. Mind and heart must be united; then wandering of thoughts will cease, and you will gain a rudder to steer the ship of your soul, a lever by which to set in movement all your inner world. But how can one unite mind and heart? Acquire the habit of praying these words with the mind in the heart, 'Lord Jesus Christ, Son of God, have mercy upon me'. And this prayer, when you learn to perform it properly, or rather when it becomes grafted to the heart, will lead you to the end which you desire. It will unite your mind with your heart, it will cut off your wandering thoughts, and give you the power to govern the movements of your soul.

THEOPHAN THE RECLUSE

From impotence to strength. An autocrat on the throne of the heart

If all goes well, a man who seeks after God will, upon reflection, decide to give up distractions and live in self-denial, inspired by fear of God and by his conscience. In answer to this decision the grace of God, which until now has acted from without, enters within through the sacraments; and the spirit of man, previously impotent, now becomes full of strength.

The man now acquires self-awareness and freedom within, and begins an inner life before God—a life truly free, reasonable and self-directed. The importunities of the soul and body and the pressure of outward events no longer distract him; on the contrary he begins to control them in accordance with the guidance of the Holy Spirit. He sits as an autocrat on the throne of the heart and from there he ordains how things should be directed and carried out. Such autocracy begins from the first moment of the inner transformation and entrance of grace, but it does not show itself at once in its full perfection. Former masters often force their way through and not only produce disturbance in the inner city, but frequently lead away the ruler of the city as a prisoner.

At the beginning such occasions often occur; but the strength of vigorous zeal, together with constancy of attention to ourselves and to our work, and wise patience in our efforts to perform it, assisted by divine grace, gradually make these occasions more and more rare. Finally the spirit becomes so strong that the attacks of those who formerly had influence over it become like a speck of dust driven against a granite wall. The spirit dwells ever within itself, standing before God; and by the power of God it reigns firm and untroubled.

THEOPHAN THE RECLUSE

Theory and practice. The dangers of too much reading and talk

He who seeks the inner kingdom of God and a living communion with Him, will naturally seek to remain continually in the thought of God. Turning his mind towards Him with all his might, his one desire will be to read only of Him, to speak only of Him. But these occupations alone will not lead to what is sought, unless accompanied by other, more practical activities. A certain type of mystic talks only of these occupations: the reason is that such teachers are people of theory and not of practice. There is some exaggeration on this subject in Roman Catholic instructions concerning spiritual life, and this is not without danger.

This practice of reading and speaking of God will, used on its own, create a facile habit for such things: it is easier to philosophize than to pray or pay attention to oneself. But since it is a work of the mind, which falls so easily into pride, it predisposes a man to self-esteem. It may altogether cool the desire for practical effort, and consequently hinder sound progress by a flattering successfulness in this mental activity.

For this reason sound-minded teachers warn their pupils of the danger, and advise them not to concern themselves too much with such reading and talk to the detriment of other things.

THEOPHAN THF RECLUSE

Do not be too much attached to reading

It is wrong to become too much attached to reading. It leads to no good and builds a wall between the heart and God. It leads to the development of a harmful curiosity and sophistry.

THEOPHAN THE RECLUSE

THE KINGDOM WITHIN US

Finding the place of the heart

At last the period of vexatious searching passes; the fortunate seeker receives what he has sought. He finds the heart and establishes himself in it with his mind before God, and stands before Him unswervingly like a faithful subject before the King, receiving from Him the power and strength to rule over all his inner and outer life, according to God's good pleasure. This is the moment when the kingdom of God enters within and begins to manifest itself in its natural strength.

THEOPHAN THE RECLUSE

The kingdom of God within us; and the spiritualization of soul and body

Now begins the task of accustoming ourselves to spiritual prayer to the Lord. The first-fruits of this prayer quicken our faith, faith reinforces our efforts and multiplies their fruits; and so the work proceeds successfully.

If we attain this habit of spiritual prayer to the Lord, we shall find that, by God's mercy, the inward longing for Him comes more frequently. And subsequently it comes about that this interior involvement is confirmed for ever, and the man dwells inwardly before God without ceasing. This is the establishing of the kingdom of God within us. But let us add that with this comes also the start of a new cycle of changes in our inner life, which may be called the spiritualization of soul and body.

From the psychological point of view, this must be said of the kingdom of God: it is born in us when the mind is united with the heart, both alike adhering steadfastly to the remembrance of God.

Then man surrenders to the Lord his consciousness and freedom as a sacrifice pleasing to Him, and receives from God power over himself; and by strength received from Him he rules over all his inner and outer life as God's vicegerent.

THEOPHAN THE RECLUSE

THE KINGDOM OF THE HEART

A Teacher within you

Instead of concentrating upon external behaviour, all those who work on themselves must have as their aim to be attentive and vigilant, and to walk in the presence of God. If God grants it, a soreness will appear in your heart; then what you desire, or even something higher still, will come of itself. A certain rhythm will set itself in motion, in virtue of which everything will progress aright, coherently and in the proper way, without your thinking about it. Then you will carry a Teacher within you, wiser far than any earthly teacher.

THEOPHAN THE RECLUSE

The new heaven of the heart

Much labour and time is needed in prayer, in order painfully to achieve a state of mind free from all disturbance—that new heaven of the heart in which Christ dwells, as the Apostle says: 'Know ye not your own selves, how that Jesus Christ dwells in you?' (2 Cor. xiii. 5).

JOHN OF KARPATHOS[1]

Three kinds of communion with God

It may seem strange that communion with God still has to be attained when it has already been given to us in the sacrament of baptism and renewed through the sacrament of confession, since it is said: 'For as many of you as have been baptized into Christ have put on Christ' (Gal. iii. 27); 'Ye are dead (that is, dead to sin through baptism or confession), and your life is hid with Christ in God' (Col. iii. 3). And we also know that God is everywhere, not far from each one of us, '. . . if haply they might feel after him. . . . . ' (Acts xvii. 27), and He is ready to dwell in everyone who is willing to accept Him. It is only

[1] John, Bishop of Karpathos (an island between Crete and Rhodes), Greek spiritual writer of the 7th century.

unwillingness, carelessness, and sinfulness that separate us from Him. Now if a person has repented and repudiated everything, and so gives himself to God, what then is the obstacle to the coming of God to dwell in him?

In order to remove misunderstanding it is necessary to discriminate between different kinds of communion with God. Communion begins from the moment when hope of it is stimulated, and it shows itself on man's side in a yearning and aspiration towards God, and on God's side in good-will, help, and protection. But God is still outside man, and man is outside God; they do not penetrate nor enter into one another. In the sacraments of baptism and confession the Lord enters into man by His grace, vividly establishes communion with him, and gives him to taste of all the sweetness of the Divine, as abundantly and intensely as those who have achieved perfection experience it; but afterwards He again conceals this manifestation of His communion, renewing it only from time to time—and then but slightly, merely as a reflection, not as the original. This leaves man in ignorance about God, and about His dwelling in man, until a certain measure of maturity or education has been attained, according to the wisdom of His direction. After this the Lord perceptibly reveals His abode in a man's spirit, which then becomes a temple filled by the Three Persons of the Godhead.

There are, in fact, three kinds of communion with God: a first in thought and intention, which happens at the time of conversion; and two others which are actual, of which one is hidden, invisible to others and unknown to oneself, and the other is evident both to oneself and to others.

The whole of our spiritual life consists in the transition from the first kind of communion with God—in thought and intention —to the third kind—a real, living, and conscious communion.

THEOPHAN THE RECLUSE

Communion with God should be our constant state

It would be wrong to think that since communion with God is the supreme aim of man, it will be granted only at some later time, for instance at the end of all our labours. No, here and now it must be our constant and unceasing state. When we have no communion with God, and do not feel Him within us, we must recognize that we have turned away from our aim and from the way chosen for us.

THEOPHAN THE RECLUSE

Grace enters within through the sacraments of initiation

A mystical communion with our Lord Jesus Christ is granted to believers in the holy sacrament of baptism. At baptism and chrismation[1] grace enters into the heart of the Christian, and thereafter remains constantly within him, helping him to live in a Christian way and to go from strength to strength in the spiritual life.

All of us who have been baptized and chrismated, have received the gift of the Holy Spirit. He is in all of us, but He is not active in all of us.

THEOPHAN THE RECLUSE

Grace and sin do not dwell together

Sin is now driven out from its stronghold and goodness takes its place, while the strength of sin is shattered and dispersed.

'Grace and sin do not dwell together in the mind,' says St. Diadochos, 'but before baptism grace incites the soul to goodness from without, while Satan lurks in its depths, endeavouring to bar all the doors of righteousness in the mind; but from the very moment that we are reborn the devil remains outside and grace dwells within.'

THEOPHAN THE RECLUSE

---

[1] *Chrismation*: according to the practice of the Orthodox Church, immediately after baptism the newly-baptized is anointed with the Holy Chrism (μύρον). The priest makes the sign of the Cross with the Chrism on the various parts of the body, saying, 'The seal of the gift of the Holy Spirit'. This sacrament of chrismation is equivalent to confirmation in the west.

Christ lives within us through the sacraments

You are making strenuous efforts to attain the habit of the Jesus Prayer. May the Lord bless you! You must believe that the Lord Jesus Christ is within us—by the power of baptism and holy communion, according to His own promise; for He is united with us through these sacraments. For those who are baptised are clothed in Christ, and those who take holy communion receive the Lord. 'He that eateth my flesh and drinketh my blood, dwelleth in me, and I in him' (John vi. 56), says the Lord. Only mortal sins deprive us of this great mercy: and even then it can be regained by those who repent and go to confession, and after receive holy communion. You must believe this. If your faith is insufficient, pray that God may increase it and establish it in you, firm and unshakeable.

THEOPHAN THE RECLUSE

Be filled with the Spirit

The Spirit of grace lives in Christians from the time of baptism and chrismation. And to participate in the sacraments of repentance and communion—is not this to receive the most abundant floods of grace?

To those who already have the Spirit it is obviously appropriate to say: 'Quench not the Spirit' (1 Thess. v. 19). But how can one say to such people: 'Be filled with the Spirit' (Eph. v. 18)? The grace of the Holy Spirit is indeed given to all Christians, because such is the power of the Christian faith. But the Holy Spirit, living in Christians, does not effect their salvation by Himself, but works together with the free actions of each individual. In this sense the Christian can offend or extinguish the Spirit—or else he may contribute to the perceptible manifestation of the Spirit's action within him. When this happens, the Christian feels himself to be in an extraordinary state which expresses itself in deep, sweet, and quiet joy, sometimes rising to the rejoicing of the spirit: this is spiritual exultation. Contrasting it with intoxication from wine, the Apostle says that we must not seek the exultation of wine, but the exultation which he calls 'being filled with the Spirit'.[1] Therefore the commandment to 'be filled with the Spirit' is simply an injunction to behave and act in such a manner as to cooperate with or allow free scope to the Holy Spirit, to make it possible for the Holy Spirit to manifest Himself by perceptibly touching the heart.

In the writings of the men of God, who were honoured with this grace of the Spirit and even lived permanently under its influence, we find that two things in particular are required if a man is to achieve this: he must cleanse his heart from passions, and turn to God in prayer. The Apostle Paul stressed these two things, as does St. John Chrysostom. Prayer, he says, allows the Holy Spirit to act freely on the heart: 'Those who sing psalms, fill themselves with the Spirit.' And he speaks later of the cleansing from the passions which leads to the same end: 'Is it in our power to be filled with the Spirit?' he asks. 'Yes, it is in our power. When we purify our soul from lies, cruelty, fornication, impurity and cupidity, when we become kind hearted, compassionate, self-disciplined, when there is no blasphemy or misplaced jesting in us—when we become worthy of it, then what will prevent the Holy Spirit from drawing near and alighting within us ? And He will not only draw near, but will fill our heart.'

THEOPHAN THE RECLUSE

Everything must be done in its own time. An orderly ascent

The Lord, having entered into union with the spirit of man, does not immediately fill him completely or dwell in him wholly. This is not because of any reluctance on His part—for He is ready to fill everything—but because of us: it is because the passions are still mixed with the powers of our nature, not yet separated from them and not yet replaced by their opposite virtues.

While fighting the passions with all zeal we must have the eyes of the mind turned towards God. This is the first principle

[1] 'And be not drunk with wine, wherein is excess; but be filled with the Spirit' (Eph. v. 18).

174

to be maintained in building a way of life pleasing to God. By it we should test the straightness or crookedness of the rules and the ascetic feats which we may have in mind and undertake.

This necessity of being turned inwardly towards God must be fully recognized, because all the errors in the active life seem to come from ignorance of this principle. Not seeing its significance, some people stop short at the exterior stage of devout exercises and ascetic efforts, others stop short at the habitual practice of good deeds, without rising any higher. Others again attempt to pass directly to contemplation. All these things are required of us but everything must be done in its own time. At the beginning there is only a seed, which afterwards develops —not exclusively, but in its general tendency—into one form of life or another. Gradualness is necessary—the orderly ascent from exterior to interior deeds, and then from both to contemplation. Such is always the sequence—never vice versa.

THEOPHAN THE RECLUSE

The parable of the leaven

Remember the Lord's parable about the leaven hidden in the three measures of meal. The leaven does not become noticeable at once, but remains hidden for a certain time, then later on its action becomes manifest, and finally it penetrates all the dough. So also the Kingdom within us is first kept secret, later it reveals itself, and finally opens out and appears in its full strength. It reveals itself, as we saw earlier, by the involuntary longing to withdraw within and stand before God. Here the soul has no power of its own, but is moved by an outside influence. Someone takes it and leads it within. It is God, the grace of the Holy Spirit, the Lord and Saviour: no matter which you say, the meaning is one and the same. God shows by this that He accepts the soul and wishes to be master of it, and at the same time He makes the soul accustomed to His mastery, revealing its true nature. Until this longing appears—and it does not appear at once—man seems to act apparently by himself; and though he is in fact being helped by grace, its action remains hidden from him. He arouses his attention and forms good intentions to be within himself, to remember God, to drive away vain and evil thoughts, and to fulfil all tasks in a way that is pleasing to God; he exerts himself and strives until he is tired, but has no success at all in this undertaking. His thoughts are distracted, movements of passion overwhelm him, there is disorder and error in his work. All this is because God has not yet revealed His mastery over the soul. But as soon as this happens (and it happens when we are overcome by this same involuntary longing to withdraw within and stand before God), immediately everything within comes into order—a sign that the King is present there.

THEOPHAN THE RECLUSE

The indwelling of Christ and the death of carnal passion

St. John Chrysostom writes, 'You will ask, "What will happen if Christ is within us?" "If Christ is in you, your body is dead to sin, but your spirit lives unto righteousness" (Rom. viii. 10).[1] You see how much evil comes from not having the Holy Spirit within you: death, enmity towards God, the impossibility of pleasing Him by submission to His Law, or of belonging to Christ and having Him dwelling in you. Look also how good it is to have the Spirit within you: really to belong to Christ, to have Christ Himself within you, to compete with the angels! For to have a body that is dead to sin, means to begin to live in eternal life, to carry within you—even here on earth—the pledge of the resurrection and the reassuring power to advance upon the path of virtue. Note that the Apostle said not only, "the body is dead", but added, "to sin", so that you should understand that it is the sins of the flesh, and not the body itself, that is mortified. It is not of the body as such that the Apostle speaks; on the contrary he wants the body, although dead, still to remain alive. When our bodies, in so far as carnal reactions are concerned,

[1] In the Authorised Version, this sentence runs, 'If Christ be in you, the body is dead because of sin, but the Spirit is life because of righteousness'. Chrysostom's argument implies a somewhat different translation, reading 'to' instead of 'because of'.

do not differ from those that lie in the grave, this is a sign that we have the Son within us, and that in us dwells the Spirit.'

As darkness cannot stand before the light, so all that is carnal, passionate, or sinful, cannot stand before our Lord Christ and His Spirit. But as the existence of the sun does not abolish the fact of darkness, so the presence within us of the Son and Spirit does not abolish the existence within us of something that is sinful and passionate, but only takes away its power. As soon as an occasion arises, the passionate and sinful elements step forward and offer themselves to our consciousness and will. If our consciousness pays attention and occupies itself with them, then our will may also turn towards them. But if, at that moment, our consciousness and will pass over to the side of the spirit and turn to our Lord Christ and His Spirit, then all that is carnal and passionate will disappear immediately like smoke before a breath of wind. This means that the flesh is dead, powerless. Such is the general rule of life for true Christians; but they are at different stages. When someone remains steadfastly with his consciousness and will on the side of the Spirit, in living and tangible union with Christ our Lord in His Spirit, then at that time nothing carnal or passionate can so much as show itself, any more than darkness before the sun or cold before flames. In such a case the flesh is quite dead and immobile. It is of this stage that St. Paul is speaking in the text quoted by St. John Chrysostom. St. Makarios of Egypt often describes this stage.

The general course to be followed in the spiritual life is well described by St. Hesychios. The essence of his teaching is this: when the flesh and passions arise, turn away from them with disregard, with contempt, with enmity; and turn with prayer to our Lord Christ who is within you—then the carnal and passionate will depart immediately.

THEOPHAN THE RECLUSE

Three kinds of activity : of the intellect, of the will, of the heart

There are three kinds of activity exercised by the powers of the soul. Each kind is adapted at the same time to the movements of the spirit, and leads to a particular type of spiritual feeling. Each leads also to the strengthening of the initial conditions for constant inwardness. These activities are: intellectual activity leading to concentration of attention; activity of the will leading to vigilance; and activity of the heart leading to sobriety. Prayer embraces all these activities at once and unites them all, for prayer in its execution is nothing other than inner activity, as we explained before. These activities, penetrated by spiritual elements, link the soul with the spirit and weld the two together. It is manifest from this how fundamentally necessary they are, and how wrong are those who disregard them. Such people are themselves the cause why their work remains fruitless: they sweat, but see no fruit; and then they quickly cool and it is the end of everything.

THEOPHAN THE RECLUSE

Dwelling in the world of God

When we achieve constant inwardness, then we are also enabled to dwell in the world of God. The reverse is equally true: when this dwelling in another world becomes habitual, only then is constant inwardness secured.

THEOPHAN THE RECLUSE

Two essential preconditions—inwardness and vision

If our mind and heart are to be rightly guided on the path to salvation, there are two essential and unavoidable preconditions —inwardness and the vision of the spiritual world. The first condition introduces man into a certain spiritual atmosphere and the second plants him there more firmly, in a climate favourable to the flame of life. Therefore it may be said that we have but to produce these two preparatory states, and what follows will come of its own accord. People often complain that the heart is hardened, and this is not surprising. Man does not collect himself within, and so is unaccustomed to inward self-awareness; he fails to establish himself where he should, and does not know the place of the heart—so how can his life and its activities be directed aright? It is as if one removed the heart from its place and then demanded that life should continue.

THEOPHAN THE RECLUSE

The eye of the spirit

The purpose of the spirit, as its manifestations show, is to keep man in contact with God and with the divine order of things, independently of all the visible phenomena that surround and flow past him. To be able properly to fulfil such a purpose, the spirit must be naturally endowed with knowledge of God and of the divine order, together with the sense of a more blessed form of existence, which shows itself in a lack of contentment with all things material. This spiritual vision existed, one must suppose, in the first man until the Fall. His spirit clearly saw God and all things divine—as clearly as with normal eyes we today see an object before us. But after the Fall the eyes of the spirit were closed, and man no longer saw what it was natural for him to see. The spirit itself remains and has eyes—but they are closed. Its condition is like that of a man whose eyelids have become stuck together. The eye is intact, it thirsts for light, it longs to see the light, feeling that the light exists; but the eyelids, being stuck together, do not allow the eye to open and to enter into direct contact with the light. Such is obviously the condition of the spirit in man since the Fall. Man has tried to replace the sight of the spirit by the sight of the mind, by abstract mental constructions, by ideologies; but this has always been without results, as we can see from all the metaphysical theories of the philosophers.

THEOPHAN THE RECLUSE

Paradise lost and Paradise regained

So you have begun to realize what real peace means. Glory be to God! Then what is the matter? Now you must advance into

179

the realm where this peace is to be found. Seek Paradise lost, in order to sing the praise of Paradise regained. That is all that matters. Everything outside and apart from this peace is emptiness. And this peace is not far, it is almost within your grasp, although you must desire it, and to desire is not so easy. May the Mother of God and your Guardian Angel help you!

THEOPHAN THE RECLUSE

Dressing and keeping the garden of Eden

The Lord took the man He created and 'put him into the garden of Eden to dress it and keep it' (Gen. ii. 15). This command to dress and keep Paradise must be understood not only in the direct physical sense, but also in its higher spiritual meaning. By 'Paradise' the Holy Fathers mean the soul of the first human beings, the place where the most abundant divine grace dwelt and where a great number of varied virtues bore their fruit. By 'dressing' this spiritual garden they meant what was later called 'spiritual work', and by the 'keeping' of this inner activity they meant the preservation of the purity already gained by the soul.

BISHOP PETER[1]

The inward rule of Christ the King

The kingdom of God is within us when God reigns in us, when the soul in its depths confesses God as its Master, and is obedient to Him in all its powers. Then God acts within it as master 'both to will and to do of his good pleasure' (Phil. ii. 13). This reign begins as soon as we resolve to serve God in our Lord Jesus Christ, by the grace of the Holy Spirit. Then the Christian hands over to God his consciousness and freedom, which comprises the essential substance of our human life, and God accepts the sacrifice; and in this way the alliance of man with God and God with man is achieved, and the covenant with God, which was

[1] Bishop Peter (Ekaterinovski): Russian spiritual writer of the 19th century.

severed by the Fall and continues to be severed by our wilful sins, is re-established. This inner alliance is sealed, confirmed, and given the strength to maintain itself by the power of grace in the divine sacrament of baptism, and for those who have fallen after baptism, in the sacrament of repentance: and afterwards it is constantly strengthened by holy communion.

All Christians live thus; and consequently they all bear the kingdom of God within themselves, that is to say they obey God as King and are ruled by God as King.

Speaking about the kingdom of God within us, one must always add: in the Lord Jesus Christ, by the grace of the Holy Spirit. This is the mark of the Christian—the kingdom of God within us. God is the King over all, He is the Creator of all things and in His Providence watches over them all: but He truly reigns in the soul and is truly professed there as King only after the re-establishment of that union of the soul with Him which was broken by the Fall. And this union is effected by the Holy Spirit in the Lord Jesus Christ, our Saviour.

THEOPHAN THE RECLUSE

(ii) THE UNION OF MIND AND HEART

The storehouse of all our thoughts

When we strive with diligent sobriety to keep watch over our rational faculties, to control and correct them, how else can we succeed in this task except by collecting our mind, which is dispersed abroad through the senses, and bringing it back into the world within, into the heart itself, which is the storehouse of all our thoughts?

ST. GREGORY PALAMAS

Outside is death: within is the kingdom

The kingdom of heaven is within you. In so far as the Son of God dwells in you, the kingdom of heaven lies within you also.

THE KINGDOM OF THE HEART

Here within are the riches of heaven, if you desire them. Here, O sinner, is the kingdom of God within you. Enter into yourself, seek more eagerly and you will find it without great travail. Outside you is death, and the door to death is sin. Enter within yourself and remain in your heart, for there is God.

ST. EPHRAIM OF SYRIA[1]

Specks of dust

You must gather yourself together within your heart and stand there before the Lord. This will show up any speck of dust. Pray, and may God grant your prayer.

THEOPHAN THE RECLUSE

Attending to the heart with discernment

Attention to what goes on in the heart and to what comes forth from it is the chief work of a well-ordered Christian life. Through this attention the inward and the outward are brought into due relation with one another. But to this watchfulness, discernment must always be added, so that we may understand aright what passes within and what is required by outward circumstance. Attention is useless without discernment.

THEOPHAN THE RECLUSE

Beware of the imagination[2]

In the natural order of things, when we try to bring our spiritual powers under control, the path from without to within is blocked by the imagination. To arrive successfully at our inward objective,

[1] St. Ephraim of Syria (c. 306–73): dogmatic and ascetic writer, author of many hymns and commentaries on the Bible. His works, originally composed in Syriac, were translated into Greek at a very early date.

[2] For the meaning of 'imagination' in this and other parallel passages, see above, p. 25.

we must travel safely past the imagination. If we are careless about this, we may stick fast in the imagination and remain there, under the impression that we have entered within, whereas in fact we are merely outside the entrance, as it were in the court of the Gentiles. This in itself would not matter so much, were it not that this state is almost always accompanied by self-deception.

It is well known that the whole purpose of those who are zealous in the spiritual life, is to place themselves in a right relationship with God: and this right relationship is realized and made manifest in prayer. Prayer is the way of ascent to God, and its stages are the stages of our spirit's approach to God. In prayer the simplest rule is not to form an image of anything: gathering the mind within the heart, stand in the conviction that God is near, that He sees and listens, and in this conviction prostrate yourself before Him who is terrible in His majesty and at the same time very close in His loving-kindness towards us. Images, however sacred they may be, retain the attention outside, whereas at the time of prayer the attention must be within—in the heart. The concentration of attention in the heart—this is the starting-point for all true prayer. And since prayer is the way of ascension to God, if our attention deviates from the heart, it means that we are deviating from the way and have ceased to ascend towards Him.

THEOPHAN THE RECLUSE

Descend from your head into your heart

You must descend from your head into your heart. At present your thoughts of God are in your head. And God Himself is, as it were, outside you, and so your prayer and other spiritual exercises remain exterior. Whilst you are still in your head, thoughts will not easily be subdued but will always be whirling about, like snow in winter or clouds of mosquitoes in the summer.

At this stage solitude and reading are two swift helpers.

THEOPHAN THE RECLUSE

THE KINGDOM OF THE HEART

A crowded rag market

When you pray with feeling, where is your attention if not in the heart? Acquire feeling, and you will acquire attention as well. The head is a crowded rag market: it is not possible to pray to God there. If at times the prayer goes well and by itself, that is a good sign. It means that it has begun to be grafted to the heart. Guard your heart from attachments; try to remember God, seeing Him before you and working before His face.

THEOPHAN THE RECLUSE

In the heart is life, and you must live there

I remember your writing to tell me that you get a headache when you try to hold fast your attention. Yes, if you work only with the head, that is what will happen; but when you descend into the heart there will be no strain at all. The head will become empty and there will be an end to thoughts. They are always in the head, chasing one another, and it is not possible to control them. But if you enter the heart, and are able to remain in it, then every time thoughts begin to confuse you, you have only to descend into the heart and the thoughts will flee. It will be a comforting and safe haven. Do not be lazy about descending. In the heart is life, and you must live there. Do not think that this is something to be attempted only by the perfect. No. It is for everyone who has begun to seek the Lord.

THEOPHAN THE RECLUSE

The whole secret mystery of the spiritual life

How should we interpret the expression, 'to concentrate the mind in the heart'? The mind is where the attention is. To concentrate the mind in the heart means to establish the attention in the heart, and mentally to see before you the ever-present and invisible God; it means turning to Him with praise, thanksgiving, and petition, while at the same time taking care that nothing extraneous should enter the heart. Here is the whole secret mystery of the spiritual life.

The most important ascetic undertaking is to keep the heart from passionate movements, and the mind from passionate thoughts. You should look into the heart and drive away from it all that is wrong. Do everything that is prescribed, and then you will be almost a nun, and perhaps completely a nun.[1] Even outside a convent, one can be a nun if one lives as a nun, while even in a convent a nun may be a laywoman.

THEOPHAN THE RECLUSE

The hermitage of the heart. Different kinds of feelings in prayer

You dream of a hermitage. But you already have your hermitage, here and now! Sit still, and call out: 'Lord, have mercy!' When you are isolated from the rest of the world, how will you fulfil the will of God? Simply by preserving within yourself the right inner state. And what is this? It is a state of unceasing remembrance of God in fear and piety, together with the remembrance of death. The habit of walking before God and keeping Him in remembrance—such is the air we breath in the spiritual life. Created as we are in the image of God, this habit should exist in our spirit naturally: if it is absent, that is because we have fallen away from God. As a result of this fall, we have to fight to acquire the habit of walking before God. Our ascetic struggle consists essentially in the effort to stand consciously before the face of the ever-present God; but there are also various secondary activities, which likewise form part of the spritual life. Here too, there is work to be done, in order to direct these activities to their true aim. Reading, meditation, prayer, all our occupations and contacts, must be conducted in such a way as not to blot out or disturb the remembrance of God. The seat of our consciousness and attention must also be concentrated on this remembrance of God.

The mind is in the head, and intellectuals live always in the

[1] Theophan's correspondent is still living in the world.

head. They live in the head and suffer from unceasing turbulence of thoughts. This turbulence does not allow the attention to settle on any one thing. Neither can the mind, when it is in the head, dwell constantly on the one thought of God. All the time it keeps running away. For this reason, those who want to establish the one thought of God within themselves, are advised to leave the head and descend with their mind into their heart, and to stand there with ever present attention. Only then, when the mind is united with the heart, is it possible to expect success in the remembrance of God.

This, then, is the aim which you should now set before yourself, and towards which you should begin to advance. Do not think that this task is beyond your strength; but also do not think that it is so easy that you have only to wish it, and it will be immediately accomplished. The first step in attracting the mind to the heart is essentially to be moved with sympathy, entering with your feelings into the meaning of the prayers which you read or hear; for it is the feelings of the heart which usually dominate the mind. If you take this first step as you should, these feelings will change according to the content of the prayers. But besides this first kind of feelings there are others, far stronger and more overwhelming—feelings which take captive both our consciousness and heart, enchaining the soul and giving it no freedom to continue reading, claiming its attention wholly for themselves. These are special feelings; and as soon as they are born, the soul too gives birth to prayers which are their very progeny. You must never interrupt these special feelings and prayers which are born in the heart—do not, for instance, go on reading, but stop at once—for you must leave them freedom to pour out until they are exhausted and emotion returns to the level of the more usual feelings during prayer. This second form of prayer is more powerful than the first, and sends the mind down into the heart more quickly. But it can only act after the first form, or together with it.

THEOPHAN THE RECLUSE

THE UNION OF MIND AND HEART

Our hearts are restless till they rest in Thee

Maybe in your case God asks for a final surrender of your heart, and your heart longs for God. For without God it can never be content but remains for ever unsatisfied. Examine yourself from this point of view. Perhaps you will find here the door to God's dwelling place.

THEOPHAN THE RECLUSE

The Lord's reception room

You seek the Lord? Seek, but only within yourself. He is not far from anyone. The Lord is near all those who truly call on Him. Find a place in your heart, and speak there with the Lord. It is the Lord's reception room. Everyone who meets the Lord, meets Him there; He has fixed no other place for meeting souls.

THEOPHAN THE RECLUSE

Inner attention and solitude in the heart

You preserve inner attention and solitude in the heart. May the Lord help you always to remain thus. This is the most important thing in our spiritual life. When consciousness is within the heart, there too is the Lord; and so the two become united and the work of salvation progresses successfully. The entry is barred to evil thoughts, and still more to emotions and moods. The Name of the Lord by itself disperses everything alien to it and attracts everything akin.

What have you to fear above all else? Self-satisfaction, self-appreciation, self-conceit, and all other things beginning with *self*.

Work out your salvation with fear and trembling. Kindle and maintain a contrite spirit, a humble and a contrite heart.

THEOPHAN THE RECLUSE

A feeling of warm tenderness

During prayer, it is essential that the spirit should be united with the mind, and that they should recite the prayer together; but whereas the mind works with words, uttered either mentally or aloud, the spirit acts through the feeling of warm tenderness[1] or tears. Union of the two is given in due course by divine grace; but for the beginner, it is enough if the spirit sympathises and co-operates with the mind. If attention is kept by the mind, the spirit is bound to feel true warmth and tenderness. The spirit is sometimes called the heart, just as the mind is sometimes termed the head.

BISHOP IGNATII

Prayer of the mind, of the heart, and of the soul

Prayer is called 'of the mind', when it is recited by the mind with profound attention, and with the sympathy of the heart. Prayer is called 'of the heart', when it is recited by the mind united with the heart, when the mind descends as it were into the heart, and sends up the prayer from its depths. Prayer is called 'of the soul', when it comes from the whole soul, with the participation of the body itself—when it is offered by the whole being, which becomes so to speak the mouthpiece of the prayer.

The Holy Fathers in their writings often include under the term 'prayer of the mind' or 'mental prayer', both prayer of the heart and prayer of the soul. But sometimes they distinguish them. Thus St. Gregory of Sinai said: 'Cry out unceasingly with the mind, or with the soul.' But nowadays, when oral teaching on this subject has greatly diminished, it is very useful to know the distinctions between definitions. In some people prayer of the mind is more active, in others prayer of the heart, in yet others prayer of the soul: it all depends how each is gifted, either naturally or through grace, by the Giver of all good. But sometimes in the same ascetic struggler first one prayer and then

[1] In Russian, *umilenie* (see above, p. 124, n. 2).

another may be active. Very often, indeed in most cases, such prayer is accompanied by tears.

BISHOP IGNATII

How to achieve discernment of thoughts

For you, the path of salvation is still dark. Read the first paragraphs of Philotheos of Sinai in the *Philokalia*, and see what is said there.[1] One act is required—and that is all: for this one act pulls everything together, and keeps everything in order. Try to organize yourself as Philotheos directs, and you will receive the right order within, as you will clearly realize. This one act is to stand with attention in your heart, and to remain there before God in worship. This is the beginning of spiritual wisdom.

You wish to grow wise in discernment of thoughts. Descend from the head into the heart. Then you will see all thoughts clearly, as they move before the eye of your sharp-sighted mind. But until you descend into the heart, do not expect to have due discrimination of thoughts.

THEOPHAN THE RECLUSE

What it means to be with the mind in the heart

You ask what it means, to be with the mind in the heart? It means this. You know where the heart is? How can you help knowing it having once learnt? Then stand there with attention and remain steadfastly within, and you will have your mind in your heart. The mind is inseparable from attention; where one is there will be the other.

You have written that you often feel a fire in your heart when you read the Akathist to our sweetest Lord Jesus. Let your attention, then, be in the place where you feel this fire; and remain there, not only during prayer but at all other times. It is not enough just to stand at prayer: you must stand with awareness that you are facing the Lord, before His all-seeing eye, which

[1] St. Philotheos of Sinai: Greek spiritual writer of ?7th–8th century, much influenced by St. John Climacus.

189

penetrates the secret depths of the heart; and in order to stand thus, endeavour to have some warm feeling towards God, of fear, love, hope, devotion, grief-laden contrition, or something akin to these. This is the basic principle of inner order. Watch, and as soon as you see that this order is disturbed, hasten to restore it.

THEOPHAN THE RECLUSE

Finding the place of the heart

When we read in the writings of the Fathers about the place of the heart which the mind finds by prayer, we must understand by this the spiritual faculty that exists in the heart. Placed by the Creator in the upper part of the heart, this spiritual faculty distinguishes the human heart from the heart of animals: for animals have the faculty of will or desire, and the faculty of zealousy or fury, in the same measure as man. The spiritual faculty in the heart manifests itself—independently of the intellect—in the conscience or consciousness of our spirit, in the fear of God, in spiritual love towards God and our neighbour, in feelings of repentance, humility, or meekness, in contrition of the spirit or deep sadness for our sins, and in other spiritual feelings; all of which are foreign to animals. The intellectual faculty in man's soul, though spiritual, dwells in the brain, that is to say in the head: in the same way the spiritual faculty which we term the spirit of man, though spiritual, dwells in the upper part of the heart, close to the left nipple of the chest and a little above it. Thus the union of the mind with the heart is the union of the spiritual thoughts of the mind with the spiritual feelings of the heart.

BISHOP IGNATII

The heart is the innermost man

The heart is the innermost man, or spirit. Here are located self-awareness, the conscience, the idea of God and of one's complete dependence on Him, and all the eternal treasures of the spiritual life.

THEOPHAN THE RECLUSE

THE UNION OF MIND AND HEART

Do not ask how

Where is the heart? Where sadness, joy, anger, and other emotions are felt, here is the heart. Stand there with attention. The physical heart is a piece of muscular flesh, but it is not the flesh that feels, but the soul; the carnal heart serves as an instrument for these feelings, just as the brain serves as an instrument for the mind. Stand in the heart, with the faith that God is also there, but *how* He is there do not speculate. Pray and entreat that in due time love for God may stir within you by His grace.

THEOPHAN THE RECLUSE

The hidden man of the heart

The spirit of wisdom and revelation, and a heart that is cleansed, are two different matters; the former is from on high, from God, the latter is from ourselves. But in the process of acquiring Christian understanding they are inseparably united, and this understanding cannot be gained unless both of them are present together. The heart alone, despite all purification—if purification is possible without grace—will not give us wisdom; but the spirit of wisdom will not come to us unless we have prepared a pure heart to be its dwelling-place.

The heart is to be understood here, not in its ordinary meaning, but in the sense of 'inner man'. We have within us an inner man, according to the Apostle Paul, or a hidden man of the heart, according to the Apostle Peter. It is the God-like spirit that was breathed into the first man, and it remains with us continuously, even after the Fall. It shows itself in the fear of God, which is founded on the certainty of God's existence, and in the awareness of our complete dependence on Him, in the stirrings of conscience and in our lack of contentment with all that is material.

THEOPHAN THE RECLUSE

THE KINGDOM OF THE HEART

The lever which controls everything

The lever which controls all our activities is the heart. Here are formed the convictions and sympathies which determine the will and give it strength.

THEOPHAN THE RECLUSE

The life of the heart

No one has power to command the heart. It lives its own special life. It rejoices of itself, it is sad of itself; and no one can do anything about this. Only the Master of all, holding all in His right hand, has power to enter the heart, to put feelings into it independently of its naturally changing currents.

THEOPHAN THE RECLUSE

At home in the heart

Congratulations on your safe return! Your own home is paradise after an absence. Everyone feels alike about this. Exactly the same feeling comes to us when, after distraction, we return to attention and to inner life. When we are in the heart, we are at home; when we are not in the heart, we are homeless. And it is about this above all that we must take trouble.

THEOPHAN THE RECLUSE

The purpose for which man was created

One must not be without work for a single moment. But there is work performed by the body, visibly, and there is work which is done mentally, invisibly. And it is this second kind that constitutes real work. It consists primarily in the unceasing remembrance of God, with the prayer of the mind in the heart. Nobody sees it, yet those who are in this state work with ceaseless vigour. This is the one thing necessary. Once it is there, do not worry about any other work.

THE UNION OF MIND AND HEART

The first divine decree about man is that he should be in living union with God, and this union consists of living in God with the mind in the heart: thus anyone who aims at such a life, and still more anyone who participates in it to some extent, can be said to fulfil the purpose in life for which he was created. Those who seek this living union should understand what they are trying to do, and not be troubled at their lack of achievement in any specially important external feats. This work by itself embraces all other action.

THEOPHAN THE RECLUSE

Union with the Lord

Every real Christian must always remember and must never let himself forget, that it is indispensable for him to be united with Our Lord the Saviour in his whole being; to let the Lord dwell in his mind and heart, and to begin to live according to His most holy life. The Lord took our flesh, and we must take on His flesh and His all-holy Spirit, accepting them and holding fast to them for ever. Only such a union with Our Lord will give us that peace and good-will, that light and life which we lost in the first Adam, and which are now renewed within us by the second Adam, the Lord Jesus Christ. And the surest way to achieve this union with the Lord, next to communion of His Flesh and Blood, is the inner Jesus Prayer.

BISHOP JUSTIN

Someone who is ever present

'I am trying to take heart.' May God help you! But do not neglect the most important thing, to be concentrated with the mind in the heart. Direct all your efforts chiefly to this. The only way is to try to stand with attention in the heart, remembering the omni-presence of God, and that His eye looks into your heart. Firmly believe that although you may be alone, you always have—not only near you, but within you—someone who is ever present, looking at you and seeing all that is in you. What I wrote to you about reciting the Jesus Prayer several times a day will prove a very powerful means towards this end. Do so for ten to fifteen minutes at a time; and it is better to stand in the position of prayer, making bows from the waist or not, as suits you best. Work in this manner, and pray to God that He may finally grant you to know in the end what it means to have a 'soreness' in the heart, as *staretz* Parthenii puts it. This is not given at once. It will take a year of concentrated work, or perhaps more, before any traces of it will begin to appear. May the Lord bless you in that work and on that path; do not think of it as a secondary activity, but regard it as your principal work.

THEOPHAN THE RECLUSE

Standing before the invisible Lord

To stand guard over the heart, to stand with the mind in the heart, to descend from the head into the heart—all these are one and the same thing. The core of the work lies in the concentration of attention and the standing before the invisible Lord, not in the head but within the chest, close to the heart and in the heart. When the divine warmth comes, all this will be clear.

THEOPHAN THE RECLUSE

Concentrated within yourself

Be concentrated within yourself and try not to leave the heart, for the Lord is there. Seek this state and work for it. When you have attained to it you will realize how precious it is.

THEOPHAN THE RECLUSE

A baby in its mother's arms

The fact that you are directed by feeling, or that you have spiritual feelings in general, does not yet mean that you are standing firmly with attention in the heart. When this last state is attained, then the mind remains in the heart permanently, standing before the Lord in fear and piety, and it has no desire to move thence, any more than a baby desires to move when resting in its mother's arms. May the Lord help you to reach this point.

THEOPHAN THE RECLUSE

The Jesus Prayer unites the mind with the heart

All your inner disorder is due to the dislocation of your powers, the mind and the heart each going their own way. You must unite the mind with the heart: then the tumult of your thoughts will cease, and you will acquire a rudder to guide the ship of your soul, a lever with which to put all your inner world in movement. How can this union be achieved ? Make it your habit to pray these words with the mind in the heart: 'Lord Jesus Christ, Son of God, have mercy upon me.' And this prayer, when you have learnt to use it properly, or rather, when it becomes grafted to the heart, will lead you to the end which you desire: it will unite your mind with your heart, it will quell the turbulence of your thoughts, and it will give you power to govern the movements of your soul.

THEOPHAN THE RECLUSE

The pool of Bethesda

So long as a state of inner disorder prevails within us, the work of prayer may be present, but the heart is almost always cold, being very seldom moved to warmth and fervent prayer. When this inner confusion is eliminated, on the other hand, the warmth of prayer is constant, and there is only occasional cooling; and this is soon overcome by patiently remaining in the order of life and occupations which arouse the feeling of warmth. There is also a great difference in the attitude of the heart towards attacks of vanity and passions. Who is free from them ? But in the former condition they entered the heart, took possession of it, and (as if by force) captured its sympathies, so that the heart was continually defiled by taking pleasure in sinful thoughts, although in this state also there were no sinful deeds. Now when the same attacks approach, the guardian—attention—stands permanently at the entrance of the heart, and in the Name of the Lord Jesus repulses the enemies; only seldom is the enemy successful in subtly insinuating some favourite temptation. This, however, is immediately noticed, and is cast out and purified by repentance, so that no trace of it remains.

During the period of seeking, before we reach this stage, we spend years sitting by the water's edge, crying out like the man at the pool of Bethesda, 'I have no one to put me into the pool' (John v. 7). Oh when will the salvation of Israel come, to put us into the pool that gives life! How is it possible that He, accepted by us within, should make us languish in this manner? The fault is ours: He is indeed within us, but we ourselves do not stand before Him in His presence. Therefore we must return within ourselves, and find Him there. We have read enough, now we must act; we have watched enough how others walk, now we must walk ourselves.

THEOPHAN THE RECLUSE

Fulfilment of the commandments—before and after the union of mind and heart

The fulfilment of the commandments that comes before the union of the mind with the heart, is different from the fulfilment of the commandments that comes after. Before the union, the ascetic wrestler fulfils the commandments with the greatest labour, having to force and compel his fallen nature. But once this union is achieved, the spiritual power that unites his mind with the heart, itself draws him on to fulfil them, making it comfortable, easy and pleasant for him to do so. 'I will run the way of thy commandments, when thou hast set my heart at liberty', as the Psalmist said (Ps. cxviii. 32. Sept.).[1]

BISHOP IGNATII

[1] Psalm cxix. 32 (B.C.P.).

THE UNION OF MIND AND HEART

The essential thing in prayer

The essential thing is to unite the mind with the heart in prayer. This is accomplished by God's grace at the proper time which He Himself determines. Our earlier techniques are completely replaced by the unhurried uttering of the Prayer; there should be a short pause after every prayer, breathing should be quiet and leisurely, and the mind should be enclosed in the words of the prayer. With such methods, we can easily attain a certain degree of attention. Very quickly the heart begins to feel in sympathy with the attention of the mind as it prays. The concord of heart and mind begins, little by little, to be transformed into the union of the mind with the heart, and the way of prayer recommended by the Fathers will then establish itself automatically. Mechanical methods of a physical kind are suggested by the Fathers exclusively as means to achieve attention in prayer quickly and easily, but not as something essential.

BISHOP IGNATII

The place of mechanical methods

The essential and indispensable part of prayer is attention. Without attention, there is no prayer. True attention, full of grace, comes from mortification of the heart towards the world. Mechanical methods always remain something secondary—simply means towards an end. The same Holy Fathers who suggest introducing the mind into the heart in conjunction with breathing, say that when the mind has acquired the habit of being united with the heart—or more correctly, when this union is achieved by the gift and action of grace—the mind no longer needs the help of these mechanical methods for such union, but simply by itself, by its own movement, unites with the heart.

BISHOP IGNATII

THE KINGDOM OF THE HEART

The way of breathing

The descent of the mind into the heart by the way of breathing is suggested for the case of anyone who does not know where to hold his attention, or where the heart is; but if you know, without this method, how to find the heart, choose your own way there. Only one thing matters—to establish yourself in the heart.

THEOPHAN THE RECLUSE

Hidden treasure

May the Lord help you to be fully alive and to preserve sobriety. But do not forget the chief thing, to unite the attention and mind with your heart, and remain there unceasingly, before the Lord. Every effort that you make in prayer must be directed towards this. Pray to the Lord, that He may give you this blessing: it is the treasure hidden in the field, the pearl beyond price.

THEOPHAN THE RECLUSE

CHAPTER VI

WAR WITH PASSIONS
from various authors

(i) WAR WITH PASSIONS

A medicine which cures all the passions

We must know that the constant invocation of the Name of God is a medicine which cures not only all the passions but also their effects. As a physician applies a cure or a poultice to the patient's wound, and these take effect though the patient himself does not know how this happens, so the Name of God when invoked kills all passions, although we do not know how.

STS. BARSANOUPHIOS AND JOHN

Flee for refuge to the Name

My brother, the passions are afflictions; and so the Lord does not excommunicate us because of them, but He says: 'Call upon me in the time of affliction; and I will deliver thee, and thou shalt glorify me' (Ps. xlix. 15. Sept.).[1] Therefore, when beset by any kind of passion, there is nothing more useful than to call upon the Name of God. All we can do, weak as we are, is to flee for refuge to the Name of Jesus. For the passions, being demons, retreat if this Name is invoked.

STS. BARSANOUPHIOS AND JOHN

[1] Ps. l. 15 (B.C.P.).

The four steps of the ladder

Remember the wise teaching of St. John of the Ladder. He describes the way of our ascension to God in the form of a ladder with four steps. Some people, he says, tame their passions; others sing, that is, pray with their lips; the third practise inner prayer; finally the fourth rise to seeing visions. Those who want to ascend these four steps cannot begin from the top, but must start from the bottom; they must step onto the first rung and so ascend to the second, then to the third, and finally to the fourth. By this ladder everyone can ascend to heaven. First you must work on taming and reducing passions; then practise psalmody— in other words, attain the habit of oral prayer; after this, practise inner prayer; and so at last reach the step from which it is possible to ascend to visions. The first is the work of the novice; the second is the work of those who are progressing; the third, of those who have progressed to the end; and the fourth is reserved for those who have achieved perfection.

THEOPHAN THE RECLUSE

Only one way to begin—by taming the passions

There is only one way to begin: and that is by taming passions. These cannot be brought under control in the soul except by guarding the heart and by attention. Those, therefore, who pass through all these stages in due order, each in its own time, can, when the heart is cleansed from passions, devote themselves entirely and wholly to psalmody, and to fighting against thoughts; and they can look up towards heaven with their physical eyes or contemplate it with the spiritual eyes of the soul, praying aright in purity and truth.

THEOPHAN THE RECLUSE

The three spiritual giants

If you wish to gain victory over the passions, enter within yourself through prayer and God's help; then descend into the depths of your heart and there track down these three powerful giants—forgetfulness, laziness, and ignorance. It is these three who uphold the ranks of our spiritual adversaries: supported by these three, all the other passions, returning to the heart, act, live, and gain strength in self-indulgent and uninstructed souls. But if by means of great attention and persistence of mind, and with help from above, you find those evil giants that are unbeknown to many, you will easily drive them away with the weapons of righteousness—with the remembrance of what is good, with the eagerness that spurs the soul to salvation, and with knowledge from heaven.

ST. MARK THE MONK[1]

Spiritual thieves

Just as thieves do not lightly attack a place where they see royal weapons prepared against them, so he who has grafted prayer into his heart is not easily robbed by the thieves of the mind.

ST. MARK THE MONK

Fighting Satan in the heart

The most important work that a spiritual wrestler can do, is to enter within the heart, there to fight Satan; to hate and repel the thoughts that he inspires and to wage war upon him.

ST. MAKARIOS OF EGYPT

Exile and restoration

After rendering man an exile from Paradise, through his trespass, and so excommunicating him from God, the devil with his demons acquired access to the reasoning power of every man, so as to sway it mentally by day and night, in some people

---

[1] St. Mark the Monk or Ascetic (also known as Mark the Hermit): Greek ascetic author of the early 5th century, who lived as a hermit in Egypt or Palestine.

more, in others less, and in yet others, to a very great degree. And the only way to protect oneself against the devil is by constant remembrance of God: this remembrance must be imprinted in the heart by the power of the Cross, thus rendering the mind firm and unyielding. This is the aim at which all our efforts in the inner spiritual life are directed. Every Christian is called to follow this path, and if he travels instead in another direction, he strives in vain. Any man who has God within him also undertakes all the varied spiritual exercises with this same purpose in view: by means of voluntary self-denial he strives to call down the bounty of the all-merciful God, that God may restore to him his former status, setting the imprint of Christ in his mind; as the Apostle says: 'My little children, of whom I travail in birth again until Christ be formed in you' (Gal. iv. 19).

ST. SIMEON THE NEW THEOLOGIAN

The protection of the virtues

He who is always at home within his own heart is a stranger to all the pleasures of this life. He walks in the Spirit, and so knows nothing of the lusts of the flesh. All the wiles of the demons against such a man remain ineffective, for he makes his way under the protection of the virtues, which stand as gatekeepers keeping guard over the city of purity.

ST. DIADOCHOS OF PHOTIKE

Separation from God and its consequences

If our spirit should sever itself from God, then the power of self-determination given to man by God will be also taken away from us. Then a man can no longer master either the inclinations of the soul, or the needs of his body, or outside contacts. Then he will be torn asunder by the desires of his soul and body and by the vanity of exterior life, although all these things on the superficial level seem to contribute to his own pleasure and happiness. Compare these two states of life and you will see that in the first man lives wholly within himself before God, and that in the second man is wholly outside himself, forgetting God. This second state of life is made much worse by the entering in of passions which take root in the ego and penetrate all the soul and body, and give an evil direction to all that is there, a direction that is not constructive but destructive, turning a man away from the path of the Spirit and the fear of God, setting him against his conscience. In this way the man becomes still more superficial than before.

THEOPHAN THE RECLUSE

Merciless and ruthless towards ourselves

Giving yourself in prayerful surrender to God and His grace, call out each of the things that incite you to sin and try to turn your heart away from them, directing it towards their opposite. In this way they will be uprooted from the heart and their violence will subside. In this task give free scope to your power of discernment and lead your heart in its wake.

This struggle against the forces of evil is absolutely essential if we are to break our own will. It is necessary to go on working on ourselves in this way until, instead of self-pity, there is born in us mercilessness and ruthlessness towards ourselves, a desire to suffer, to torture ourselves, to tire out our soul and body. This must be continued until, instead of trying to please men, we form a feeling of repulsion against all bad habits and connections—until we form a hostile and fierce resistance against them, at the same time submitting ourselves to all the wrongs and disparagements which men inflict upon us. It is necessary to go on working until our appetite exclusively for things material, sensory, and visible disappears completely, and is replaced by a feeling of disgust for such things; and instead we begin to thirst and to search only for what is spiritual, pure, and divine. Instead of earthliness—the limitation of life and happiness solely to this earth—the heart comes to be filled with a sense of being but a pilgrim on earth, whose whole longing is for his heavenly home.

THEOPHAN THE RECLUSE

I will rise up and go forth

After the initial awakening by grace, the first step belongs to man's free will. Exercising this free will, he journeys into himself in three ways. First, his will inclines towards good and chooses it. Secondly, it removes obstacles: in order to disrupt the ties which bind him to sin, it banishes from his heart self-pity, the desire to please men, the inclination towards things sensory and earthy, and in their stead it stirs up mercilessness to himself, absence of desire for things of the senses, acceptance of every kind of disgrace. It makes him feel that his true home lies in the world to come, whereas here he is but a wanderer and an exile. Thirdly, free will is inspired to start at once on the right path, permitting no self-indulgence, and making man hold himself constantly on the alert.

In this way everything calms down in the soul. Incited by grace, the man is freed from all shackles, and with complete readiness says to himself: I will rise up and go forth.

From this moment another movement starts in the soul—a movement towards God. Having mastered himself by understanding the motives of all his inclinations, thus regaining inner freedom, he must now sacrifice the whole of himself to God. Yet only half of the work has so far been achieved.

THEOPHAN THE RECLUSE

Our campaign against the passions

From the moment when your heart starts to be kindled with divine warmth your inner transformation will properly begin. This slight flame will in time consume and melt everything within you, it will begin and continue to spiritualize your being to the full. Indeed, until this flame starts to burn, there will be no spiritualization, in spite of all your strivings to achieve it. Thus the engendering of its first flicker is all that matters at this moment, and to this end be sure to direct all your efforts.

But you must realize that this kindling cannot take place in you while the passions are still strong and vigorous, even though they may not in fact be indulged. Passions are the dampness in the fuel of your being, and damp wood does not burn. There is nothing else to be done except to bring in dry wood from outside and light this, allowing the flames from it to dry out the damp wood, until this in its turn is dry enough to begin slowly to catch alight. And so little by little the burning of the dry wood will disperse the dampness and will spread, until all the wood is enveloped in flames.

All the powers of the soul and activities of the body are the fuel of our being, but so long as man does not pay heed to himself these are all saturated and rendered ineffective by the soggy dampness of his passions. Until the passions are driven out, they obstinately resist spiritual fire. Passions penetrate into both the soul and the body, and overpower even man's spirit itself, his consciousness and freedom; and in this manner they come to dominate him entirely. As they are in league with devils, through them the devils also dominate man, although he falsely imagines that he is his own master.

Delivered by the grace of God, the spirit is the first to tear itself out of these fetters. Filled with the fear of God and under the influence of grace, the spirit breaks every bond with passion, and repenting of the past, firmly resolves henceforward to please God alone in everything, to live only for Him, to walk according to His commandments. With the help of the grace of God, the spirit is able to stand firm in this resolution, banishing passions from the soul and body, and spiritualizing all within itself.

And now in you too, the spirit has been liberated from the bonds which held it. You are standing on the side of God, consciously and by deliberate choice. Your desire is to belong to God and to please Him alone, and this is the mainstay of your spiritual activity. But while your spirit has been re-established in its rightful freedom, the soul and body are still under the sway of passions and suffer violence from them. You have now to arm yourself against your passions and to conquer them. Drive them out of your soul and body. This struggle against the passions is unavoidable, for they will not willingly yield up their illegal possession of your being.

Recollection of God is the life of the spirit. It fires your zeal to please God, and makes unshakeable your decision to belong to Him. It is, I repeat, the mainstay of the spiritual life; and it is, I will add, the base for your campaign against every passion that invades the heart.

THEOPHAN THE RECLUSE

How the enemy attacks us through other people

Defeated in the heart itself, the enemy has his own methods of attacking us through external influences. I shall point out the chief instances. Suppose that someone, having learnt wisdom, does not allow himself to be lightly swayed by thoughts and impulses which have the appearance of being right, but immediately cuts them off, following either his own power of discernment or the advice of more experienced men, and acts in this way with such resolution that there seems to be no possibility of catching him by this method: the enemy then drops this trick, and begins to act from the outside through people he can use. Then come flattering compliments, calumnies, persecutions and unpleasantnesses of all kinds. It is for this that you must keep both eyes open, this that you must foresee and understand. To prevent this altogether does not lie in our power, but it does lie in our power to be more intelligent than the enemy. The chief thing is to endure everything while still preserving, unbroken in our hearts, a sense of love and peace. Our helper is the Lord. We should beg Him to bring peace to our heart and, if this is His will, to put external things right as well. On our part we must not forget where the storm comes from and by whom it is raised, nor should we direct our feeling of enmity towards people, but towards him who, standing behind, encourages them and directs the whole affair.

THEOPHAN THE RECLUSE

WAR WITH PASSIONS

How to preserve within you the peace of God

If you have felt that your mind has come to be at one with the soul and body, that you are no longer cut into pieces by sin but are something unified and whole, that the hallowed peace of Christ is breathing in you, then watch over this gift of God with all possible care. Let prayer and the reading of religious books be your principal occupation; give to other works only a secondary importance, be cold towards earthly activities, and if possible eschew them altogether. Sacred peace, fine as the breath of the Holy Spirit, immediately withdraws from the soul which behaves carelessly in its presence; the soul which lacks reverence, proves disloyal by indulging in sin, and permits itself to grow negligent. Together with the peace of Christ, grace-given prayer withdraws likewise from the unworthy soul: then the passions invade it like hungry beasts, and begin to torment the victim who has given himself to them, and who has been left to himself by God, who has withdrawn from him. If you become surfeited with food, or still more with drink, the peace of God will cease to act in you. If you are angry, you will lose this peace for a long while. If you allow yourself to become irreverent, the Holy Spirit will no longer work within you. If you begin to love something earthly, if you become infected by a passionate attachment to some object or skill, or by a special liking for some person, holy peace will certainly withdraw from you. If you allow yourself to take pleasure in impure thoughts, peace will leave you for a long time, because it does not tolerate the evil stench of sin—and especially the sins of lust and vanity. You will seek this peace and find it not; you will weep for its loss; but it will pay no attention to your tears, that so you may learn to give due value to the divine gift, and to guard it with proper care and reverence.

Hate everything that draws you down into distraction or sin. Crucify yourself on the cross of the Gospel commandments; keep yourself always nailed to it. Rebuff all sinful thoughts and wishes with courage and vigilance; cast away earthly cares; try to live the Gospel by zealously fulfilling all its commandments. When you pray, once more crucify yourself on the cross of prayer. Push aside all the memories, however important they may be, which come to you during prayer: ignore every one of them. Do not theologize, do not be carried away by following up brilliant, original, and powerful ideas which suddenly occur to you. Sacred silence, which is induced in the mind at the time of prayer by a sense of God's greatness, speaks of God more profoundly and more eloquently than any human words. 'If you pray truly,' said the Fathers, 'you *are* a theologian.'

BISHOP IGNATII

The dangers of satiety

Flee from satiety—the state when the heart says cunningly to itself: Enough! I need nothing more; I have worked hard, I have established order in myself, now I can allow myself a little rest. It was said about Israel, 'Thou art waxen fat, thou art grown thick, thou art covered with fatness'. (Deut. xxxii. 15). What more contentment was there to seek for? But what was the result? 'He forsook God.' In its original context this verse refers to physical satiety and to satisfaction with one's external conditions. But it is equally applicable to spiritual satiety and to satisfaction with one's inner state. The result is the same— a forsaking of God. When there is enough of everything, why pray to God and think of Him? Although self-satisfied people do not reach this stage all at once, the germ of it is in them already. The direct effect of satiety is weakening of attention and allowing of exemptions to oneself. Whoever permits this will begin to slide downhill like a man on a slippery slope. This is the danger. So watch!

THEOPHAN THE RECLUSE

The evil 'troika'

It seems to me that at every moment you are putting others on trial and passing judgement on them in your soul. Look carefully. Even if this only happens from time to time and is not a permanent state of mind, it brings considerable harm. High opinion of ourselves gives rise to two things: blowing our own trumpet and censuring others. These three make up the evil 'troika' which drives us full speed to perdition. We must unharness these spirited horses and get rid of them. And then the result will be that the slower you drive, the further you go.[1] Please watch yourself more carefully.

Physical labour is a good thing; the same labour done as part of your monastic obedience is a work of sanctity. Let memory of God never leave your heart. We should see the Lord before us just as we see the light; and in our heart we should prostrate ourselves before Him in a spirit of humility and contrition. A sobering fear will come.

It is a good thing when someone rebukes you: rejoice if this happens. It is a bad thing when people all round you are praising you and no one is telling you the truth. It does not take long for this snare to entangle you. At such times you cannot help considering yourself a saint, and starting to censure all those around you.

May the Lord give you strength to do what is right. Take care not to fall into the way of those who walk coldly along with correct outward behaviour, yet lack the inner feelings which sanctify a man and attract the grace of God. Yet this will happen as soon as you give in to high opinion of yourself and to self-satisfaction, which are marks of vanity.

THEOPHAN THE RECLUSE

Judging others

We have to discriminate between different kinds of judging. Sin begins when we start to despise a person in our heart because of some fault which he has committed. It is possible to judge quite simply, without bringing in a verdict against the person we judge. And if at the same time we feel pity in our heart for the person at fault, sincerely desiring his amendment of life and

[1] A Russian proverb.

praying that he may do better in future, then there will be no sin in judging but, on the contrary, to judge him would be as much an act of love as is possible in such a case. The sin of judging is more in the heart than on the lips. Talking about a particular thing may be a sin or not, depending upon the feeling with which the words are said. Feeling gives the speech its character. But it is best to refrain from any kind of judging, for fear of becoming censorious; in other words, it is best not to come too close to the fire and the soot so as not to be burned and blackened. We should do better to direct our censure and criticism against ourselves.

THEOPHAN THE RECLUSE

Your own dead and other people's funerals

In order to prevent your thoughts from wandering, you should acquire a feeling of being constantly with God in the heart. Then there will be no room for alien thoughts. To stop condemning others you should become deeply conscious of your own sinfulness and grieve over it, mourning for your soul as if it were dead. As someone said: With your own dead in the house you will not trouble about other people's funerals.

THEOPHAN THE RECLUSE

An inner thief in collusion with thieves outside

They say that vanity is an inner thief who is in collusion with thieves outside. He opens the doors and windows to them; they enter and cause great devastation within. Who knows? Maybe the time of darkness which you have experienced and which left you as soon as you prayed is a ruse of the enemy to engender thoughts of vanity—to make you say to yourself, 'How good I am at prayer! The moment I prayed all the devils ran away!' Take heed: if thoughts of vanity come to you after prayer, this shows that the enemy is trying to fan your pride.

THEOPHAN THE RECLUSE

The flames of anger and the fire of hell

'Let not the sun go down upon your wrath: neither give place to the devil' (Eph. iv. 26–27).

The devil has no access to the soul, if the soul itself harbours no passions. In such a state it is transparent and the devil cannot see it. But when it admits the movement of a passion and consents to this movement, it becomes darkened and the devil sees it. He approaches it boldly and assumes control over it. Two evil passions principally trouble the soul—lust and irritability. When the devil manages to captivate someone through lust, he leaves him alone in its turmoils: the devil does not bother him any more, except perhaps to disturb him a little with anger. But if a man does not give in to lust, the devil hastens to incite him to anger, and gathers round him a quantity of irritating things. A man who fails to discern the devil's wiles allows himself to become annoyed at everything, permitting anger to master him, and so he 'gives place to the devil'. But a man who stifles every upsurge of anger resists the devil and repels him, and gives no place to him within himself. Anger 'gives place to the devil', as soon as it is regarded as something just and its satisfaction is felt to be lawful. Then the enemy immediately enters the soul and begins to suggest thoughts, each more irritating than the last. The man starts to be aflame with anger as though he were on fire. This is the fire of hell; but the poor man thinks that he is burning with zeal for righteousness, whereas, there is never any righteousness in wrath (James i. 20). This is the form of illusion[1] peculiar to wrath, just as there is another form of illusion[1] peculiar to lust. A man who speedily overcomes wrath disperses this illusion and thus repels the devil as though by a strong blow in the chest. Is there anyone who, after extinguishing his anger and analysing the whole business in good faith, does not find that there was something wrong at the basis of his irritation? But the enemy changes the wrong into a sense of self-righteousness and builds it up into such a mountain that it seems as though the whole world would go to pieces if our indignation is not satisfied.

[1] *prelest* (see p. 40, n. 2).

WAR WITH PASSIONS

You say that you cannot help being resentful and hostile? Very well then, be hostile—but towards the devil, not towards your brother. God gave us wrath as a sword to pierce the devil—not to drive into our own bodies. Stab him with it, then, right up to the hilt; press the hilt in as well if you like, and never pull it out, but drive another sword in as well. This we shall achieve by becoming gentle and kind towards each other. 'Let me lose my money, let me destroy my honour and glory—my fellow-member is more precious to me than myself.' Let us speak thus to each other, and let us not injure our own nature in order to gain money or fame.

THEOPHAN THE RECLUSE

It is never worth while to lose your temper

On the face of it, there is nothing at all in the world over which it is worth losing our temper; for what is more valuable than the soul and its peace? This peace is destroyed by anger. When a man is angry, he assumes the rôle of a slanderer and fans the flames into a great blaze, in his imagination magnifying the offence of another. The reason for all this is that he does not keep his attention turned on himself—and so ill-feeling bursts out. Deep in the heart we cling to our right to judge and punish others for their sins, instead of ourselves. That is all there is to it. If a man saw himself as a sinner, being vividly conscious of all the consequences of sin, anger would be far from him.

THEOPHAN THE RECLUSE

Extinguishing all feelings of anger

Not to utter a single angry word is a great achievement, which is made possible by the absence of irascibility in the heart. Irascibility is extinguished, like a spark, by surrender to God's will. We recognize that God permits troubles to come in order to try us and thus demonstrate the strength of our virtue; and this helps us to preserve our temper in such cases, for we believe that God Himself is watching us at such a moment.

WAR WITH PASSIONS

Your idea that people who bring trouble may be tools of the enemy is right. So whenever anyone causes you trouble, always assume that the devil stands behind them, inciting them and suggesting offending words and deeds to their minds.

THEOPHAN THE RECLUSE

How the temptations of the enemy act

Let us remind ourselves of the manner in which the temptations of the enemy act. The sweep of the enemy's sword is the introduction of a thought into the heart: the devil expects that the heart will respond to it, and on this assumption proceeds to build up a strong temptation. For example, you think of a person who has offended you: that is the sweep of the enemy's sword. When the heart responds to this thought by harbouring an unpleasant feeling towards the offender, this means the sword has penetrated as far as the soul and has wounded it. Immediately the enemy closes with the soul and stirs up there a storm of enmity and revengefulness. But when the heart is always ready to forgive offences, keeping itself in a state of serene meekness and peace towards everyone, then no matter how vividly the enemy presents an idea of the offender to the soul, there is no response in the heart; and so the enemy will have no opening through which to introduce his temptation. The sweep of his sword will rebound from the heart as from a warrior clad in armour.

THEOPHAN THE RECLUSE

The inner traitor

There is one method which, if practised with full attention, will seldom allow anything passionate to slip unnoticed into the heart. This is to examine our thoughts and feelings, so as to discover which way they tend: towards pleasing God or towards pleasing ourselves. It is quite easy to determine this. All you have to do is to watch yourself. Know that so long as you do not pander to yourself in what you do, there is no fault in it. One of the *starets* said to his disciple, 'Watch, lest you harbour a traitor in yourself.' 'Who is the traitor?' asked the disciple. 'Self-gratification,' answered the *staretz*. And this is indeed so. Self-gratification is the cause of all evils. If you examine all the bad things that you have done, you will see that in each case they originated from pandering to yourself.

THEOPHAN THE RECLUSE

A glass of poison

As a general rule, decide whether a thing is permissible by the effect it produces within. Permit yourself what is constructive, but never what is destructive. Would any man in his right senses stretch out his hand for a glass into which he knows that poison has been poured?

THEOPHAN THE RECLUSE

A calm place in your heart at the feet of the Lord

When bad thoughts come you should avert your mind's eye from them. Turn to the Lord and cast them out in His Name. If a thought has already moved the heart and, little by little, induced you to take an evil pleasure in it, you should blame yourself, beg the Lord's forgiveness, and chastise yourself until the opposite feeling is born in your heart. For instance, instead of censuring somebody, you should have in your heart a feeling of praise or at least of respect for that person.

Prepare beforehand a calm place in your heart where you are at the feet of the Lord. As soon as trouble comes, hasten there and call ceaselessly upon Him, as though exorcising some evil pest. And God will help—everything will quieten down.

THEOPHAN THE RECLUSE

WAR WITH PASSIONS

In league with the passions

A man who is in league with the passions in his consciousness and heart is passionate through and through: such a state is abhorrent to God. But when a man sincerely desires passionlessness, even though violent emotions surge up in him and attack him, yet his state is not abhorrent to God, for he hates the passions and longs to act according to God's will instead of being enslaved by them.

THEOPHAN THE RECLUSE

Always at home

You have to discriminate between feelings which are part of your make-up and fleeting emotions which come and go. So long as the passions are not completely destroyed, wrong thoughts and feelings, wrong impulses and intentions will not cease. They lessen with the lessening of the passions, their source being the passionate side of our nature; so we must direct all our attention to this warfare against the passions. There exists one method to train us—and that is constant remembrance of the Lord and prayer to Him. The *startsi* knew how to drive out everything evil by this means, establishing in its place a state acceptable to God. Acquiring the habit of the Jesus Prayer is the external aspect of this weapon. In its inner reality, it may best be described as 'being always at home'. We must stay always in our heart with the Lord, calling to Him; and this banishes everything evil. Read St. Hesychios on sobriety. In this task constancy and persistence always prove victorious.

THEOPHAN THE RECLUSE

Jesus present and absent

When the Jesus Prayer is absent, all manner of harmful things assail us, leaving no room for anything good in the soul. But when our Lord is present in the prayer, everything alien is banished.

ST. GREGORY PALAMAS

How the demons enter

The demons have no means of taking possession of a man's spirit or body, no power forcibly to enter his soul, unless they first deprive him of all holy thoughts, and make him empty and devoid of spiritual contemplation.

ST. JOHN CASSIAN[1]

The time of hidden martyrdom

It is of the nature of inner prayer to reveal the hidden passions concealed in the human heart and to tame them. Inner prayer shows us our captivity to the fallen spirits, making us realize our imprisonment and freeing us from it.

There is no need, then, to be disturbed and perplexed when passions rise up from our fallen nature or when they are spurred on by evil spirits. Since passions are tamed by prayer, when they arise we should practise the Jesus Prayer inwardly, very quietly and without haste: little by little this will allay the upsurging passions. At times the onset of passions and the invasion of hostile thoughts is so powerful that it leads to a great struggle in the soul. This is the time of hidden martyrdom. When assailed by passions and devils, we should proclaim our faith in the Lord by devoting ourselves with the utmost persistence to prayer. This will invariably bring us victory.

BISHOP IGNATII

[1] St. John Cassian (c. 360–435) was originally professed as a monk in Bethlehem. After spending more than seven years at Scetis in Egypt, he travelled first to Constantinople (where he came under the influence of St. John Chrysostom) and then to the west. Around 415 he founded two monasteries in France near Marseilles, and in later life composed various works in Latin. A bridge figure between east and west, he was instrumental in spreading a knowledge of Egyptian monastic spirituality in the Latin world.

The rule of fasting

The rule of fasting is this: to remain in God with mind and heart, relinquishing all else, cutting off all pandering to self, in the spiritual as well as in the physical sense. We must do everything for the glory of God and for the good of our neighbour, bearing willingly and with love the labours of the fast and privations in food, sleep, and relaxation, and foregoing the solace of other people's company. All these privations should be moderate so as not to attract attention and not to deprive us of strength to fulfil the rule of prayer.

THEOPHAN THE RECLUSE

A time to speak and a time to keep silence

You ask whether you should talk with others about the spiritual life. Do so, only do not talk to them about your own personal experience. Discuss the question generally, but adapting your remarks to the state of those who have asked the question. Sometimes people bring up spiritual questions only as a subject of conversation. Even this is better than talking about worldly matters or having an idle chat. To keep silence, as you say you would prefer, is possible when you are alone, or when the conversation does not concern you. As to praying to the Lord to guard your tongue when you have to visit someone and are on your way there, that is a good thing. The best thing is to be always with the Lord. It is possible, however, to talk and yet still to remain with the Lord. Try to accustom yourself to that.

When you talk to someone, above all refrain from upsetting him by aggressiveness, or by expressing an opinion directly opposed to his, from an obvious desire to have your own way. It is the enemy who inspires you to do this, in order to start an argument and by this means to bring about discord. Avoid equally speaking of spiritual things in order to display your own wisdom. This too is a suggestion of the enemy, and if you follow it you will be laughed at by men and will gain God's displeasure.

THEOPHAN THE RECLUSE

WAR WITH PASSIONS

The ascetic battle. Victory comes by grace alone

The first victory over oneself—the condition and basis of all other inner victories, which alone makes them possible—lies in breaking our own will and in surrender to God, rejecting and detaching ourselves from everything sinful. This act of self-surrender leads us to turn aside in loathing and aversion from the passions. With this spiritual resource to fight for us in the battle, we are as strong as a whole army. Where there is no such surrender to God, victory is already in the hands of the enemy before any battle is joined. But when this act of surrender is present, victory is often conceded to us without a fight. From this we can see that, since the point of departure in any positive activity is our innermost state, this is also the point against which the enemy's campaign is launched. Consciousness and will, if attracted to the side of good, in their hatred strike out at all evil and all passions, especially those that are within ourselves. The decisive moment is precisely this attraction of the will to the side of good. Here, as always, the force which wages war on the passions is the mind or spirit in which lie consciousness and freedom—the spirit, that is to say, supported and strengthened by grace. It is grace which heals our faculties, crowning all our ascetic struggles. Again it is grace that endues our mind and spirit with strength to attack the passions and strike them down. And conversely, when the passions grow stronger, they aim directly at the mind or spirit—in other words they strive to subjugate our consciousness and freedom. Against this inner sanctuary where consciousness and freedom dwell, the enemy directs his flaming arrows, attacking us through the passions and using our body and soul as a place of ambush. But as long as our consciousness and freedom remain unimpaired, standing on the side of good, the victory is ours, no matter how strong the assault.

This, however, does not mean that the whole power to conquer comes from us and not from God—it only indicates the point through which this power to conquer operates. The immediate combatant in the warfare is our regenerated spirit. But it is grace that is the victorious and destroying force against the passions. It creates one thing in us and destroys another—acting always through the spirit, in other words, through the consciousness and will. The man who struggles prostrates himself before God with a cry for help, full of loathing and hatred against the enemies. Acting through him, God then puts them to rout and strikes them down.

THEOPHAN THE RECLUSE

Turn for help to God

What do we do when attacked by some criminal? We strike out at him and shout for help. Our cries are answered by the police, who then rescue us from danger. We must do the same in inner warfare with the passions. Filled with anger against them, call for assistance: Help me, O Lord! Jesus Christ, Son of God, save me! O God, make speed to save me! O Lord make haste to help me! Having thus called on the Lord, do not allow your attention to wander from Him, do not let it turn to what is happening within you, but go on standing before the Lord and imploring His help. This will make the enemy run away as though pursued by flames.

Without entering into altercation with passionate thoughts, let us turn directly to God, with fear, devotion, and trust, surrendering ourselves to His influence. By doing this we already push everything passionate away from our mind's eye, and look only at the Lord. Because we pay no attention to it, the passionate thought is cut off from the soul: it withdraws of its own accord if it has been aroused by some natural cause. But if the enemy is also present in it, he is struck down by the ray of inner light which comes from contemplation of the Lord. Thus as soon as the soul turns to God and appeals to Him, it is freed from the onslaught of passions.

THEOPHAN THE RECLUSE

Work without haste

We should work without haste, increasing our efforts gradually so as not to overtax our strength. Otherwise our work will resemble a new patch on an old garment. The decision to adopt some ascetic endeavour should come from within. In the same way a sick man sometimes finds a remedy or antidote by intuition, by a kind of spontaneous craving for it.

THEOPHAN THE RECLUSE

War of the mind and war of action

The war with the passions that is required of us is essentially a war of the mind. We succeed in it by denying all sustenance to the passions and so starving them out. But there is also the war of action, which consists in deliberately undertaking and performing what is diametrically opposed to our passions. For instance, to conquer avarice we should give money away freely; to fight pride we should choose some degrading occupations; to overcome a craving for amusements we should stay at home, and so on. It is true that this method used by itself does not lead directly to the aim; for when suppressed the passion may force its way inwards, or retire only to give place to some other passion. But when this active struggle is united with the inner one, the two together are quickly enabled to overcome any kind of passionate attack.

THEOPHAN THE RECLUSE

Inner warfare and active opposition

If warfare is conducted only inwardly it drives the passion out of man's consciousness; but the passion still remains alive, although not in evidence. But active opposition stabs this snake straight through its head. This does not mean that inner warfare should be abandoned. It should remain constant; otherwise the whole struggle may bear no fruit and our inclination towards the passions may even increase rather than decrease. If we abandon inner warfare, we shall find, as we struggle with one passion, that another comes and cleaves to us: for example, we expel gluttony by fasting, and then vainglory takes it place. If we fail to give due attention to inner warfare, no effort, however strenuous, will bear any fruit. Inner warfare coupled with active opposition to the passions strikes at them alike from within and without, and so destroys them as quickly as an enemy is destroyed when he is surrounded and attacked both in front and from the rear.

THEOPHAN THE RECLUSE

Impurity and innocence

Make it a rule never willingly to encourage any passionate thought, feeling, or desire, but to drive them away with hatred the moment you notice them. Then you will always be innocent before God and your conscience. You will still have the impurity of passions in you, but you will also have innocence.

THEOPHAN THE RECLUSE

The two opposing forces

Two completely opposing forces influence me: the force of good and force of evil, the force of life and the force of death. Being spiritual powers, both are invisible. Aroused by my free and sincere prayer, the good force always chases away the evil one, for the evil force derives its strength only from the evil concealed in me. To avoid the chilling influence of the evil spirit, we should always have in our heart the Jesus Prayer: 'Jesus, Son of God, have mercy upon me.' Against the invisible devil stands the invisible God, against him who is powerful stands He who is the most Powerful of all.

ST. JOHN OF KRONSTADT[1]

[1] St. John of Kronstadt (1829–1908), Russian priest, a member of the married parish clergy: celebrated for his charitable work and gifts of healing, and also

(ii) KNOW YOURSELF

Seeing oneself

Until the soul is established with the mind in the heart, it does not see itself, nor is it properly aware of itself.

THEOPHAN THE RECLUSE

How to find out what you are worth

I have come to the conclusion that you are still in the head and not in the heart. Descend into the heart and you will know at once what you are worth. You expressed the wish to attain a sense of your own unworthiness. This you will begin to see and feel as soon as you descend into the heart. The deeper you go, the clearer it will appear.

THEOPHAN THE RECLUSE

True self-knowledge

True self-knowledge is to see one's own defects and weaknesses so clearly that they fill our whole view. And mark this—the more you see yourself at fault and deserving of every censure, the more you will advance.

THEOPHAN THE RECLUSE

The measure of progress in the spiritual life

Pay heed to yourself. I will say just one thing, or rather repeat what I have already said. Progress in the spiritual life is shown by an ever-increasing realization of our own worthlessness, in the full and literal sense of this word. The moment that we ascribe

---

as a preacher and spiritual director. His remarkable diary *My Life in Christ*, has appeared in many languages, including English (translated by E. E. Goulaeff, London, 1897). He was proclaimed a saint in 1964 by the Holy Synod of the Russian Orthodox Church in Exile, and is the only person to have been canonized by the Russian Church since the Revolution of 1917.

some value to ourselves, in any sense whatever, it will mean that things have gone wrong. It is also dangerous; the enemy will draw close and begin to divert our attention, throwing stumbling blocks in our path. A soul that thinks highly of itself is like the crow in the fable who listened to the fox's flattery, and let the piece of cheese drop in order to show off. May the Lord help you to become more thorough in the task of attributing no value to your labours. See to it, as well, that there are fewer images in your soul and more thought and feeling. Persevere with the inner prayer you have begun; this is the way to reduce the flow of images through the mind. The moment will come when you will feel the issue of them stanched, like the issue of blood in the woman (Luke viii. 44).

THEOPHAN THE RECLUSE

'*I am not like others*'

What a panegyric you have composed—calling yourself bad, sly, inconstant, ungrateful, proud, ill-tempered, ignorant of how to pray to God! Very well—but you should add one thing more: good for nothing and worthless. Repeat this often to yourself, making your whole soul say it, not just reciting it mechanically by rote. For deep down we can and do value ourselves very highly.

When we do so value ourselves, the tongue or the memory repeats the words you mention, or similar ones, while in the soul lives the conviction that we are not like others. The strange thing is that it is almost impossible for the soul to notice this self-deceit. And so it remains hidden until the Lord brings it out in one way or another and shows it up in all its hideousness. Perhaps we may guess the presence of such a state of affairs inside us, when we see that words of criticism said either directly or behind our backs provoke in us displeasure or annoyance against those who spoke them. Try to discern the state of your soul at such times. But beware of self-justification which is a great hindrance.

THEOPHAN THE RECLUSE

WAR WITH PASSIONS

The feeling of sinfulness

A sense of our own righteousness does us great harm. Keep firmly in mind the point that the moment this feeling arises, however feebly, it is a sure sign that our efforts have gone wrong. The greater your conviction that you are a sinner, the more certain it is that you are travelling on the right path. But this feeling of sinfulness should spring from the depths of the soul in a natural way, instead of being suggested from without by our own reflections, or by some remark from another person.

There are many good feelings, but the feeling of worthlessness is the most fundamental; and when it is absent everything else is of no use. Commit this carefully to your memory.

THEOPHAN THE RECLUSE

The smoke and stench of hell

Picture the other nuns as walking on a hill or on the roof, while you are far, far below them. And if your soul happens to look down on another nun as being inferior, you should reproach yourself vigorously and hasten to beg the Lord's forgiveness. The worst thing of all is self-exaltation, vanity, condemnation of others. It is the smoke and stench of hell. Accustom yourself to rejoice more when you are treated with contempt, reproached, and even wronged, than when you are welcomed and kindly treated. In this lies the surest way to humility.

THEOPHAN THE RECLUSE

Judge yourself and you will stop judging others

Why do we criticize others? Because we do not try to know ourselves. Whoever is busy trying to know himself has no time to notice the faults of others. Judge yourself and you will stop judging others. Regard every man as better than you are, for without this thought a man is far from God, even though he performs miracles.

THE NUN MAGDALINA

An unbroken chain of acts of self-denial

Imprint this, I beg you, on your memory. From the moment of awakening to the moment of closing our eyes in sleep, we should behave in such a way that the whole day becomes an unbroken chain of acts of self-denial, undertaken always for the sake of the Lord, before His face and to His glory. There is nothing so very unusual about acts of self-denial; they occur in the daily activities of life and consist in an inner decision and turning of the will. They can lie behind any word, look, movement, or trifling matter. Their distinctive feature is a refusal to pander to oneself in anything big or small, a constant resistance against self-will.

THEOPHAN THE RECLUSE

A feeling of self-importance

Examine yourself to see whether you have within you a strong sense of your own importance, or, negatively, whether you have failed to realize that you are nothing. This feeling of self-importance is deeply hidden, but it controls the whole of our life. Its first demand is that everything should be as we wish it, and as soon as this is not so we complain to God and are annoyed with people.

The high value we set on ourselves, in consequence of this feeling of importance, not only upsets our relationship with other men but also our attitude to God. Self-importance is as wily as the devil and cleverly conceals itself behind humble words, settling itself firmly in the heart so that we swing between self-deprecia-tion and self-praise.

THEOPHAN THE RECLUSE

Grace works secretly. Unceasing repentance and unceasing tears

It must be understood that a man struggling towards perfection is not himself aware of the progress which he makes on his path. He toils with the sweat of his brow, but (so far as he can see) his labour bears no fruit. This is because grace works secretly. The eye of human vision does not discern the good which he is doing. The only thing that the man himself can see is his own worthlessness. The way to perfection is through the realization that we are blind, poor, and naked. This sense of nakedness is closely linked with contrition of the spirit, when in unceasing repentance we pour out before God our grief and sorrow at our impurity. Penitent feelings are an essential element of true spiritual progress, and whoever evades them is deviating from the right way. Repentance is the starting point and foundation stone of our new life in Christ; and it must be present not only at the beginning but throughout our growth in this life, increasing as we advance. On reaching spiritual maturity man becomes acutely conscious of his sinfulness and corruption, and his sense of contrition and repentance grows ever more profound. Tears are the measure of progress, and unceasing tears are a sign of coming purification.

THEOPHAN THE RECLUSE

Re-creation through the Holy Spirit

But you are still wavering in doubt! Looking at me, and seeing such a sinner before you, you ask involuntarily—is it possible that the Holy Spirit acts in this sinner, in whom the movement of passions is so evident and so strong?

A just question! And it leads me to perplexity and horror. I am carried away, I sin; I commit adultery with sin, I betray my God, I sell Him for the abominable price of sin. And in spite of my continuous betrayal, my treacherous and perfidious behaviour, He remains unchanging. Ever gracious, He waits for my repentance with long-suffering, and draws me by every means to penitence and amendment of.life. You heard what the Son of God says in the Gospel? 'They that are whole have no need of the physician, but they that are sick: I came not to call the righteous, but sinners to repentance' (Mark ii. 17). So spake the Saviour, and so He acted. He ate with publicans and sinners, converting their hearts to faith and virtue, and so leading them into spiritual companionship with Abraham and other righteous men. Does the endless goodness of the Son of God astonish you? Know that the All-Holy Spirit is equally good and equally anxious for the salvation of mankind; He is equally meek, gentle, long-suffering, and altogether merciful. The Holy Spirit is one of the three equal Persons of the Holy Trinity, which constitute, without confusion and without division, the unique Divine Being, three Persons in one nature.

Yet sin attracts the Holy Spirit to man! The sin which was seen by man but not committed, which he recognized and deplored—that kind of sin attracts Him! The more man contemplates his sin and the more he laments over himself, the more pleasing and accessible he is to the Holy Spirit, who like a physician approaches only those who recognize themselves as being ill. On the other hand He turns away from those who are rich in vain self-conceit. Look upon your sin, and search it out. Do not turn your eyes away from it. Deny yourself, do not over-value your soul. Give yourself up entirely to the contemplation of your sin, and weep over it. Then in due time you will become conscious of your re-creation through the incomprehensible and inexplicable action of the Holy Spirit. He will come to you when you expect Him not. He will act in you when you have recognized yourself as quite unworthy of Him.

THEOPHAN THE RECLUSE

Continual repentance

It is impossible to live at peace with God without *continual repentance*. The Apostle John lays down the following condition for peace with God: 'If our heart condemn us not' (1 John iii. 21). If you have nothing on your conscience, you can have boldness of access to God with a feeling of peace, but if you have something, then the peace is disturbed. To have something on our conscience—this is due to the awareness of sin. But according to the same Apostle we are never without sin: and he feels this so strongly that he calls anyone who imagines otherwise a liar (1 John i. 8). Consequently, there is never a single moment when we have nothing on our conscience, either voluntary or involuntary, and therefore there is never a single moment when our peace with God is assured. It follows from this that it is absolutely essential to cleanse our conscience in order to be at peace with God. The conscience is cleansed by repentance: consequently it is necessary to repent unceasingly. For repentance cleanses all pollution from the soul and makes it pure (1 John i. 9). Repentance does not just consist in the words, 'Forgive, O Lord; have mercy, O Lord'. To receive remission of sins we must also realize to the full the definite impurity of each thought, glance, and word, of each kind of allurement, we must be conscious of our own guilt and of our own lawlessness and absence of justification, we must recognize our need to pray for God's forgiveness, until the spirit attains peace. As far as great sins are concerned, they must be confessed immediately to our spiritual father and pardon obtained, because in the case of such sins we cannot restore peace to our spirit simply by daily acts of repentance in our private prayers. Therefore the duty of continual repentance is the same as the duty of keeping our conscience pure and irreproachable.

THEOPHAN THE RECLUSE

Resign yourself to life-long friction

Make the following a rule—first of all, anticipate trouble at every moment and when it comes encounter it as something expected. Secondly, when something happens that conflicts with your will and is on the point of irritating or upsetting you, hasten to bring your attention into your heart and strive with all your might to prevent such feelings from arising: steel yourself against them and pray. If you succeed in preventing feelings of irritation and disturbance from arising within you, then you are finished with your trouble, for these feelings are its starting point. But if even a small feeling is brought to birth, resolve, if possible, not to do or say anything until you have managed to drive it away. If you find it impossible not to say or do something, try not to talk and act according to those feelings but according to God's commandment, in the manner that He ordains, meekly and quietly, as though nothing had happened. In the third place, put out of your mind all expectation that the nature of things will change, and resign yourself to life-long friction. Do not forget this or underrate its importance, for unless you act in this way patience cannot be firmly established. Finally, with all this, preserve a good-humoured expression, an affable tone of speech, friendly behaviour, and above all avoid reminding people in any way about their unjust words or deeds. Behave as though they had done nothing wrong. Accustom yourself to preserve the remembrance of God unceasingly.

THEOPHAN THE RECLUSE

Wipe out all alien impressions

I forgot to remind you that any impression alien to the inner state to which you are committed should be immediately wiped out as soon as it comes. Do not put the matter off till the evening, let alone for a long time. It is quite simple to do this: descend into your heart where the impression has remained, repel it by refusing to harbour it, and at the same time pray to the Lord to protect you against it. Do this until it leaves you.

THEOPHAN THE RECLUSE

Scrutinizing our thoughts

Do not let the eye of the mind turn away from the heart; and when anything comes forth from there, at once catch it and examine it. If it is good, let it be; if it is not good, it must be killed at once. In this way, learn to know yourself. If some thought emerges more often than others, it signifies a passion stronger than the rest. This means that you must combat it with greater energy. Yet do not place any reliance on yourself and do not expect to achieve anything by your own efforts. All means of healing and all remedies are sent by the Lord. So give yourself up to Him—and this at all times. Strive and go on striving; but expect all good to come only from the Lord.

THEOPHAN THE RECLUSE

Self-knowledge and reading the Fathers

Look to yourself, and have more concern with the heart. To discriminate between movements of the heart, read and reflect on the writings of Sts. John of the Ladder, Isaac of Syria, Barsanouphios and John—also of Diadochos, Philotheos, Abba Isaias, Evagrios,[1] Cassian, and Neilos[2] in the *Philokalia*; and apply what they say to yourself. When you read, do not just leave impressed on your mind a general idea of the author's argument, but always turn what he says into a personal rule to be applied to yourself. When you do this, the general idea you have formed always undergoes some shades of change.

THEOPHAN THE RECLUSE

Passing from one perception to another

From now on, your deliberation with yourself will not be as before. Unless animated by grace, human reasoning usually drifts into generalities; now, on the contrary, guided by grace and under its sway, it will relate everything directly to yourself without any excuse or prevarication, and it will present matters to you in the aspect which is most relevant to your own situation. Thus in reality you will not so much meditate as pass from one perception to another.

THEOPHAN THE RECLUSE

[1] Evagrios of Pontus (346–99), monk at the Cells in the Nitrian Desert of Egypt. Although some of his works are of doubtful doctrinal orthodoxy, he remains one of the most important of all Greek spiritual writers. The works of Evagrios included in the *Philokalia*, which Theophan here recommends to his correspondent, are entirely free from heresy.

[2] St. Neilos the Ascetic (died c. 430), founder and head of a monastery near Ancyra in Asia Minor: nearly a thousand of his letters survive, together with various treatises on the monastic life. Several works by Evagrios have been incorrectly ascribed to him.

KNOW YOURSELF

The cleansing path of ever-increasing sufferings

We must continually accept trials and tribulations at God's hand, and also the spirit of contrition which He imparts: for these and other such things are a most powerful instrument in our purification. In their effect these experiences are as great a help as a spiritual director, and when a spiritual director is lacking they can and do replace him, provided the person in question has faith and humility. For in such instances it is God Himself who acts as director, and He is certainly wiser than man. St. Isaac of Syria describes in detail the gradual process whereby the Lord leads a man who is being purified into the cleansing path of ever-increasing sufferings, and how He arouses within him the spirit of contrition. All that is required on our side is faith in God's loving providence, and a ready, joyful, and grateful acceptance of everything sent by Him. Lack of faith and acceptance deprives these bitter experiences of their cleansing power, hindering it from reaching the heart and the ground of our being. Without external afflictions and annoyances, it is hard for a man to resist pride and to avoid a high opinion of himself. Without tears of contrition how can we shake ourselves free from pharisaical egotism and self-righteousness?

THEOPHAN THE RECLUSE

Good for nothing

A soul untried by sorrows is good for nothing.

THEOPHAN THE RECLUSE

The road to the kingdom

There is but one road to the kingdom of God—a cross, voluntary or involuntary.

THEOPHAN THE RECLUSE

The Holy Spirit shows us what we are

The Holy Spirit confers true humility. However intelligent, sensible, and clever a man may be, if he does not possess the Holy Spirit within him, he cannot know himself properly; for without God's help he cannot see the inner state of his soul. But when the Holy Spirit enters the heart of man, he shows him all his inner poverty and weakness, the corruption of his soul and heart, and his remoteness from God. The Holy Spirit shows a man all the sins that coexist with his virtues and righteousness: his laziness and lack of zeal for salvation and for the good of others, the selfishness that informs what appear to be his most unselfish virtues, the crude self-love that lurks where he never suspected it. In brief, the Holy Spirit shows everything in its true aspect. Enlightened by the Holy Spirit, a man begins to experience true humility, distrusting his own powers and virtues and regarding himself as the worst of mankind.

The Holy Spirit teaches true prayer. No one, until he receives the Spirit, can pray in a manner truly pleasing to God. This is so, because anyone who begins to pray without having the Holy Spirit in him, finds that his soul is dispersed in all directions, turning to and fro, so that he cannot fix his thoughts on one thing. Moreover he does not properly know either himself, or his own needs; he does not know how or what to ask from God; he does not even know who God is. But a man with the Holy Spirit dwelling in him knows God and sees that He is his Father. He knows how to approach Him, how to ask and what to ask for. His thoughts in prayer are orderly, pure, and directed to one object alone—God; and by his prayer he is truly able to do everything.

METROPOLITAN INNOCENT OF MOSCOW[1]

---

[1] Innocent (Veniaminov) (1797–1879), the greatest Russian missionary during the 19th century. For a major part of his life (1824–68) he served in eastern Siberia and in Alaska, where he preached to the Eskimos and Red Indians: he was the first Orthodox bishop to work on the American continent.

WORK, INNER AND EXTERNAL

(iii) WORK, INNER AND EXTERNAL

Inner work

Unless a man is assisted by inner work according to the will of God, he labours in vain at what is external.

STS. BARSANOUPHIOS AND JOHN

Leaves and fruit

A brother asked Abba Agathon[1]: 'Tell me, Abba, which is greater, physical work or guarding what lies within?' The Abba replied: 'Man is like a tree; physical work is the leaves and guarding what lies within is the fruit. Now it says in the Gospel, "Every tree which bringeth not forth good fruit is hewn down and cast into the fire" (Matt. iii. 10): clearly, then, all our care should be about the fruit, that is, about guarding the mind. But we also need the protection and adornment of leaves, that is, physical work.'

SAYINGS OF THE FATHERS[2]

The two orders of life in a monastery

Two orders of life go on in a monastery: one external, the other internal. Rules imposed in a monastery all relate to the external life. These rules are necessary simply because we bring our bodies into a monastery as well as our souls: but the work of the soul's salvation must proceed in its own way side by side with these exterior rules. If a man does not realize this he may turn away from the first steps of the monastic life, considering these rules and tasks inconsistent with his purpose and his inclination. Alternatively, while remaining in the monastery, he may think that the whole of the monastic life is contained in these rules. In

[1] Monk of Scetis in Egypt during the 4th century, and friend of St. Makarios.

[2] *The Sayings of the Fathers*: a collection of stories relating for the most part to 4th and 5th century monks of Egypt (especially Scetis).

233

this case he will strive in vain, making not a single step towards the purification and perfection of his soul.

Dedicate yourself to a life where hands and feet do one thing, while the soul in her desire for salvation is occupied with something else.

THEOPHAN THE RECLUSE

The chief enemy of life in God

The chief enemy of life in God is a profusion of worldly cares. This profusion of cares impels a man into an endless round of secular activities. Every day, from morning till night, it drives him from one job to another, not giving him a moment's rest, leaving him no time to turn to God and to remain for a while uplifted in prayer to Him.

This profusion of cares has no place among monks. Those who understand this enter a monastery simply in order to free themselves from this torture of cares. And they are freed. When the multitude of cares subsides, the mind and heart are left completely free and there is nothing to hinder them from remaining in God and taking their joy in Him. Those who practise the monastic life in an intelligent way, quickly gain success in this and become firmly established in their purpose. All that remains thereafter is to maintain this treasure of freedom from cares; and such people do in fact manage to maintain it. Every monk or nun has a task to carry out in the course of the twenty-four hours. Since these tasks are a matter of routine, they do not demand any special attention; and so the hands can be at work while the mind converses with God and thus feeds the heart. This norm for the inner order of things was long ago recommended by St. Antony the Great. So you see that even monks have an active life, similar to the active life of laymen. Only their activities are not accompanied by the multitude of cares which gnaw at the minds of laymen. It is this freedom from anxiety, resulting from the ordered sequence of the monastic life, that enables them to hold fast to their aim—in other words, to remain constantly with God and in God.

THEOPHAN THE RECLUSE

Inner peace and bodily health

Do not overlook the fact that health does not depend on food alone, but above all on inner peace. Life in God, cutting us off from worldly turmoil, brings peace to the heart and, through this, keeps the body also in good health.

Activities are not the main thing in life. The most important this is to have the heart directed and attuned to God.

THEOPHAN THE RECLUSE

Contemplation and action must go hand in hand

We cannot limit ourselves to the active life alone, but should combine it with intellectual occupations, so that with their help we can remorselessly keep the inner state in its right order. We should invariably link contemplation to action and action to contemplation. When the two are so joined they quickly enable the soul to advance, cleansing it from evil and strengthening it in good. See the writings of Abba John Kolobos and Abba Poemen[1]; but the same teaching can also be found in all the ascetic writers.

THEOPHAN THE RECLUSE

Living the contemplative life in the world

There are two ways to become one with God: the active way and the contemplative way. The first is for Christians who live in the world, the second for those who have abandoned all worldly things. But in practice neither way can exist in total isolation from the other. Those who live in the world must also keep to the contemplative way in some measure. As I told you before, you should accustom yourself to remember the Lord always and to walk always before His face. That is what is meant by the contemplative way.

The question arises: how can we hold the Lord in our attention while busy with various activities? This is how it can

[1] Monks of Scetis in Egypt during the 5th century.

235

be done. Whatever your occupation, great or small, reflect that it is the omni-present Lord Himself who orders you to perform it and who watches to see how you are carrying it out. If you keep this thought constantly in mind you will fulfil attentively all the duties assigned to you and at the same time you will remember the Lord. In this lies the whole secret of Christian conduct for one in your position, if you are to succeed in your chief aim. Please think it over carefully and adjust yourself to this practice. When you have done this your thoughts will cease to wander hither and thither.

Why is it that things are not going well with you just now? I think it is because you wish to remember the Lord, forgetting worldly affairs. But worldly affairs intrude into your consciousness and push out the remembrance of the Lord. What you should do is just the reverse: you should busy yourself with worldly affairs, but think of them as a commission from the Lord, as something done in His presence. As things are now, you fail both on the spiritual and on the material level. But if you act as I have explained, things will go well in both spheres.

THEOPHAN THE RECLUSE

The body at work, the thought with God

The body at work but the thought with God—such should be the state of a true Christian.

We should set in order our inner state as soon as we open our eyes each morning. In this same state of inner order we should keep ourselves all day, and in the evening warm and strengthen it and so fall asleep. It is a good thing to set limits to our personal affections, avoiding particular friendships, and making all our relationships with others of the same nature.[1] When inner prayer comes, it can partially replace attendance in church. Yet nothing increases the fervour of inner prayer so much as being in church.

THEOPHAN THE RECLUSE

[1] Theophan's correspondent is probably a monk.

WORK, INNER AND EXTERNAL

Freedom from cares

Strive to keep in order your thoughts about worldly concerns. Try to arrive at a state in which your body can carry out its usual work, while leaving you free to be always with the Lord in spirit. The merciful Lord will give you freedom from cares, and where this freedom prevails everything is done in its own time, and nothing is a worry or a burden. Seek, ask—and it will be given.

THEOPHAN THE RECLUSE

The need for concealment

Try to carry out all your ascetic endeavours, whatever they may be, in such a way that no one in the monastery knows about them. If other people learn about any of them, this is already a bad thing. Do not regard concealment—to prevent others from seeing or knowing—as something not strictly necessary. No, it is very strictly necessary indeed. Spiritual effort, if blazoned abroad, is empty and nothing worth.

THEOPHAN THE RECLUSE

Ascetic efforts are means, not ends. No salvation without humility

External labours and ascetic endeavours are means, and not ends in themselves; they are valuable only when they bring us to our aim and contribute expressly to it. Do not dwell on them in your thoughts as though they were something important. The main thing is our feelings and inward dispositions. Turn your whole attention to these, once you have established your exterior order of life. Above all preserve humility and pray to be given it, and find fault with yourself as often as you can, so as to attain self-abasement. As soon as you wake up, try to realize your own worthlessness, and then strive to remain in this feeling all day. Abase yourself even more when facing the Lord in prayer. Who am I, and Whom have I the temerity to address in human speech?

237

Rejoice if you happen to meet with external humiliation that is not of your own seeking. Accept it as a special mercy of God. Make it your criterion that when you are displeased with yourself you are in a good state. But as soon as a feeling of self-satisfaction creeps in, however slight, and you begin to rate yourself highly, know that you are not in a right state and begin to reprove yourself. For the Lord's sake, I pray you, do not forget this. If self-abasement is lacking all the rest is nothing. There have been people who attained salvation by humility alone, without ascetic endeavours. But without humility no one has ever been saved or ever will be saved.

THEOPHAN THE RECLUSE

The scaffolding and the building

Think as little as possible about external ascetic feats. Although they are necessary, they are nothing but a scaffolding inside which the building is erected. They are not the building itself; the building is in the heart. Turn all your attention, then, on what is to be done in the heart.

The first tempting thought which will begin to attack you will be self-satisfaction or self-righteousness. It will be followed by inner self-praise, by blowing your own trumpet, and after this by arrogance before others. Understand the nature of these temptations. Read St. Makarios the Great and especially the Ladder of St. John Climacus, where much is written about discrimination between thoughts. One and the same action may be either pleasing or displeasing to God, depending on the thoughts that accompany it. Learn from their teachings.

THEOPHAN THE RECLUSE

Distraction and captivation of the heart. Why we sometimes feel sad

You tell me that you are subject to distraction. This is the first attack of the enemy which is harmful for our inner order. When you enter into communication with other people or busy yourself with secular affairs, do so in such a way that you still remember the Lord at the same time. Act and speak always with the awareness that the Lord is near and directs everything according to His pleasure. Therefore, if there is something that requires your attention, prepare yourself beforehand so that you will not be withdrawn from the Lord in the course of attending to it, but will remain in His presence all the while. You should pray to be granted this. It is certainly possible to acquire this habit; simply make it a rule from now on always to act in this way.

The second snare of the enemy that prevents us from dwelling within, is the cleaving of the heart to some particular thing, and its captivation by this object. This is worse than distraction. Captivation of this type did not in fact happen in your case and you soon returned to your former condition. But if your heart had cleaved to something, you would have had a long drawn-out struggle to shake yourself free. In that case it would have been necessary first to tear the heart away from the thing it was cleaving to, and secondly to engender a revulsion against it. Keep this in mind and protect yourself in every way against distraction and, still more, against captivation of the heart. The remedy is one and the same—not to let the attention withdraw from the Lord and from consciousness of His presence.

Why does a long conversation with someone make you feel sad afterwards? Because during the conversation your attention withdraws from the Lord. This is unacceptable to the Lord and He makes you aware of it by rendering you sad. Accustom yourself to be with the Lord unceasingly, whatever you may be doing, and do everything for Him, striving to bring it to harmony with His commandments. Then you will never feel sad, for you will know that you are always doing His work.

THEOPHAN THE RECLUSE

Work with your hands, and yet remain with God in mind and heart

Whatever you are told to do, do it without inner argument, with complete willingness, as though it were *a command from God*. Set these words which I have underlined deep in your heart and act in their spirit. Accept every order as coming directly from God Himself, and execute it with all zeal and attention as a work given by God and performed in His presence. Act as though you were obeying not men but the all-seeing God; and stand in fear of the judgement which awaits those who do the work of God negligently (Jer. xlviii. 10). Please keep this firmly in your mind.

And now consider the change in God's design concerning you, so as to prevent yourself from acting in a way contrary to God's intention. What was your position before? In church you stood apart, at your ease, with nothing to do except pray and comfort yourself with the warmth of prayer. In your cell too, the chief thing was prayer and prayer alone. Now in church you have work to do, and in your own room also you have work to do. Do you think there is no reason for this? Far from it. The Lord is offering you the chance of moving forward to a second stage. Before, you spent your time in fervent prayer, without any occupations being imposed by the monastic rule. Now you have to learn to remain in prayer just as before, only with the addition of occupations. That is what the Lord asks from you. Contrive to do it. You had some work to do before, but now you have much more. You must do what you have to do, and at the same time not allow your mind to withdraw from God; that is, you must be as though you were standing at prayer. This must be your guiding principle: work with your hands and yet remain with God in mind and heart. Write, but do not let your mind withdraw from God, and do not allow your warmth of prayer to lessen, or your sobriety to weaken. The same must happen when you assist in church. Experience will teach you how to succeed in this. And in this way you will acquire new experience and new strength in remaining within.

THEOPHAN THE RECLUSE

True obedience for the sake of the Lord

You have termed unwilling obedience 'mechanical obedience'. In actual fact, the only kind of obedience that effectively shapes our character is obedience performed against our own will and our own ideas.

If you do something because that is the way your heart is inclined, where is the obedience? You are merely following your own will and your own tastes. If you recognize your motives, you make such self-willed action slightly better. But in true obedience you obey without seeing the reason for what you are told to do, and in spite of your own reluctance. A special blessing is promised for such an obedience—the blessing of being preserved free from all harm when the duty imposed on you is fulfilled. When this obedience is performed for the sake of the Lord, then the Lord takes His obedient servant under His own care and looks after him.

THEOPHAN THE RECLUSE

Unquestioning obedience is more valuable than any ascetic feat

You thought that things were better when you were not required under obedience to do secretarial work. You deceive yourself. Unquestioning obedience which goes against our inclinations is more valuable than any ascetic feats: it can be harmful only when practised in an ill-judged and generally superficial way, as it was by you. In actual fact the Lord always rewards the labour of self-denial. You do not seem at all disturbed by this resistance of yours against the duty of obedience. Yesterday you took the vow to obey the Abbess in everything, and now you refuse to bear a light duty for which you are well fitted. Is this the way to carry out a vow? The vow of obedience is your covenant with the convent, the very basis of your life ás a nun. And now this covenant is destroyed, and you have cast yourself out of the order into which you had already stepped with one foot. You should repent and shed tears over this. For as a result of this your inner order is bound to be disarrayed and perhaps has been despoiled already, even though externally it may seem to be in the process of formation. For this you must do penance.

You are to make three prostrations at a time, begging the Lord with tears to forgive you for your deceitfulness and disobedience, in promising one thing in words while in deed doing something entirely different. Repent of this sin in confession: it is a sin not merely of intention but of fact. Pray God to move your superior to give you the same obedience once more. When it is again given you, stop the prostrations.

THEOPHAN THE RECLUSE

A healing mud-bath

You write: 'I work like a beginner among novices.' I do not understand what kind of work you mean; but whether work is good or inadvisable depends entirely on the spirit in which it is performed. Watch that spirit and judge the work accordingly.

When you find that you are being maligned, accept it: it is a kind of healing mud-bath. You do well not to lose the feeling of brotherly friendliness towards those who apply this medicine to you.

THEOPHAN THE RECLUSE

Too much absorbed in work

Your laziness in spiritual occupations arises from the enthusiasm with which you have taken up physical work. Do not be too much carried away by your work, otherwise your head will become confused. And if your head is confused, your heart will become confused as well.

THEOPHAN THE RECLUSE

Manual labour

Manual labour leads to humility, fills up odd intervals, and keeps the thoughts from wandering. To replace it with prostrations is good—this is a better form of work. But is such a course always possible? The anchorites of Egypt sat at manual labour from morning to night, immersed in inner prayer and thoughts of God. They performed their external rule of prayer at night.

St. Isaac the Syrian, on the other hand, does not favour manual labour, saying that it distracts one from God. This is true of complicated work but simple work does no harm.

THEOPHAN THE RECLUSE

Excessive attachment to rules

Any type and sequence of occupations is good, so long as it helps to keep our attention directed towards God. There is no need to describe what occupations I mean. If an occupation does not enrich our life of prayer, it should be abandoned and something else taken up instead. For instance, you open a book and begin to read, but things do not go right. Put this book aside and take up another. If that one is no good, take a third one. If things don't go well with this one either, drop reading and make prostrations or meditate. You should have some handicraft that does not distract the attention. When your attention towards God is awake and prayer is going on within you, it is better not to start doing anything—if at home, that is to say—but to sit or walk about, or, better still, to stand before the icons and pray. When prayer begins to grow weak, increase its fervour by reading or meditation. Rules are necessary for those who enter a monastery, in order to make them accustomed to monastic activities and occupations. But later, when they have attained certain inner perceptions and especially warmth in the heart, rules cease to be strictly necessary for them. Generally speaking we should not be too much attached to rules, but should preserve freedom in regard to them, having only one intention: to keep our attention directed in adoration towards God.

Our body should always be kept as tight as a string, like a soldier on parade, and we should not let it relax, and this not only when walking or sitting down, but also when standing up or lying down.

All the things we have to do, great or small, should be done as though the eye of God were looking at us. Every visitor or every person we meet should be welcomed as a messenger from God. The first question we should always ask inwardly is this: what does the Lord wish me to do with or for this person? We should receive everyone as though they were the image of God, reverencing them and ready to help them all we can.

Mercilessness towards self, willingness to undertake any service for others, and complete self-surrender to the Lord, abiding in Him in prayer—these are the things which build up spiritual life.

THEOPHAN THE RECLUSE

External activities must not distract you from inner work

You have broached the question of occupations. Since what you do depends not on the monastic rule but on your own decision, you can arrange your activities so that they do not distract you from inner work. In this follow the advice of St. Isaac the Syrian. He is not in favour of manual labour and only allows it occasionally when there is a need for it; for it distracts the attention of our mind. We should especially train ourselves to prevent this. To do no work at all is an impossibility—work is a necessity of our nature. Yet we should not be too much caught up in it either. The monks of Egypt worked all day, yet their mind did not leave God.

THEOPHAN THE RECLUSE

Keeping the inner stove hot

Learn to perform everything you do in such a way that it warms the heart instead of cooling it. Whether reading or praying, working or talking with others, you should hold fast to this one aim—not to let your heart grow cool. Keep your inner stove always hot by reciting a short prayer, and watch over your feelings in case they dissipate this warmth. External impressions are very rarely in harmony with inner work.

THEOPHAN THE RECLUSE

WORK, INNER AND EXTERNAL

These are the various means whereby the passions are destroyed within us. Sometimes they are overcome by our own mental and active efforts, sometimes by our spiritual director and sometimes by the Lord Himself. It has already been said that without inner mental struggle, our external efforts cannot be successful. The same is true of the efforts which we make under the guidance of a director, and also of the purification effected in us by Providence. Inner struggle should therefore be unceasing and unremitting. By itself it is not very powerful, but when it is absent all the other means are ineffective and of no use. Those who work actively and those who suffer, those who weep and those who obey the rules imposed upon them—in every group alike many have perished and are perishing now because they do not engage in inner warfare, guarding their mind and heart.

Remember what we said about the positive value of inner work—that it is inner work which gives to all our external activities their purpose and their effectiveness. This shows us how very important inner work is: it will be clear to everyone that it constitutes the starting point, basis, and aim of all kinds of spiritual and ascetic effort.

Our whole task may be reduced to the following rule: collecting yourself within, recover your spiritual self-awareness, set to work inwardly, and, prepared in this way, practise the external duties imposed upon you either by your spiritual director or by Providence. But while doing this you must watch and notice with strict and unwavering attention everything that arises within you. As soon as some passion is awakened, chase it away and strike it down, both mentally and actively, not forgetting to rekindle within yourself and rouse to warmth the spirit of contrition and of sorrow for your sins.

It is to this that the whole attention of the spiritual wrestler should be directed. In this way, through continuous concentration he will prevent himself from being distracted, but will as it were gird up the loins of his mind. As he follows this inward path, ever watchful over himself, he will learn the virtue of sobriety.

Now you can understand why spiritual wrestlers have always considered the chief virtue in all spiritual work to be sobriety, and why they regarded those who lacked it as barren.

THEOPHAN THE RECLUSE

Self-education. Read, feel, act

Each man, then, must train himself, and instil into himself the truths contained in the words of Christ, so that they enter and dwell within him. With this purpose in view he should read them and reflect on them, and commit them to memory; he should learn to be in inward sympathy with them, feeling a deep love for them, and then he should put them into practice. This last is the whole aim of self-education. So long as this is lacking we cannot say of a man that he has taught himself, even if he knows the words of Christ by heart and is good at reasoning. It is precisely for their lack of this that St. Paul reproached the Jews in his Epistle to the Romans: 'Thou therefore which teachest another, teachest thou not thyself?' (Rom. ii. 21). If a man preaches Christ but does not himself live in Him, then the word of Christ has not entered him.

It is clear that any kind of education by others only brings fruit when combined with a man's own teaching of himself. Each must make himself realize the sense of what he is taught, so that after hearing or reading something he persuades himself not only to think exactly like that, but also to feel and to act so. For the word of Christ enters a man to dwell in him, only if he succeeds in persuading himself to believe and to live according to it.

A man is indeed unwise if he reads diligently the words of God but fails to ponder over them, not making himself feel their meaning and not practising them in actual life. For then the word of God flows through him like water in a gutter, without entering him or leaving a trace. We can know all the Gospels and Epistles by heart and yet not have the word of Christ dwelling within, because we have not studied them in the right way. Thus a man acts foolishly if he feeds only his mind with the word of Christ, but does not bother to bring his heart and his life into correspondence with it. And so it stays in him like sand poured into his head and memory, which lies there dead instead of living. The word of Christ lives only when it passes into feeling and life; but in such a man this does not happen, and so we cannot say that the word of Christ dwells in him.

THEOPHAN THE RECLUSE

Do all in the Name of the Lord Jesus

'And whatsoever ye do in word or deed, do all in the name of the Lord Jesus, giving thanks to God and the Father by him' (Col. iii. 17).

Here St. Paul speaks of the third way whereby we prove that our hidden abode is in God—and that is by doing everything in the Name of the Lord. As for the other two methods, by means of the first—the reading of Holy Scripture and the assimilation of the revealed truths which it contains—we banish vain and unclean imaginings and fill our minds with good thoughts, wholly concerned with things divine; and by means of the second—prayer—we establish in ourselves the habit of remembering God always and walking continually in His presence. Both these methods keep our attention and feeling absorbed in God. It seems, perhaps, that this should be enough? It seems so, but it is not. If these two methods alone are used they will not lead us to the aim which we desire. Man is not only thought and feeling, but above all he is action. He is ever moving, constantly active. But every action involves attention and feeling. The man who acts is entirely wrapped up in his action. Consequently the man who seeks God will find that because of certain things he cannot avoid doing, he will inevitably deviate from God in his thought, and after thought, in his feeling. Occupations bring him down from heaven to earth, or lead him from his seclusion in God into external relationships with other human beings. For our occupations are almost all visible, since they are carried out among fellow creatures and the things of the senses. It follows from this that if man's occupations are not so directed as to enable him to keep his life secluded in God, the first two methods will remain fruitless and it will even become impossible for him to practise them as he should. Occupations keep on distracting us—even the practice of studying the Holy Scriptures and the practice of prayer. And so the Apostle, in the passage which we quoted, teaches us how to turn all our actions into a means of preserving our secret life in God: this can be achieved by 'doing all in the Name of the Lord'. If we succeed in attuning ourselves in this way, we shall not withdraw from the Lord either in thought or feeling. For to do all in the Name of the Lord means to do everything to His glory, in the desire to please Him, having understood His will correctly even in some trivial matter. In this the members of the body, like tools, will do the work; and thought and feeling will be turned towards the Lord, anxious to carry out their task in a manner pleasing to God and obedient to His glory.

This method is more effective than the first two in securing our purpose; success in the first two depends on success in the last. For the first two are mental in character, and what is of the mind enters into our whole being through action. When our action is sanctified by its dedication to God, then in the process of doing it, a certain divine element enters into all the organs and powers which take part in the work. The greater the number of such deeds, the more are the divine elements entering the being of a man. And later they fill him completely so that his whole nature is immersed in the divine, and abides in God. Gradually, as this God-ward orientation is established, prayer and worship of God, accompanied by thoughts of what is good, become more firmly established too. Prayer and worship influence the work being done for the glory of God; and because we are abiding in the divine, as a reward our deeds themselves are endowed with greater strength and effectiveness.

All our activities St. Paul embraced in two terms: word and deed. Words are uttered by the mouth, deeds are performed by other members. From the moment of waking up to the moment of falling asleep we are continually engaged in both. Our speech flows almost without stopping, while the various movements of the body continue unceasingly. What a rich offering to God if all of this could be directed to His glory! By making our speech serve the glory of God not only is evil speaking banished but also vain or idle talk, and only one kind of speech remains—that which serves to edify our brethren or at least (to put it at its lowest) does not bring them any harm. We should also consecrate our speech to God by reciting prayers. Furthermore, by turning our deeds to the glory of God, not only can we rid ourselves of evil deeds done from lust or irritation—such things should be not so much as thought of among Christians—but we are also enabled to see in what spirit we should perform such deeds as are permissible, necessary, and useful. This rids our actions of all pandering to self and of all servitude to the world and its evil ways.

To do everything in the Name of the Lord means to turn all to His glory, to try to perform everything in such a way as to please Him, conscious that it is His will. It means also to surround every deed by prayer to Him; to begin it with prayer and to end it with prayer; as we begin, to ask His blessing; as we proceed, to beg His help; and as we finish, to give Him thanks for accomplishing His work in us and through us.

THEOPHAN THE RECLUSE

The chain of suffering

The life of a Christian on earth is a chain of suffering. It is necessary to fight against our own body, against passions and evil spirits. Our hope lies in this fight. Our salvation is from God. Having put our reliance on Him, we must bear with patience the time of struggle. We are ground between the millstones of temptation as grain that is ground into flour. Divine Providence permits these trials to assail us for the great benefit of our soul; from them we acquire a contrite and humble heart which God will not despise.

BISHOP IGNATII

WAR WITH PASSIONS

(iv) SOLITUDE

In a monastery you have to face solitude

Once you go to a monastery you have to face solitude. Life in a monastery is hard for anyone who would like to live there in company with many others, as he would in society. In a monastery you must know only one person—the abbot, or else your father confessor and *staretz*. Towards the others your attitude should be as though they were not present. Then everything will go well; otherwise the commotion is worse than at a ball in St. Petersburg.

THEOPHAN THE RECLUSE

Only God and the soul

Only God and the soul—this is to be truly a monk. But how can one attain to this ? By any way that you like, so long as you do attain to it; for so long as a man has not reached this state, he is not yet a monk. But difficult though it is to become a true monk, do not be discouraged: the spirit of zeal will come and will disperse all your fears. This spirit is irresistible. It comes, is accepted by the heart, and effects great changes within. This is the origin of all true monastic life. It would be more accurate to say that no one makes himself a monk—he is made such by an outside force.

There are quiet natures which are not suited to rigorous feats of self-denial. It is more natural for them to live humbly, in the simplicity of their heart, doing good and helping all who need help.

THEOPHAN THE RECLUSE

The world can still be with us in the heart

This friend, this lady of whom you write to me, does she think that in renouncing the tumult of the world she has already done all that is necessary? Does she not realize that the world can still be with us in the heart, so long as we are simply living as we please, solely to gratify ourselves?

THEOPHAN THE RECLUSE

'Give and take'

Try to compose yourself in such a way that you do not readily go out to meet other people, and do not willingly receive visitors at home. The *startsi* write that so long as there is a desire in us to give and take, we must not expect any peace. This expression 'give and take' embraces everything—all kinds of communication with others. Such a degree of detachment cannot be achieved all at once, but the foundations should be laid now. May the sweetness of dwelling with the Lord fill you with His grace.

THEOPHAN THE RECLUSE

Seeking the will of God in solitude

You know, of course, that your whole purpose at the moment is to change yourself inwardly. And so, corresponding to these inward changes and obeying the impulse that comes from them, external things must be changed as well. My advice to you in your present position is this. Begin retreating into solitude at your own home, and dedicate these hours of solitude to praying above all for one thing: 'Make known to me, O Lord, the way wherein I should walk' (Ps. cxlii. 8. Sept.).[1] Pray thus not merely in words and thought, but also from your heart. For this time of solitude, set aside certain hours every day, which is the better way; or else certain days of the week. And then observe this time of solitude properly, seeking above all for enlightenment, and to be shown the right way by God. To this add the practice of fasting, which affects the flesh: it will be a good aid to prayer. And during this time try, by way of experiment, to make acts of inward renunciation—now of one thing, now another—in order to

[1] Ps. cxliii. 8 (B.C.P.).

become indifferent to everything; and retreat into seclusion in such a way that nothing can draw you back. The aim is to bring your soul to a state in which it longs to escape from its present way of life as a prisoner seeks to break loose from his fetters.

THEOPHAN THE RECLUSE

How to use moments of solitude

You should devote your moments of solitude exclusively to working for God—to prayer and the thought of God. These practices, if followed even reasonably aright, will not allow you to grow bored. For they bring spiritual consolation such as nothing else on earth can give.

THEOPHAN THE RECLUSE

What it means to be a recluse

You say you would like to become a recluse. It is too soon for this; and there is no need. After all, you live alone, and your visitors are few and far between. Going to church does not interrupt your solitude but intensifies it, and gives you the strength to pass your time in prayer at home as well. From time to time you could perhaps stay indoors for a day or two, endeavouring to be with God all the time. But in your case this already happens of itself, so there is no need to make plans about becoming a recluse. When your prayer has gained such stability that it keeps you always face to face with God in your heart, you will have seclusion without being a recluse. For what does it really mean to be a recluse? It means that your mind, enclosed in the heart, stands before God in reverence and feels no desire to leave the heart or to occupy itself with anything else. Seek this kind of seclusion and do not worry about the other. Even behind closed doors one can wander about the world, or let the whole world invade one's room.

THEOPHAN THE RECLUSE

SOLITUDE

Keeping your thoughts within the monastery walls

Someone once said: 'See that your thoughts do not wander outside the walls of the monastery, and you will soon find the sweet rest of monastic seclusion.' This is the most blessed part chosen by Mary—to arrive at the stage when you have nothing in your thoughts but church and cell. How excellent this is! I think the beatitude of this state is past description.

THEOPHAN THE RECLUSE

War with passions—in community and in solitude

You are assured, so you tell me, that there is more merit in striving to serve God in the hubbub of daily life than in working for salvation in solitude. Do not argue against this conviction. Those who truly strive to serve God do not aim at gaining merit. All they care about is to purify themselves from the passions, from all passionate thoughts and feelings. For this purpose life lived in common with others is more suitable, because it provides us with practical experience in struggling with the passions and overcoming them. These victories strike the passions in the chest and the head, and repeated victories quickly kill the passions completely. In solitude, on the other hand, the struggle goes on only in the mind, which is often as weak in its effect as the impact of a fly's wing. This is why it takes longer to kill the passions in solitude. Besides, in such a struggle it is practically always the case that the passions are not wholly killed but merely forced to subside for a time, until the object of passion is again encountered. And so it sometimes happens that the passion suddenly flashes out like lightning: in that case a man who has long enjoyed peace from passions, through fighting them not only mentally but in actual fact, will not be shaken by their sudden attack. This is why men of experience in the spiritual life advise others to overcome the passions by battling against them in a definite form whilst living in community, and only later to retreat into solitude.

THEOPHAN THE RECLUSE

WAR WITH PASSIONS

Being annoyed when our solitude is disturbed

To be vexed and annoyed if someone interrupts your solitude is very wrong. This comes of thinking too highly of yourself: it is as if you said, 'Do not *dare* to hinder *me*!' Here the enemy triumphs within you. Make it a rule not to give in to this feeling of annoyance. Exasperation and anger are permissible only when directed against our own evil thoughts and feelings.

THEOPHAN THE RECLUSE

Lack of inner order

You complain of a lack of inner order. Without such order nothing you do can be of much profit. It is easier to gain it and to establish yourself in it, if you are living in the desert. Fear of God, a contrite and humble heart—these are its first manifestations.

THEOPHAN THE RECLUSE

The true wilderness

How should you order yourself inwardly so as to enjoy peace of soul? Secure for yourself inner solitude. But such solitude is not a mere vacuum nor can it be gained simply by creating complete emptiness in oneself. When you retreat into yourself, you should stand before the Lord, and remain in His presence, not letting the eyes of the mind turn away from the Lord. This is the true wilderness—to stand face to face with the Lord. This state of standing before the Lord is something that supports and maintains itself. To be with the Lord is the aim of our existence, and when we are with Him we cannot fail to experience a feeling of well-being; this feeling naturally attracts our attention to itself, and through this, to the Lord from whom the feeling comes.

THEOPHAN THE RECLUSE

Old acquaintances

It is good to withdraw from distractions under the protection of four walls, but it is even better to withdraw into solitude within onself. The first without the second is nothing, whereas the last is of the utmost value even without the first.

It is an excellent thing to go to church, but if you can accustom yourself to pray at home as if in church, such prayer at home is equally valuable.

Just as a man sees another face to face, try thus to stand before the Lord, so that your soul is face to face with Him. This is something so natural that there should have been no need to mention it specially, for by its very nature the soul should strive always towards God. And the Lord is always near. There is no need to arrange an introduction between them for they are old acquaintances.

THEOPHAN THE RECLUSE

External and inward seclusion

You wish to withdraw into seclusion. When the right time comes it will be possible. But first make the necessary preparation. Speaking generally, it seems to me that complete isolation is not good for you, but it is all right for you to withdraw into seclusion from time to time. There is no need for you to seek more than that. When the small flame is kindled in the heart, and you begin to dwell in the heart with your attention, you already possess true inner seclusion. External seclusion will also be necessary, but it seems to me that even then you would do well to withdraw into solitude only from time to time.

THEOPHAN THE RECLUSE

Preserving inner concentration among outward cares

You were granted a great favour from the Lord. Through it He is expressing His approval of your past labours and encouraging you to undertake greater labours still. But maybe He is also teaching you this: are not inner temptations, or external sorrows and burdens, approaching to face you? Such is the thought of St. Isaac. He says that whenever you happen to feel a special action of grace, you should look well on all sides, lest any calamity should befall you and cast you down. But attacks of boasting are more likely to assail you than sorrowful misfortunes. In that case recollect from your former life all that your conscience forbids you to praise, and thus damp down the thoughts that arise within you, just as one sometimes damps a fire down with earth, in order to prevent a big blaze being born from a small flame. Self-praise and self-esteem are followed by sinful thoughts and sinful movements, and other such failings which are far from negligible. May the Lord save you from them all!

The Lord approves your desire for solitude, but does not indicate the time. You must wait for precise indications: until they are given, keep inner silence, and continue to do all you can to look after your convent properly.

How can you keep inner concentration amongst outward cares? Do your work with zeal and attention, unremittingly and without haste. Every piece of work which you have to do, accept as given you by God Himself, and do it as such. Your thoughts will then be with the Lord. You can acquire this habit with God's help.

THEOPHAN THE RECLUSE

Retreat within yourself

You thirst for a definite seclusion. It would be better to wait. External seclusion will come of itself once inner seclusion is established. God will arrange about that. Yet do not forget that you can be alone amid the noise of the world; and equally you can be surrounded by the hubbub of the world whilst withdrawn in your cell. You will have something better than external seclusion if you retreat in this way within yourself, thus making it impossible for any external turmoil to distract you. Pray that you may be granted this.

THEOPHAN THE RECLUSE

TIMES OF DESOLATION

(v) Times of Desolation

Two kinds of withdrawal

The abiding of our soul with the Lord, which is the whole essence of inner work, is not something that depends upon us. The Lord visits the soul, and the soul dwells with Him; the soul rejoices before Him and He fills it with spiritual warmth. Then the Lord withdraws and at once the soul is empty, nor does it lie at all within its power to make the Good Visitor of souls return. The Lord withdraws to put the soul to the test, or sometimes to punish it, not so much for external trespasses but for some inner evil to which the soul has granted admission. When the Lord withdraws to put the soul to the test, He quickly returns once more when it begins to call out to Him. But when He withdraws as a punishment, He does not soon return—not until the soul has realized the sin it has committed, has repented, has wept over it and done penance.

Theophan the Recluse

Why does the soul grow cool?

Above all, watch carefully when the soul grows cool. This is a bitter and dangerous state. The Lord uses it as one of His means of guidance, instruction, and correction. But it can also be a kind of punishment. The reason is usually an open sin, but since in your case no such sin is in evidence, the cause should be sought in inner feelings and dispositions. It may be that a high opinion of yourself has stolen into you, and you think that you are not like the others? Maybe you are planning to tread the path of salvation by yourself and to ascend on high by your own efforts?

Theophan the Recluse

Periods of dryness and insensitivity are inevitable

You undertake different tasks, so you tell me, 'in most cases unwillingly and without any eagerness—I have to force myself'.

But this, after all, is a basic principle in the spiritual life—to set yourself in opposition to what is bad and to force yourself to do what is good. This is the meaning of the Lord's words, 'The kingdom of heaven suffereth violence, and the violent take it by force' (Matt. xi. 12). This is why following the Lord is a yoke. If all were done eagerly, where would be the yoke ? Yet in the end it so comes about that everything is done easily and willingly.

You say, 'A dull insensitivity holds me fast; I become like an automaton—without thoughts or feelings.'

Such states come sometimes as a punishment because we have inclined in thought or feeling to something evil; and sometimes they come as an education—chiefly to teach us humility, to accustom us not to expect anything from our own powers, but to wait on God alone. A few such experiences undermine confidence in self; and so, when we are delivered from heaviness we know where the help comes from, and we realize on whom to rely in everything. This is a depressing state, but it must be endured with the thought that we do not deserve anything better, that we have earned it. There are no remedies against it and deliverance from it depends on God's will. All we can do is to cry to the Lord: Thy will be done! Have mercy! Help me! But on no account should we allow ourselves to grow slack, for this is harmful and destructive. The Holy Fathers describe such states as cooling off or dryness; and they agree in regarding them as something inevitable for anyone trying to live according to God's will, for without them we quickly become presumptuous.

THEOPHAN THE RECLUSE

A punishment for anger

During times of dryness we should look to see whether there has been any feeling of conceit or self-presumption in the soul; and having found it, we should repent before the Lord and resolve to be more cautious in future.

This dryness is most often a punishment for anger, lying, spitefulness, censoriousness, or pride. The cure is to return to the state of grace. Since grace comes by the will of God, all we can do is to pray that He will free us from this dryness and stone-like insensitivity.

THEOPHAN THE RECLUSE

Failure to trust in God

As soon as you turn away—however slightly—from God, and no longer place your trust in Him, things go awry; for then the Lord withdraws, as though saying: 'You have put your trust in something else—very well, rely on that instead.' And whatever it may be it proves utterly worthless.

THEOPHAN THE RECLUSE

How cold it is without grace!

You see how cold it is without grace, and how listless and inert the soul is towards anything spiritual. This is the state of good pagans, of Jews faithful to the Law, and of Christians who lead blameless lives but do not think about their inner life and its relation to God. Yet they do not feel an ache like yours, because (unlike you) they know nothing of the effects of grace. Since from time to time it falls to their lot to experience a kind of spiritual consolation—natural, not grace-given—they remain at peace.

What keeps grace in the soul more than anything else? Humility. What makes it withdraw more than anything else? Feelings of pride, a high opinion of oneself, self-reliance. Grace departs as soon as it senses this evil stench of inner pride.

THEOPHAN THE RECLUSE

The reasons for our coldness

We grow cold within when our heart is distracted, when it cleaves to something other than God, worrying about different things, getting angry and blaming someone—when we are discontented and pander to the flesh, wallowing in luxury and wandering thoughts. Guard against these things, and the coldness will diminish.

As to the heart—where else is life if not in the heart?

THEOPHAN THE RECLUSE

No self-indulgence and no self-pity

You say that you have no success. Indeed, there will be no success so long as you are full of self-indulgence and self-pity. These two things show at once that what is uppermost in your heart is 'I' and not the Lord. It is the sin of self-love, living within us, that gives birth to all our sinfulness, making the whole man a sinner from head to foot, so long as we allow it to dwell in the soul. And when the whole man is a sinner, how can grace come to him? It will not come, just as a bee will not come where there is smoke.

There are two elements in the decision to work for the Lord: first a man must *deny himself*, and secondly he must *follow Christ* (Mark viii. 34). The first demands a complete stamping out of egoism or self-love, and consequently a refusal to allow any self-indulgence or self-pity—whether in great matters or small.

THEOPHAN THE RECLUSE

Always expect sudden changes

Take courage! When the warmth of the spirit grows weak, we should strive in every way to restore it, cleaving to the Lord with fear and trembling. Everything comes from Him. Despondency, boredom, heaviness of spirit and body may occasionally oppress us and remain for a long time. You should not lose heart, but should stand firm, zealously working according to the rules you have undertaken. And do not expect the soul to be freed quickly from its attraction towards the wrong state; do not expect it always to preserve an equal warmth and sweetness. This never happens.

On the contrary, always expect sudden changes. When dullness and heaviness come, realize that this is you, the true you, as you are; as to spiritual sweetness, accept it as an undeserved bonus.

THEOPHAN THE RECLUSE

Light and darkness in the soul

How many times already have you been made aware of the duty which your conscience dictates to you—the duty to remain with the Lord, not preferring anything else to Him? Perhaps your awareness of this duty no longer ever leaves you. May the actual practice of it likewise prevail constantly within you; for this, after all, is our true aim. When we are with the Lord, the Lord too is with us; and everything is bright. When the window curtains are drawn apart in a room and the sun shines, the room is full of light. If you draw the curtain over one window it will be darker, and when you draw them all the room will be in total darkness. It is the same with the soul. When it is turned towards God with all its powers and feelings, everything in it is bright, joyful, and calm. But when it turns its attention and feeling to something else this brightness diminishes. The greater the number of things that occupy the soul, the greater the darkness that invades it; and then complete darkness may result. It is not so much thoughts that bring this darkness, as feelings; while a single instance of being carried away by the feelings is less likely to bring darkness than is a continued passionate attachment to some object. The greatest darkness of all comes from external acts of sin.

THEOPHAN THE RECLUSE

Joy and fear. The preservation and the withdrawal of grace

The whole of your letter manifests the joyful state of your soul. You rejoice in God's mercy towards you, and at the same time you are afraid. It would appear that you have learnt from experience the truth that one must 'Serve the Lord with fear, and rejoice in him with trembling' (Ps. ii. 11). You must keep both these two things and hold them together inseparably, in order not to allow joy to lead to negligence, nor fear to quench your joy. It follows that you must hold yourself in extreme reverence before God, regarding Him as the Father who is most merciful and watches over us with loving care, but who is at the same time strict without any indulgence.

It is only natural that you should feel a sense of fear that all this joy may leave you again. Under the influence of this fear, you are anxious and ready to find a way of keeping your joy. But do you expect to succeed in this by yourself? Because of this one thought alone, all that you have gained may be taken away again. Make every effort on your own side to preserve this joy, but entrust the actual task of safeguarding it into the hands of the Lord. If you do not strive, God will not safeguard it for you. But if you put your hopes on your own efforts and struggles, God will withdraw, seeing that you regard His aid as superfluous, and you will be met by the same difficulties as you encountered originally. Work until you are ready to fall, force yourself to the utmost degree, but still expect the actual safeguarding to be in the hands of God alone. You must not relax either your work and efforts, or your hopes in God alone. Let one strengthen the other —and then both together will form a strong defence.

The Lord always wants us to have whatever will help us most towards salvation, and He is ready to give it to us at all times: He only waits for our readiness or capacity to receive it. Therefore the question of what we must do to safeguard this help is transformed into another: what must we do to keep ourselves in readiness to receive the protecting power of God, which is waiting to enter into us? And how in fact does this power enter into us? It is essential to recognize ourselves as empty, an empty vessel containing nothing; to add to this the consciousness of our own powerlessness to fill this emptiness by any effort of our own; to crown this by the certitude that the Lord alone can do it, and not only can but wants to and knows how; and then, standing with the mind in the heart, to cry out: 'Bring me into good order by the means that Thou knowest, O Lord'. Do all this with unshakeable hope, confident that He will guide you into the paths of righteousness and will not let your feet stray.

You are delighted because the feeling of joy and consolation returned to you. That is natural. But with this, be careful not to allow yourself fanciful conjectures: 'Ah! here it is! This is what it is! This is what it is like, and I did not know it!' Such ideas are thoughts from the enemy, leaving emptiness behind them, or leading up a blind alley. All the time you must repeat only: 'Glory to Thee, O Lord', adding 'God, be merciful!' If you dwell on these vain conjectures, immediately along with them there will come memories as to how you worked and struggled, what you did and from what you abstained, in which of your states the sense of joy and well-being appeared and in which it left you, and in which it endured and was firmly established. And afterwards you will make a decision always to act in some particular way. Thus you will fall into fanciful self-conceit, believing that at last the secret of spiritual progress has been revealed to you and lies in your grasp. But the very next time you pray, all the falsity of such dreams will be made evident, the prayer will be empty, inconstant, and of little comfort. The comfort will lie only in the memory of your former good state, and not in its present possession. And you will have to sigh and condemn yourself. But if the soul cannot induce itself to sigh, then the false mood will last and grace will withdraw again. For such a mood of fantasy shows that the soul has leaned again on its own efforts and not on God's mercy. Grace is always grace, and is independent of all work. He who confuses it with work may be deprived of it for this reason. Remember this well. Withdrawals of grace, sent by God's providence to chasten us, are especially intended to help us in learning this saving lesson.

THEOPHAN THE RECLUSE

WAR WITH PASSIONS

(vi) ILLUSION[1]

How to recognize the illusion of the devil

The true beginning of prayer is warmth of heart, which scorches the passions and fills the soul with joy and gladness, strengthening the heart with an unshakeable love and with a firm assurance that leaves no room for doubt. The Fathers say that whatever enters the soul, whether visible or invisible, is not from God so long as the heart is in doubt about it and so does not accept it: in such cases, it is something that comes from the enemy. In the same way if you see your mind attracted by some invisible force to wander outside or to soar on high, do not trust it and do not allow the mind to be enticed by it; but immediately force your mind to continue with its proper work. Whatever is of God comes by itself, says St. Isaac, whilst you are ignorant even of the time of its coming. Thus the enemy tries to produce an illusion of some spiritual experience within us, offering us a mirage instead of the real thing—unruly burning instead of true spiritual warmth, and instead of joy, irrational excitement and physical pleasure which in turn give rise to pride and conceit—and he even succeeds in concealing himself from the inexperienced behind such seducements, so that they think his diabolic illusion is really the working of grace. Yet time, experience, and feeling will reveal him to those who are not altogether ignorant of his evil wiles. 'The palate discriminates between different foods', say the Scriptures. In the same way spiritual taste shows all things as they are, without any illusion.

ST. GREGORY OF SINAI

Confusion and peace

When there is confusion in the soul, of whatever kind, do not at such a time trust its judgement; for what the soul tells you

[1] In Russian, *prelest*.

then will not be the truth. At such moments its counsellor is Satan, and his advice is certainly not for its salvation—the poor soul is torn this way and that.

'The wrath of man worketh not the righteousness of God' (James i. 20). What comes from God is wholly peaceful, calm and sweet; and it leaves this sweetness in the soul as well as pouring it out in abundance all around, even though at first sight it sometimes has a forbidding appearance.

THEOPHAN THE RECLUSE

Wandering thoughts

You are subject to wandering thoughts because you listen to idle talk, and memories of it remain with you. Out of these memories the enemy weaves a web in front of your mind's eye in order to enmesh it. When this happens, you should descend into your heart, turning your eyes away from the illusory images presented by the enemy, and call to the Lord.

THEOPHAN THE RECLUSE

Conceit masquerading as zeal

To make progress in prayer and to escape from illusion, self-denial is needed, which teaches us that nothing should be sought in prayer except attention. Then the work of prayer will become more simple and easy. Temptations will also become less strong, although they always accompany any endeavour. St. Nil Sorski and other Holy Fathers tell us that powerful temptations coming from the devil—temptations far beyond our strength—attack us if we seek to experience in ourselves the fruits of prayer of the heart prematurely. We seek these fruits too soon because—unknown to ourselves—we suffer from an exaggerated opinion of our own abilities, and from conceit masquerading as zeal.

BISHOP IGNATII

WAR WITH PASSIONS

The origin of illusion

Many people understand about the ultimate effects of illusion, for these are clearly manifest. What is more important is to learn how this illusion originally arises. It starts from a false thought, which serves as the foundation of all the delusions and all the disastrous infirmities that afflict the soul. A false thought in the mind already contains the whole structure of illusion, just as a seed sown in the earth contains the whole plant which will grow out of it.

BISHOP IGNATII

Joyful sorrow and true prayer, free from illusion

If a man holds fast to tears of contrition, to prevent himself being carried away by the joy which he experiences in prayer, and so forming a high opinion of himself, then he possesses a mighty weapon against the enemy. He who preserves this joyful sorrow will escape all harm. True prayer, free from illusion, is prayer in which spiritual warmth, coupled with the Jesus Prayer, brings fire into the depths of our heart and burns up the passions like tares. Such prayer brings gladness and peace to the soul, and comes neither from right nor left, nor even from above, but wells up in the heart like a spring of water from the life-giving Spirit. This kind of prayer and this alone should you love and seek to keep in your heart, always preserving your mind from dreaming. Fear nothing once you have it, for He who said, 'Be of good cheer; it is I; be not afraid' (Matt. xiv. 27), is Himself with us. Whoever is attuned to this inner harmony and lives righteously and sinlessly, who has turned his back upon sycophancy and arrogance, will stand firm and suffer no ill even if a whole army of devils rises against him and brings innumerable temptations.

THEOPHAN THE RECLUSE

ILLUSION

Does the practice of the Jesus Prayer lead to illusion?

Some people assert that the Jesus Prayer is always, or nearly always, followed by illusion, and strictly forbid the use of this prayer.

To accept such an idea and to make such a prohibition constitutes a terrible blasphemy—illusion of an utterly deplorable character. Our Lord Jesus Christ is the one source of our salvation, the only means whereby we can be saved: and His human Name has received from His divinity an unlimited and holy power to save us. How can this power, working for salvation—the only power that gives salvation—become distorted and work for perdition? Such a suggestion is absurd. It is melancholy, blasphemous, soul-destroying nonsense. Those who adopt this line of argument are indeed beguiled by the devil, and deceived by the spurious reasoning which comes from Satan.

Examine all the Holy Scriptures: you will find the Name of the Lord exalted and glorified everywhere in them, and its saving power extolled throughout. Study the writings of the Fathers and you will see that all of them, without exception, suggest and advise the practice of the Jesus Prayer, calling it a weapon stronger than any other in heaven or on earth; a gift of God, an inalienable heritage, one of the culminating and most exalted bequests of the God-Man, a solace most sweet and full of love, a sure pledge. Finally, turn to the canonical decrees of the Eastern Orthodox Church and you will find that in the case of all its illiterate children, both monks and laymen, the Church has established the recitation of the Jesus Prayer as a substitute for the reading of psalms and prayers in one's own cell or room. What weight, then, can there be in the recommendations of a few blind men, extolled and applauded by others equally blind, as compared with the unanimous testimony of the Holy Scriptures, of all the Holy Fathers, and of the canonical decrees of the Church concerning the Jesus Prayer?

BISHOP IGNATII

WAR WITH PASSIONS

The enemies of the Jesus Prayer

Certain people have developed an unfortunate prejudice against the Jesus Prayer, although they lack the personal knowledge that comes from a correct and long practice of the Prayer. It would have been much more safe and sensible for such people to refrain from making any judgement on the subject: they should realize their complete ignorance of this sacred task, rather than take upon themselves the mission of preaching against the practice of the Jesus Prayer, and of denouncing this holy prayer as the cause of diabolic illusion and the soul's perdition. I must say to them by way of warning that to censure the prayer which uses the Name of Jesus, and to ascribe a harmful effect to this Name, is as bad as the censure which the Pharisees passed upon the miracles accomplished by Our Lord. This ignorant and blasphemous theorizing against the Jesus Prayer has all the character of heretical pseudo-philosophy.

BISHOP IGNATII

The need for experienced direction (i)

You ask why illusion comes during the practice of the Jesus Prayer? It comes not from the prayer itself but from the manner in which it is practised—and here we should observe the directions prescribed in the *Philokalia*. These directions should be followed under the eye of a teacher who knows the correct way of performing the Prayer. But if anyone tries to practise it by himself, merely from descriptions in books, he cannot escape illusion. In any description only an external outline of the work is given: a book cannot provide all the detailed advice which is supplied by the *staretz*, who understands the inner state that should accompany the Prayer, and so can watch over the beginner and give him the further guidance that he needs. He who practises this method of prayer without a guide to help him, is of course left with only the external activity and the various physical exercises. He conscientiously performs everything laid down in the books about the posture of the body, breathing, and

268

ILLUSION

looking into the heart. But since methods of this kind naturally
lead to a certain degree of concentrated attention and warmth,
whoever does not have by him a reliable judge, capable of explaining to him the nature of the change that has taken place in him,
may come to imagine that this limited warmth is indeed what he
is seeking and that grace has descended upon him, whereas in
fact it is not there as yet. And so he begins to think that he possesses grace, without actually having it. Such is the nature of
illusion; and this illusion will thereupon distort all the subsequent
course of his inner life. That is why nowadays we find the *startsi*
advising people not to undertake these physical methods at all,
because of the danger involved in them. By themselves they cannot
give anything of grace, for grace is not connected with external
exercises, but comes down only into the inner being: on the
other hand, the proper inner state will attract the action of grace
even without such methods.

This proper inner state consists in practising the Jesus Prayer
in such a way that we walk in God's presence: at the same time
we must kindle to fervour within ourselves the feelings of
adoration and the fear of God, ceasing to pander to ourselves in
anything, listening to our conscience always and in everything,
keeping it unpolluted and at peace, and placing the whole of
our life, both inner and outer, in God's hands. When these
spiritual elements are present, the grace of God, coming in its
own time and absorbing them all into one, kindles from them
the spiritual fire which is the token of the presence of grace in
the heart. If we follow this way, it is difficult to fall into self-
conceit. But even so it is better to have a guide whom we meet
personally and who can see our face and hear our voice; for these
two things reveal what is within.

THEOPHAN THE RECLUSE

The need for experienced direction (ii)

Inner prayer brings salvation. But in our inner prayer we stand
in great need of experienced direction, so long as we are still
praying by our own efforts and labour. It is precisely during this

269

period of practising inner prayer that people, who lack a skilful hand to guide them, are mostly liable to go astray.

THEOPHAN THE RECLUSE

Why the Jesus Prayer sometimes leads to insanity

Insanity can come from the Jesus Prayer only if people, while practising it, fail to renounce the sins and wicked habits which their conscience condemns. This causes a sharp inner conflict which robs the heart of all peace. As a result the brain grows confused and a man's ideas become entangled and disorderly.

As to your first question asking about the small flame: when God gives it you will understand. Without having tasted the sweetness of honey a man cannot know what it is like. So also here. We must acquire a constant feeling of love for God, and then the flame will become manifest.

THEOPHAN THE RECLUSE

The illusion of those who do not practise inner prayer

There are good grounds for regarding as self-deception and illusion the inner state of those monks who, having rejected the practise of the Jesus Prayer and inner work in general, are satisfied with external prayers alone—with continual attendance at church services and with the unrelenting observance of a cell rule, consisting exclusively in the reading of psalms and in verbal and oral prayers. They cannot avoid being self-opinionated, as *staretz* Basil explains. This is the mark of the self-opinionated state of mind: people under its influence come to regard themselves as leading a life of attention, and often, out of pride, despise others. Verbal and oral praying is certainly fruitful when it is linked with attention, but this happens only very occasionally: for we learn to preserve attention chiefly through the practice of the Jesus Prayer.

BISHOP IGNATII.

HUMILITY AND LOVE

(vii) HUMILITY AND LOVE

Where humility and love are absent, everything spiritual is absent

You say that you have no humility or love. So long as these are absent, everything spiritual is absent. What is spiritual is born when they are born and grows as they grow. They are the same for the soul as mastery of the flesh is for the body. Humility is acquired by acts of humility, love by acts of love.

THEOPHAN THE RECLUSE

The measure of humility

Keep both eyes open. This is the measure of humility: if a man is humble he never thinks that he has been treated worse than he deserves. He stands so low in his own estimation that no one, however hard they try, can think more poorly of him than he thinks himself. This is the whole secret of the matter.

THEOPHAN THE RECLUSE

Defects of character

The Lord sometimes leaves in us some defects of character in order that we should learn humility. For without them we would immediately soar above the clouds in our own estimation and would place our throne there. And herein lies perdition.

THEOPHAN THE RECLUSE

The path to humility—obedience

There is no need for me to repeat to you that the invincible weapon against all our enemies is humility. It is not easily acquired. We can think ourselves humble without having a trace of true humility. And we cannot make ourselves humble merely by thinking about it. The best, or rather, the only sure way to humility is by obedience and the surrender of our own will. Without this it is possible to develop a satanic pride in ourselves, while being humble in words and in bodily postures. I beg you to pay attention to this point and, in all fear, examine the order of your life. Does it include obedience and surrender of your will? Out of all the things you do, how many are done contrary to your own will, your own ideas and reflections? Do you do anything unwillingly, simply because you are ordered, through sheer obedience? Please examine it all thoroughly and tell me. If there is nothing of this type of obedience, the kind of life you lead will not bring you to humility. No matter how much you may humble yourself in thought, without deeds leading to self-abasement humility will not come. So you must think carefully how to arrange for this.

THEOPHAN THE RECLUSE

Conceit and censoriousness

Humbling oneself is not yet humility, but only the desire and search for humility. May the Lord help you to acquire this virtue. There is a spirit of illusion which in some unknown way deceives the soul by its guile. It so confuses our thoughts that the soul thinks itself humble, whereas inwardly it conceals an arrogant and conceited opinion of its own worth. So we have to go on looking carefully into our heart. External relationships which lead us to humility are the best means here.

You have been somewhat negligent. The fear of God left you, and soon after that attention left you too, and you fell into the habit of censuring people. You say that you have sinned inwardly, and this is true. Repent quickly and beg God's forgiveness. Such a fault as that brings its own retribution: the fault is inward, and so is the punishment. We can condemn others not only in words but also with an inner movement of the heart. If the soul, when thinking of someone, criticizes them adversely, then it has already condemned them.

THEOPHAN THE RECLUSE

HUMILITY AND LOVE

Taking offence, and turning the other cheek

You say that you are offended. To be offended at lack of attention is to consider oneself worthy of attention, and consequently to set a high value upon oneself in the heart; in other words, to have a heart swollen with pride. Is this good? Is it not our duty to endure wrongful accusations? Certainly it is. How then shall we start practising this duty? After all, when we are commanded to endure, we have to endure every unpleasantness without exception, and endure gladly, without losing our inward peace. The Lord told us, when smitten on one cheek, to turn the other also, but we are so sensitive that if a fly so much as brushes us with its wing in passing we are immediately up in arms. Tell me, are you prepared to obey this commandment of the Lord about being smitten on the cheek? You will probably say, Yes, you are prepared. Yet the instance you describe in your letter is precisely an occasion where this commandment applies. Being smitten on the cheek should not be taken literally. We should understand by it any action of our neighbour in which, it seems to us, we did not receive due attention and respect—any action by which we feel degraded, and our honour, as people call it, wounded. Every deed of this kind, however trivial—a look, an expression—is a blow on the cheek. Not only should we endure it, but we should also be ready for some greater degradation which would correspond to turning the other cheek. What happened in your case was a very light slap on one cheek. And what did you do? Did you turn the other? No; so far from turning it, you retaliated. For you have already retaliated; you have made the other person feel that you are somebody, as though saying, 'Keep your hands off me!' But what are we good for, you and I, if we do this? And how can we be regarded as disciples of Christ if we do not obey His commandments? What you should have done is to consider: do I deserve any attention? If you had had this feeling of unworthiness in your heart you would not have taken offence.

THEOPHAN THE RECLUSE

WAR WITH PASSIONS

Take up the sword of humility

Spiritual unrest and passions harm the blood and effectively damage our health. Fasting and a general abstinence in our daily life are the best way to preserve our health sound and vigorous.

Prayer introduces the human spirit into God's realm where the rock of life dwells; and the body also, led by the spirit, partakes of that life. A contrite spirit, feelings of repentance, and tears—these do not diminish our physical strength but add to it, for they bring the soul to a state of comfort.

You wish that contrition and tears would never leave you, but you had better wish that the spirit of deep humility should always reign in you. This brings tears and contrition, and it also prevents us from being puffed up with pride at having them. For the enemy manages to introduce poison even through such things as these.

There is also spiritual hypocrisy which may accompany contrition. True contrition does not interfere with pure spiritual joy, but can exist in harmony with it, concealed behind it.

And what of self-appreciation? Take up the sword of humility and meekness, hold it always in your hand, and mercilessly cut off the head of our chief foe.

THEOPHAN THE RECLUSE

CHAPTER VII

TEACHINGS OF THE STARTSI OF VALAMO MONASTERY

(i) SCHEMA MONK AGAPII

Oral prayer

In the beginning the Jesus Prayer is mostly uttered with unwillingness and constraint. But if we have a firm intention to subdue all our passions, through prayer and with the help of divine grace, then with frequent practice of the Prayer and perseverance, as the passions grow less, the Prayer itself will become gradually easier and more attractive.

In oral prayer we must try in every possible way to keep our mind fixed on the words of the prayer, saying it without haste and concentrating all our attention on the meaning of the words. When the mind becomes distracted by alien thoughts, we must bring it back undiscouraged to the words of the prayer.

Freedom from distraction is not given to the mind quickly, nor whenever we wish it. It comes when we have first humbled ourselves, and when God chooses to grant this blessing to us. This divine gift does not depend upon the length of time we pray or the number of prayers we recite. What is needed is a humble heart, the grace of Christ, and constant effort.

From oral prayer recited with attention we pass over to inner or mental prayer. This is so called because in such prayer our mind is swept towards God and sees Him alone.

TEACHINGS OF THE STARTSI OF VALAMO

Inner prayer (prayer of the mind)

To practise inner prayer, it is essential to keep our attention in the heart before the Lord. In response to our zeal and humble striving in prayer, the Lord bestows upon our mind His first gift—the gift of recollection and concentration in prayer. When attention is directed towards the Lord effortlessly and without interruption, this is attention given by grace, whereas our own attention is always forced. This inner prayer, if all goes well, in due time passes into prayer of the heart: the transition is easily made, provided we have an experienced teacher to guide us. When the feelings of our heart are with God and love for God fills our heart, such prayer is called prayer of the heart.

Prayer of the heart

It is said in the Gospels: 'If any man will come after me, let him deny himself, and take up his cross, and follow me' (Matt. xvi. 24). When we pray, then, we must first give up our own will and our own ideas, and then take up our cross, which is the labour of body and soul that is unavoidable in this spiritual quest. Having surrendered ourselves entirely to the never-sleeping care of God, we should joyfully and humbly endure the sweat and labour, for the sake of the true reward God will grant to the zealous when the right time comes. Then God, imparting His grace to us, will put an end to the wanderings of our mind and will place it—together with the remembrance of Himself—immovably within the heart. When this dwelling of the mind in the heart has become something natural and constant, the Fathers call it 'union of mind and heart'. In this state the mind has no longer any desire to be outside the heart. On the contrary, if outward circumstances or some long conversation keeps the mind away from its attention to the heart, it experiences an irresistible longing to return within, a craving and spiritual thirst: its one desire is to set to work once more with renewed zeal in building its inner house.

When this inner order is established, everything in a man passes

276

from the head into the heart. Then a kind of inner light illumines all that is within him, and whatever he does, says, or thinks, is performed with full awareness and attention. He is able to discern clearly the nature of the thoughts, intentions, and desires that come to him; he willingly submits his mind, heart, and will to Christ, eagerly obeying every commandment of God and the Fathers. Should he deviate from them in any respect, he expiates his fault with heart-felt repentance and contrition, humbly prostrating himself before God in unfeigned sorrow, begging and confidently awaiting help from above in his weakness. And God, seeing this humility, does not deprive the suppliant of His grace.

Prayer of the mind in the heart comes quickly to some people, while for others the process is slow. Thus of three people known to me, it entered into one as soon as he was told about it, in that same hour; to another it came in six months' time; to a third after ten months, while in the case of one great *staretz* it came only after two years. Why this happens so, God alone knows.

Know also that before the passions are destroyed prayer is of one kind, and after the heart has been purified of passions it is of another kind. The first kind helps to purify the heart of passions, while the second is a spiritual token of future bliss. This is what you should do: when you can actually feel the mind entering the heart and are consciously aware of the effects of prayer, give full sway to such a prayer, banishing all that is hostile to it; and so long as it continues active within you, do nothing else. But when you do not feel thus carried away, practise oral prayer with prostrations, striving in all possible ways to keep your attention in the heart before the face of the Lord. This manner of praying will also enable the heart to acquire warmth.

Watch and be sober, and especially during the prayer of mind and heart. No one pleases God more than he who practises the prayer of mind and heart aright. When outward surroundings make prayer difficult, or when you have no time to pray, at such times, whatever you may be doing, strive to preserve the spirit of prayer in yourself by all possible means, remembering

God and striving in every way to see Him before you with the eyes of your mind, in fear and love. Feeling His presence before you, surrender yourself to His almighty power, all-seeing and omniscient, in worshipful submission laying all your activities before him, in such a way that in every action, word and thought you remember God and His holy will. Such, in brief, is the spirit of prayer. Whoever has a love for prayer must without fail possess this spirit, and, as far as possible, must submit his understanding to God's understanding by means of constant attention of the heart, humbly and reverently obeying the commands of God. In the same way he should submit his wishes and desires to God's will, and surrender himself completely to the designs of God's providence.

In all possible ways we should combat the spirit of arbitrary self-will and the impulse to shake off all restraint. It is a spirit that whispers to us: This is beyond my strength, for that I have no time, it is too soon yet for me to undertake this, I should wait, my monastic duties prevent me—and plenty of other excuses of like kind. He who listens to this spirit will never acquire the habit of prayer. Closely connected with this spirit is the spirit of self-justification: when we have been carried away into wrong-doing by the spirit of wilful arbitrariness and are therefore worried by our conscience, this second spirit approaches and sets to work on us. In such a case the spirit of self-justification uses all kinds of wiles to deceive the conscience and to present our wrong as being right. May God protect you against these evil spirits.

(ii) Igumen Varlaam

The Apostle writes: 'For our rejoicing is this, the testimony of our conscience' (2 Cor. i. 12). Simeon the New Theologian says: 'If our conscience is pure, we are given the prayer of mind and heart; but without a pure conscience we cannot succeed in any spiritual endeavour.'

TEACHINGS OF THE STARTSI OF VALAMO

(iii) Igumen Nazarii[1]

With reverence call in secret upon the Name of Jesus, thus: 'Lord Jesus Christ, Son of God, have mercy upon me, a sinner.'

Try to make this prayer enter ever more deeply into your soul and heart. Pray the prayer with your mind and thought, and do not let it leave your lips even for a moment. Combine it, if possible, with your breathing, and with all your strength try through the prayer to force yourself to a heart-felt contrition, repenting over your sins with tears. If there are no tears, at least there should be contrition and mourning in the heart.

[1] Igumen Nazarii (1735–1809), *starets* at the Sarov monastery, sent by Metropolitan Gavriil of St. Petersburg in 1782 to take charge of Valamo: he remained abbot until 1801. On arrival he found the community in a grave state of decline, with only a few monks left. Under Nazarii's leadership the number of monks rapidly increased, and the spiritual life of the monastery was once more raised to a high level.

279

Further Reading

St Theophan the Recluse and St Ignatii Brianchaninov did not see themselves as innovators, but sought to base their teaching upon the Greek Fathers. Anyone interested in exploring the Patristic background of their ascetic theology should consult in the first instance the great collection of spiritual texts known as *The Philokalia*, edited by St Nicodemus of the Holy Mountain and St Makarios of Corinth. A full translation of this, made from the original Greek, is in process of publication: *The Philokalia: The Complete Text*, translated by G. E. H. Palmer, Philip Sherrard and Kallistos Ware. Volumes 1–4 have so far appeared (Faber, London/Boston, 1979–95); a fifth and final volume is in preparation. There is an earlier two-volume translation of selected portions, based on the Russian version of *The Philokalia* made by St Theophan: *Writings from the Philokalia on Prayer of the Heart* (Faber, London, 1951), and *Early Fathers from the Philokalia* (Faber, London, 1954), both translated by E. Kadloubovsky and G. E. H. Palmer.

A number of St Theophan's writings have been translated into English. Among the more recent volumes to appear are *The Path of Prayer* and *The Heart of Salvation*, both translated by Esther Williams and published by the Praxis Institute Press (Newbury, MA/Robertsbridge); and *The Spiritual Life and how to be attuned to it*, translated by Alexandra Dockham (St Herman of Alaska Brotherhood, Platina, 1995). Theophan's adaptation of Lorenzo Scupoli's works *Spiritual Combat* and *Path to Paradise* has appeared in English with the title *Unseen Warfare*, translated by E. Kadloubovsky and G. E. H. Palmer, with an interesting introduction by H. A. Hodges (Faber, London, 1952).

FURTHER READING

St Ignatii Brianchaninov's most important work has been published in English as *The Arena: An Offering to Contemporary Monasticism*, translated by Archimandrite Lazarus (Moore) (3rd printing, Holy Trinity Monastery, Jordanville, 1991). Also available in English is St Ignatii's work *On the Prayer of Jesus*, likewise translated by Archimandrite Lazarus (Watkins, London, 1952; 2nd impression, London, 1965).

The best introduction to the Jesus Prayer is by the French Orthodox author Archimandrite Lev Gillet, who wrote under the *nom de plume* 'A Monk of the Eastern Church': *The Jesus Prayer*, revised edition with a foreword by Bishop Kallistos Ware (St Vladimir's Press, Crestwood, 1987). More scholarly, but often less perceptive, is the study by the French Jesuit Irénée Hausherr, *The Name of Jesus*, translated by Charles Cummings (Cistercian Studies Series 44, Kalamazoo, 1978). For a vivid and moving example of what the Jesus Prayer can mean in personal use, see the anonymous nineteenth-century Russian work *The Way of a Pilgrim*, translated by R. M. French (SPCK, London, 1954).

On St Paisii Velichkovskii, who forms the link between the Greek *Philokalia* and the nineteenth-century Russian teachers, see Fr Sergii Chetverikov, *Starets Paisii Velichkovskii: His Life, Teachings, and Influence on Orthodox Monasticism* (Nordland, Belmont, 1980); and the work edited by the St Herman of Alaska Brotherhood, *Blessed Paisius Velichkovsky* (Platina, 1976). Consult also Bishop Seraphim Joantă, *Romania: Its Hesychast Tradition and Culture* (St Xenia Skete, Wildwood, 1992).

On the more general background, consult:

Nicholas Arseniev, *Russian Piety* (Faith Press, London, 1964)

Sergius Bolshakoff, *Russian Mystics* (Cistercian Studies Series 26, Kalamazoo/London, 1977)

John B. Dunlop, *Staretz Amvrosy: Model for Dostoevsky's Staretz Zossima* (Nordland, Belmont, 1972)

Sergei Hackel, 'The Eastern Tradition from the Tenth to the Twentieth Century. B. Russian', in Cheslyn Jones, Geoffrey Wainwright and Edward Yarnold (eds.), *The Study of Spirituality* (SPCK, London, 1986), pp. 259–76

Archimandrite Lazarus (Moore), *St. Seraphim of Sarov: A Spiritual Biography* (New Sarov Press, Blanco, 1994)

FURTHER READING

Vladimir Lossky, *The Mystical Theology of the Eastern Church* (James Clarke, London, 1957)

Macarius, Starets of Optino, *Russian Letters of Spiritual Direction 1834–1860*, translated by Iulia de Beausobre (Dacre Press, London, 1944)

John Meyendorff, *St Gregory Palamas and Orthodox Spirituality* (St Vladimir's Seminary Press, Crestwood, 1974)

Archimandrite Sophrony (Sakharov), *Saint Silouan the Athonite* (Monastery of St John the Baptist, Tolleshunt Knights, 1991)

Thomas Špidlík, *La doctrine spirituelle de Théophane le Reclus. Le Coeur et l'Esprit* (Orientalia Christiana Analecta 172, Rome, 1965).

INDEX

PERSONS

INDEX

PLACES AND SUBJECTS

INDEX

INDEX

INDEX